"A Warm & Zealous Spirit"

"A Warm & Zealous Spirit"

John J. Zubly and
the American Revolution,
A Selection of His Writings

Edited by

Randall M. Miller

**Mercer University
Press**
Macon, Ga. 31207

All books published by Mercer University Press are produced
on acid-free paper which exceeds the minimum standards set by the
National Historical Publications and Records Commission.

Library of Congress Cataloging in Publication Data

Zubly, John Joachim, 1724-1781.
  "A warm & zealous spirit".

  Bibliography: p. 201
  Includes index.
  1. United States — History — Revolution, 1775-1783 — Pamphlets.
2. Zubly, John Joachim, 1724-1781. I. Miller, Randall M. II. Title.
III. Title: "Warm & zealous spirit."
E203.Z8   1982   973.3   81-22367
ISBN 0-86554-028-4   AACR2

For Inez and H. Leroy "Pat" Patterson, my "other" parents

A Father's Tribute (to his family). From the album of John Joachim Zubly, as reproduced in Joseph Henry Dubbs, *The Reformed Church in Pennsylvania* (Lancaster: Pennsylvania-German Society, 1902), p. 216.

Better is a dry morsel, and quietness therewith,
than an house full of sacrifices with strife.
                    —Proverbs 17:1

And even things without life giving sound,
whether pipe or harp,
except they give a distinction in the sounds,
how shall it be known what is piped or harped?
For if the trumpet give an uncertain sound,
who shall prepare himself to the battle?
                    —1 Corinthians 14:7-8

So the servants of the householder came and said unto him,
Sir, didst not thou sow good seed in thy field?
from whence then hath it tares?
He said unto them,
An enemy hath done this.
The servants said unto him,
Wilt thou then that we go and gather them up?
But he said,
Nay; lest while ye gather up the tares,
ye root up also the wheat with them.
Let both grow together until the harvest:
and in the time of harvest I will say to the reapers,
Gather ye together first the tares,
and bind them in bundles to burn them:
but gather the wheat into my barn.
                    —Matthew 13:27-30

Contents

Acknowledgments

Even in a small enterprise a scholar accumulates many debts. My experience has been no different. My work on this book went smoothly because librarians at the following institutions were unfailingly cordial and helpful: the American Philosophical Society; the Balch Institute in Philadelphia; the British Museum; the William L. Clements at the University of Michigan; the Free Library of Philadelphia; the Georgia Department of Archives and History in Atlanta; the University of Georgia, Athens (rare books and manuscripts); the German Society of Pennsylvania; Harvard University (rare books and manuscripts); Haverford College; the Henry E. Huntington Library, San Marino, California; the Historical Society of Pennsylvania; the Library Company of Philadelphia; the Library of Congress; the Presbyterian Historical Society; Princeton Theological Seminary; Princeton University (rare books room); Saint Joseph's University; the South Carolina Department of Archives and History in Columbia; the University of Pennsylvania (rare books room); the University of South Carolina (South Caroliniana Collection); Williams College; and Yale University (rare books and manuscripts). Anthony R. Dees and the staff at the Georgia Historical Society in Savannah deserve special thanks for providing a congenial environment and efficient assistance over two summers.

The book benefited much from the encouragement of Mills Lane IV of Savannah. Lawrence Cress (Texas A & M University), Michael Lofaro (University of Tennessee), my wife Linda Patterson Miller (Pennsylvania State University), John M. Mulder (Louisville Presbyterian Seminary), and William E. Pauley commented on earlier versions of my introduction and improved its style and argument. I also learned much from students in John Mulder's American church history seminar at Princeton Theological Seminary in 1976, where I first presented my ideas about Zubly. Anita Schorsch was particularly perceptive in her remarks. James T. McDonough (Saint Joseph's University) helped me with Latin translations and transcriptions. Paul A. Cimbala (Emory University) early on assisted me in bibliographical searches. Doris Leisch and Joseph Casino provided copy-editing and proofreading assistance. To all of these individuals and institutions, I offer my thanks, and, of course, I absolve them all from responsibility for any errors that might have crept into this book.

The publication of this book was made possible by support from the Balch Institute, the German Society of Pennsylvania, the Miller Foundation, and Saint Joseph's University.

I dedicate this book to my mother-in-law and father-in-law, loving Christian parents who became good friends and patient supporters of my work.

Havertown, Pennsylvania   R.M.M.

June, 1981

Introduction

by
Randall M. Miller

On the face of it, the colony of Georgia did not seem ripe for revolution in the years following the French and Indian War in America. Much of the colony remained a raw, unclaimed wilderness. According to the governor's 1773 report, roughly thirty-three thousand persons, almost half of them black slaves, lived in the colony. They inhabited sparsely an area in the shape of a triangle—from the mouth of the Saint Mary's River extending up the littoral to Savannah, the principal town and hub of economic and political life in Georgia, and filling the area west to Augusta. Exposed to hostile Indians and threats from the French and especially the Spanish, the colony looked to London for protection, partially supplied in the form of presents to propitiate the Indians and a war to remove the Spanish and French menace. The colony produced little in the way of manufactures, beyond some backwoods homespun, shingles, and staves. Indeed, Georgia required an annual Parliamentary subsidy to meet the costs of administration. It was a mobile, fluid society in the seedtime of its economic development. When the Trustees abdicated power in 1752, the legal and moral strictures against slaveholding fell so that the indigo and rice plantation system rapidly emerged. Land and slaves became the preoccupation of many white Georgians. The prosperity of the 1750s created an expanding gentry class who, along with the wealthy Savannah merchants, set the tone of life in the colony. It was a tone that too often sounded of prices current and slave imports rather than political acuity.[1]

---

[1] For general descriptions of eighteenth-century Georgia see James E. Callaway, *The Early Settlements of Georgia* (Athens, 1948); Carl Bridenbaugh, *Myths & Realities: Societies of the Colonial South* (Baton Rouge, 1952), chapters 2 and 3 on Savannah as a pale reflection of Charleston and on the multi-ethnic, vibrant backcountry of Georgia and the Carolinas; W. W. Abbot, *The Royal Governors of Georgia, 1754-1775* (Chapel Hill, 1959), especially pp. 3-33; and Harold E. Davis, *The Fledgling Province: Social and Cultural Life in Colonial Georgia, 1733-1776* (Chapel Hill, 1976), the best discussion of Georgia's rapid maturation. See also, "Report of Sir James Wright on the Condition of the Province of Georgia, on 20th September, 1773," in Georgia Historical Society *Collections*

The crown appointment of Sir James Wright as governor in 1760 promised the youthful colony sober administration and a rigorous attention to its economic growth. Wright was intelligent, diligent, and politically savvy, and owing to his immense holdings in real estate and slaves, he was responsive to Georgia's propertied interests. He easily established himself as the dominant political force in the colony for most of his long prewar administration (1760-1775). As a royal colony, Georgia also had a council composed of local elites appointed by the crown and a commons, or lower house, in the assembly, which was largely made up of merchants and gentry elected by the colony's freeholders. The former body functioned both as an appeals court and the upper house of the assembly, while the latter was in theory confined to legislative duties. Members of the council and the commons were men of property who shared a common appreciation of deferential politics and a hunger to penetrate and exploit America's rich interior. These were preoccupations of the governor as well. Except for his attempts to enforce Parliamentary revenue and trade acts and to honor his royal instructions, Wright rarely pursued issues inimical to local planter and merchant interests. Politically inexperienced, economically and militarily dependent on Great Britain, and flushed with prosperity under royal management, the legislators could be expected to sustain Wright in his authority. They generally did so.[2]

A keen observer, however, might hear rumblings of disquietude beneath the surface calm. The elimination of the Spanish threat in the

(Savannah, 1873), 3:158-79. The growth of the colony after 1738 was largely due to the immigration of foreign Protestants and planters and slaves from other British colonies. A good brief summary of the census data on colonial Georgia—taken from the Colonial Office Group, class 5, at the Public Record Office, London—is in Robert V. Wells, *The Population of the British Colonies in America before 1776: A Survey of Census Data* (Princeton, 1975), pp. 169-71. No student of southern colonial history can afford to miss Richard Beale Davis, *Intellectual Life in the Colonial South, 1585-1763*, 3 vols. (Knoxville, 1978). Although thin on Georgia developments, Davis demonstrates that the southern colonies had a rich cultural life and contributed much to the shaping of the American mind.

[2]On Wright's career and tenure see Abbot, *Royal Governors*, pp. 84-183; Kenneth Coleman, "James Wright," in Horace Montgomery, ed., *Georgians in Profile: Historical Essays in Honor of Ellis Merton Coulter* (Athens, 1958), chapter 3; and Coleman, "James Wright and the Origins of the Revolution in Georgia," in James Kirby Martin, ed., *The Human Dimensions of Nation Making: Essays in Colonial and Revolutionary America* (Madison, 1976), pp. 105-20.

Floridas and the pacification of the Indians, however temporary, allowed Georgians to fix their gaze on domestic political concerns. Unluckily for the British, a mild postwar depression occurred simultaneously with George Grenville's attempt to tax the colonists directly. The Stamp Act of 1765, taxing all printed matter and demanding specie payment, threatened to stagnate trade further and to drain the colony of what little specie it possessed. Forced to defend this and other unpopular revenue acts, Wright antagonized his traditional mercantile and planting allies who depended on the coastal and imperial trade for their maintenance and profits. Other men of lesser station and lesser loyalty to Wright, whether seeking personal advantages by fomenting discord or truly faithful to the principle of local rule, came forward during and after the Stamp Act resistance to challenge Wright, Parliament, and the planter-merchant hegemony.[3]

Weaned on the memory of their fathers' successful contest with the Trustees on questions of rum, slaves, and land,[4] the ambitious, grasping planter-merchant parvenus also sought to wrest greater political power for themselves. The lower house of the assembly offered them a convenient forum to voice their discontents and to extend their political and pecuniary fortunes. During the politically charged 1760s and 1770s, the clashes between governor and council on the one side and the commons on the other formed the leitmotif for much of the colony's political history. Imitating the progress of other lower houses of assembly in the British mainland colonies, the Georgia commons—with mixed success—pressed for the Parliamentary privileges of free speech and debate, exemption from arrest, control over membership, the

---

[3]The Revolutionary awakening in Georgia is discussed in Randall M. Miller, "The Stamp Act in Colonial Georgia," *Georgia Historical Quarterly* 56 (Fall 1972): 318-31; Abbot, *Royal Governors*, pp. 103-83; Lawrence Henry Gipson, *The Triumphant Empire: Britain Sails into the Storm, 1770-1776.* Volume 12 of *The British Empire Before the American Revolution* (New York, 1965), pp. 226-38; and, especially, Kenneth Coleman, *The American Revolution in Georgia, 1763-1779* (Athens, 1958).

[4]For the heritage of dissidence from the Trustees' period see Randall M. Miller, "The Failure of the Colony of Georgia Under the Trustees," *Georgia Historical Quarterly* 53 (March 1969): 1-17. For an insightful introduction to the literature and a handsome, accurate edition of the malcontents' writings see Trevor R. Reese, ed., *The Clamorous Malcontents: Criticism & Defenses of the Colony of Georgia, 1741-1743* (Savannah, 1973). For a different interpretation see Clarence L. VerSteeg, *Origins of a Southern Mosaic: Studies of Early Carolina and Georgia* (Athens, 1975), chapter 3.

exclusive right to frame money bills, and in what caused the most volatile exchanges with the governor and council, the power to appoint the colonial agent. Although the young Georgia commons lagged far behind those of other colonies, especially that of neighboring South Carolina, her members manifested a growing political confidence and maturity. In the midst of Parliamentary designs to restrict westward movement and to usurp their taxing function, they demonstrated an increasing willingness to take on the governor and the king's agents in a struggle for the people's affections.[5]

The polyglot, multireligious composition of the colony also invited internecine rivalries. German Lutherans, transplanted New England Puritans, Scotch-Irish Presbyterians, Quakers, a sprinkling of Jews in Savannah, and Baptists and Methodists on the frontier all stood outside the established Church of England. The religious convulsion known as the Great Awakening, which swept the backcountry and reached some of Savannah's unchurched citizens, had abated but not wholly spent its force by the 1760s. However, the enthusiastic evangelicals—the "New Light" Presbyterians, Baptists, and Methodists—were generally located on the fringes of settlement and so posed no immediate danger to the social and religious establishment in Georgia. The dissenting sects quarreled among themselves and as a rule fared well at the hands of the Anglicans, who were beset by internal problems of poor staffing and low maintenance. Still, the dissenters had a congenital distrust of the established church which, if grafted onto a political controversy, made any conflict of church and state potentially contagious.[6]

[5]Jack P. Greene, *The Quest for Power: The Lower Houses of Assembly in the Southern Royal Colonies, 1689-1776* (New York, 1972ed.), pp. 68-71, 84-86, 105-106, 119-20, 166-68, 184-85, 188-91, 202-204, 211-16, 424-28, 433-36.

[6]The best treatment of religion in Georgia during the colonial and Revolutionary periods is Davis, *Fledgling Province*, pp. 193-232. See also Reba C. Strickland, *Religion and the State of Georgia in the Eighteenth Century* (New York, 1939); and for a good, brief survey, Kenneth Coleman, *Colonial Georgia: A History* (New York, 1976), pp. 144-59, 230-36.

For an understanding of the anti-authoritarian cast of the Awakening see Richard L. Bushman, *From Puritan to Yankee: Character and the Social Order in Connecticut* (Cambridge, Mass., 1967); and Alan Heimert, *Religion and the American Mind: From the Great Awakening to the Revolution* (Cambridge, Mass., 1966). For a different assessment of the Awakening and religion's impact on America see Richard Hofstadter, *America at 1750: A Social Portrait* (New York, 1971), chapters 6-8. My interpretation also differs in emphasis from Carl Bridenbaugh, *Mitre & Sceptre: Trans-Atlantic Faiths, Ideas, Personalities & Politics, 1689-1775* (New York, 1962).

Georgia lacked only an issue to stir any latent animus toward the religious and political establishment. The crisis came with a rush after the French and Indian War. Parliament was determined to raise a revenue in the North American colonies, to exercise a closer review of colonial political affairs, and to bind the colonial economies tightly to British home interests. In rapid succession Parliament pushed through the Sugar Act, the Stamp Act, the Declaratory Act, a revised Mutiny Act, a reorganization and expansion of the American customs service, the Townshend Acts, the Tea Act, the Coercive or "Intolerable" Acts, and a spate of lesser known but to many colonists at least equally obnoxious measures which provoked a constitutional debate on both sides of the Atlantic Ocean. By invading the taxing powers of the colonial assemblies, Parliament threatened to reverse the assemblies' century-long "quest for power," as, indeed, the new customs regulations, the attacks on colonial paper currency, and the direct taxes disrupted the fragile colonial economies. The colonists met these challenges with mobs, boycotts, angry words, and a profusion of political and constitutional arguments. Although tardier and tamer than the rest, Georgians eventually joined in the clamor for redress.

Throughout the developing crisis, Governor Wright complained that the modest anti-British agitation in Georgia was the handiwork of a scattering of déclassé malcontents who fed on radical ideas and examples of lawlessness imported from the north. According to Wright, the weak, trimming enforcement of crown policy in other colonies, particularly South Carolina, encouraged dissidence everywhere in the empire. He was not wholly wrong in this assessment, but he miscalculated badly the extent and depth of local discontent.[7]

While most planters and merchants opposed the Parliamentary innovations, many shrank from the specter of violence and anti-authoritarianism they perceived in the American resistance movements. The mass rallies and provocative language of the Georgian "Sons of Liberty" during the Stamp Act days drove some of the propertied class to a reluctant alliance with Parliamentary authority. Confident of this support, Wright persisted in his attempts to enforce the laws. Initially, to

---

[7]See for example, James Wright to Henry Seymour Conway, 2 February 1766, in Allen D. Candler, comp., "Unpublished Colonial Records of the State of Georgia" (Georgia State Archives, Atlanta) 37:112; and Wright to William Legge, Earl of Dartmouth, 24 August 1774, in Georgia Historical Society *Collections* 3:181.

the disgust of radicals in other colonies and to their own acute embarrassment at home, Georgia's "patriots," as they celebrated themselves, accommodated Wright on the Stamp Act, and during the Townshend Acts furor of 1768 to 1770, they failed to coerce Savannah merchants to participate in a general boycott against British goods. Even the assembly eschewed radicalism. It protested British policy through memorials and correspondence with other assemblies in America. Wright thus showed remarkable staying power in Georgia.

But the resistance refused to retire from the field. Congeries of small merchants, rising planters, artisans, shopkeepers, religious dissenters, and backcountry farmers—men closed off from the inner circles of power in Georgia and suspicious of Wright and his friends—propelled the resistance in Georgia, which moved by fits and starts from one political and constitutional crisis to another after 1765. The commons used the opportunity to claim wider prerogatives, and Wright's strength rested ever more precariously on the doubtful loyalties of local gentlemen of property and standing.[8]

What finally gave shape and meaning to the inchoate American resistance, both in Georgia and elsewhere, were the constitutional musings of contemporary American pamphleteers. Every revolution has its pamphleteer. In America there were many. In Georgia there was only one—the Reverend John Joachim Zubly of Savannah. In his widely circulated pamphlets written between 1765 and 1775, Zubly sorted out the sometimes confused and only dimly perceived tenets of American Whiggism. He presented both a comprehensive theory of American constitutions and a compelling rationale for opposition to Parliament's pretensions to power in America. His pamphlets pulled Georgians from their provincial eddies into the mainstream of American Revolutionary thought. Expressive of ideas current and palatable to Georgia's Whigs, Zubly's pamphlets measure the degree to which the southerly outpost of British benevolence had matured politically.

Zubly consciously linked Georgia with the patriot cause in other colonies, and he built upon the arguments of northern Whig writers. He particularly admired the *Letters from a Farmer in Pennsylvania* by John Dickinson, in many ways Zubly's intellectual kin. Zubly wanted to reprint the *Letters* in Georgia in order to "catch a spark" of Dickinson's flame

---

[8]The general discussion follows Abbot, *Royal Governors*, pp. 103-83; Gipson, *The Triumphant Empire*, pp. 226-38; and Coleman, *Revolution in Georgia*, 16-54.

and so "bring Some of that fire" southward.[9] Zubly identified then the wide areas of intellectual consanguinity with Georgia's older sister colonies.

Zubly was born in St. Gall, a town in northeastern German-speaking Switzerland, on 27 August 1724. He studied at the local *gymnasium* and prepared for his life's work in the ministry. After his ordination at the German Reformed church in London in 1744, he emigrated to British America to join his father and other Zubly family members who had settled among Swiss Germans and Salzburgers in South Carolina and Georgia as early as 1736. Zubly's early years in America remain shrouded in obscurity. In 1745 he appeared in Savannah, where he occasionally assisted another German Swiss minister, the Reverend Bartholomew Zouberbuhler. Zubly never received a regular appointment from the Georgia Trustees, largely due to Zouberbuhler's opposition, and so shuttled back and forth between South Carolina and Georgia preaching to English and German settlements as far south as St. Simon's Island.[10]

---

[9]Zubly's writings circulated as far north as Massachusetts and were reprinted in London and Philadelphia. On Zubly's "American ties" see, for example, Ezra Stiles to J. J. Zubly, 24 November 1766; and Zubly to Stiles, 10 October 1768, 19 April 1769, Ezra Stiles Papers (Yale University). On Zubly's admiration for Dickinson see Zubly to [John Dickinson?] n.d., "Dickinson Correspondence," 12:118, Logan Papers (Historical Society of Pennsylvania, Philadelphia).

[10]The only known full-length biography of Zubly is Roger A. Martin, "John J. Zubly: Preacher, Planter, and Politician" (Ph.D. dissertation, University of Georgia, 1976). An excellent short treatment of Zubly's life and thought is William E. Pauley, Jr., "Tragic Hero: Loyalist John J. Zubly," *Journal of Presbyterian History* 54 (Spring 1976): 61-81. A good brief overview of Zubly's writings is M. Jimmie Killingsworth, "John Joachim Zubly," in *American Writers Before 1800* (forthcoming). There is much information in William J. Hinke, *Ministers of the German Reformed Congregations in Pennsylvania and other Colonies in the Eighteenth Century* (Lancaster, Pa., 1951), pp. 345-52. Hinke also includes a list of Zubly's publications. With varying degrees of accuracy, the following trace the lineaments of Zubly's life: Roger A Martin, "John Zubly Comes to America," *Georgia Historical Quarterly* 61 (Summer 1977): 125-39; Marjorie Daniel, "John Joachim Zubly—Georgia Pamphleteer of the Revolution," *Georgia Historical Quarterly* 19 (March 1935): 1-16; Daniel, "John Joachim Zubly," in Allen Johnson and Dumas Malone, eds., *The Dictionary of American Biography*, 20 vols. (New York, 1928-1936), 20:660-61; and Eunice Ross Perkins, "John Joachim Zubly: Georgia's Conscientious Objector," *Georgia Historical Quarterly* 15 (December 1931): 313-23. See also the *Georgia Gazette,* 3 June 1767; the *Royal Georgia Gazette,* 26 July 1781; and Allen D. Candler, comp., *Colonial Records of the State of Georgia,* 26 volumes (Atlanta, 1904-1913), 23:484, 25:125, 280.

Sometime in 1746 he first met the evangelist George Whitefield. They became friends for life, and Whitefield converted Zubly to support his Bethesda orphanage project in Georgia. In 1753 Zubly traveled north to Pennsylvania and New Jersey to raise money for the orphanage. This trip introduced him to many prominent political and religious figures in the middle colonies, and he returned from his tour with a keen interest in religious affairs outside Georgia. Zubly also revealed his love of contention during his northern tour because he was drawn into several local congregational disputes.

In Georgia the strong-willed and sometimes refractory young minister also had a falling out with Zouberbuhler and departed for the Orangeburg District of South Carolina in 1747. There he joined his father, David Zubly, who had established his ministry in the colony in 1736 and induced the congregation at Purrysburg to invite his son to fill the pulpit. Following a brief stint at Purrysburg, Zubly removed to Wando Neck. He prospered there. In November 1746 he married Anna Tobler, a German Swiss immigrant. After bearing Zubly three children—John (d. 1780), Anne (b. 1756), the favorite, and David (d. 1790)—Anna Zubly died in 1765. Zubly later wed Anne Pyne, but they had no children together.

In 1760 Zubly answered a call from the Independent Presbyterian Church in Savannah, a small church of dissenters which had many leading Georgians in the congregation. Except for a short, unhappy exile in South Carolina during the American Revolutionary War, he made Savannah his home until his death in 1781. Zubly's mastery of homiletics, his firm grasp of modern and classical languages, and his spirited defense of religious dissenters from what he termed "Episcopal oppression" combined to make him a formidable and controversial figure in Georgia life. His strong preaching and liberal admission policies in his church caused dissension and once threatened a schism. In religion and in politics, Zubly would not have an easy tenure in Savannah.[11]

Zubly quickly acquired the prerequisites of social and political power in his adopted home. Through shrewd investments, some of which engendered rancor and disputes, he amassed a fortune in land and slaves. He also established a profitable ferry connecting Charleston and

---

[11]On the potential schism see Davis, *Fledgling Province*, pp. 203-204; and Zubly to Ezra Stiles, n.d. [1769], Stiles Papers.

Savannah at Middlesex, near Purrysburg, on the Savannah River. Zubly's hand was everywhere in the economic development of Georgia, and he acted the part of a gentleman. He lived in a handsome brick house in Savannah, one of the few in the city. He also entered politics. He did so unobtrusively at first by accepting several minor civil offices, such as clerk of Christ's Church Parish. In time, however, his refinement, his wealth, and his intimacy with Governor Wright gave him access to the finest tables of the great men of state in colonial Georgia.[12]

By correspondence and reading, Zubly quenched his intellectual thirst and escaped the barren intellectual desert of Georgia. He won respect as a scholar widely read in history and political theory as well as in theology.

The College of New Jersey (Princeton), the leading Presbyterian institution in the colonies, recognized his learning by conferring honorary A.M. and D.D. degrees on him. Zubly's inquisitiveness and reputation drew him into America's intellectual community and acquainted him with social and political currents in other colonies. He exchanged letters and ideas with Ezra Stiles and other northern divines, and occasionally tilted against them as he kept a close watch on religious and political developments to the north. He also kept his friends apprised of Georgia's affairs.[13]

[12]Zubly engaged in a lively dispute with Lachlan McGillivray over land titles, and incidentally over religious issues as well. He related his side of the land dispute in a series of sharp, biting articles, "An Apology for a Law Suit," in the *Georgia Gazette* from 3 June 1767 to 6 April 1768. On Zubly's holdings see Charles G. Cordle, ed., "The Will of Dr. John Joachim Zubly," *Georgia Historical Quarterly* 22 (December 1938): 384-90, from the original Will of J.J. Zubly, 25 May 1781, in Will Book WW, 1780-1783, pp. 190-94 (South Carolina Department of Archives and History); Marion Hemperley, comp., *English Crown Grants in Christ Church Parish in Georgia, 1755-1775* (Atlanta, 1973), pp. 214-15; Davis, *Fledgling Province*, pp. 36, 51; Martin, "Zubly," pp. 41-42.

[13]See, for example, Ezra Stiles to Zubly, 25 April 1767, Stiles Papers; Zubly to Stiles, 12 February 1767, Gratz Collection (Historical Society of Pennsylvania); Zubly to Stiles, 10 October 1768, 30 April and 9 October 1771, 30 January 1772, Stiles Papers. Zubly was particularly attentive to religious issues and Whitefield's projects. In his northern travels he embroiled himself in several local religious disputes. For an example of Zubly at his most acerbic, see Zubly to Conrad Beissel [founder of the Convent of "The Solitary" at Ephrata, Pennsylvania], 9 January 1755, Dreer Collection (Historical Society of Pennsylvania). See also Zubly's *The Nature of that Faith without which It is Impossible to please God . . . .* (Savannah, 1772), pp. 59-60, for his wrestling with a New England minister on definitions of faith. On Zubly's northern trips and his connections with Reformed and Lutheran German communities see Joseph H. Dubbs, *The Reformed Church in Pennsylvania* (Lancaster, Pa., 1902), pp. 206-13, which includes several Zubly

At home he accumulated a large book collection, amply supplied with political treatises, histories, and religious tracts. The Reverend Henry Melchior Muhlenberg described Zubly's library as "a fine collection of old and new books, the like of which I have seldom seen in America."[14] Zubly's library provided him with samples of the best in Western thought, and in the swirl of events leading up to the American Revolution, Zubly often found occasion to exploit this rich resource.

As was common among stationed clergy, Zubly sought to preserve his sermons in print. He also scrawled out letters and articles for the Savannah *Georgia Gazette* and published broadsides. But he found his medium in that happy English invention, the pamphlet. Then in its heyday of influence, the pamphlet was large enough to develop an argument, yet short and cheap enough to be read at one sitting and then passed along to another individual.[15]

Zubly's early religious writings reveal a strong debt to Continental European pietism. They often turned on Zubly's fascination with death. In his book-length work, *The Real Christians Hope in Death*, published in English in Germantown in 1756, for example, Zubly compiled numerous deathbed scenes from Christian lives to demonstrate the

letters to Pennsylvania Germans. For some useful observations on Zubly's conceptions of death and his ties to the allegorical icongraphy of eighteenth-century American and German Reformed/Calvinism see Anita Schorsch, "A Key to the Kingdom: The Iconography of a Mourning Picture,"*Winterthur Portfolio* 14 (Spring 1979): 52, 54, 55.

[14]Theodore G. Tappert and John W. Doberstein, eds. and trans., *Journals of Henry Melchior Muhlenberg*, 3 vols. (Philadelphia, 1942), 2:645, 679, 682. When Zubly lost all his property during the Revolutionary War, he expressed regrets only for the loss of his library. See Zubly to ?, 9 April 1780, and "Extracts of Letters, &c Found among the Papers of Rev. John J. Zubly, D.D.," pp. 3-4, John Joachim Zubly Papers (Georgia Historical Society, Savannah). Zubly's library fit the pattern of other southern book collectors and readers. Richard Beale Davis, *A Colonial Southern Bookshelf: Reading in the Eighteenth Century* (Athens, Ga., 1979), demonstrates that the libraries of southern individuals were not very much different from their northern counterparts in selection of books on classics, poetry, and by foreign writers, although southern readers showed a greater affinity for books on politics and agriculture.

[15]My discussion of Revolutionary pamphlets and ideology owes much to the excellent analysis in Bernard Bailyn, *The Ideological Origins of the American Revolution* (Cambridge, Mass., 1967). Although it concentrates on Boston and ignores the southern colonies altogether, Thomas C. Leonard's article, "News for a Revolution: The Exposé in America, 1768-1773," *Journal of American History* 67 (June 1980): 26-40, shows the prevalence of "conspiracy" theories and fears of social decline in America.

sweetness and liberation of mortal death for the Christian. He returned to this theme in his funeral sermons and his correspondence. Zubly's religious orientation also derived from his deep interest in European history, particularly the experiences of the Swiss and Germans who became his principal examples of Christian piety and bravery.

Zubly's political pamphlets, which some contemporaries dismissed as softheaded and verbose,[16] were no better or no worse than most political scribblings of the day—when considered as literary pieces. Zubly, after all, wrote for purpose, not profession, and his works retained an amateurish flavor common to the genre in America. He generally dispensed with literary devices and relied on logic to carry his points. He wasted little effort in satire or copying the polished modes of the popular English polemicists, for he set out to persuade and instruct, not to raise fevers or amuse. Indeed, in his first political offering, *The Stamp-Act Repealed* (1765), he warned that passion consumed reason, and so he much preferred dry debate to heated words, however eloquent. He generally honored his own advice. Save his angry *Letter to the Reverend Samuel Frink* (1770) and his appeal *To the Grand Jury* contesting his banishment in 1777, his political pamphlets are distinguished by their moderation and reason.

Zubly's religious beliefs mixed with his sometimes fierce anti-Anglicanism to accent all his writing and became both the cause and the consequence of his involvement in Georgia's Revolutionary struggles. He never successfully separated the religious from the political, nor, indeed, did he believe them to be discrete. Surveying the religious landscape of Georgia, this self-proclaimed sentinel of religious dissent feared the worst. In 1773, for example, he confided to Ezra Stiles that dissenters suffered from untold burdens imposed by the established church. Questions of oath requirements, burial privileges, clergymen's fees, and marriage rites all vexed and perplexed relations between local

---

[16]James Habersham, while acting governor of the colony in 1772, leveled the most devasting criticism at Zubly's writing. He dismissed the "Per Lock" essays in the *Georgia Gazette*, which he attributed to Zubly, as "mere Sophistry, and a jingle of Words without meaning, unless to puzzle and blind the Minds of the People, who are not capable of judging the Subject." Habersham to James Wright, 13 June 1772, in Georgia Historical Society *Collections* (Savannah, 1904), 6:185. Contrariwise, Ezra Stiles wrote that Zubly's *Stamp-Act Repealed* gained him "great Applause, with the best Judges of Composition in New England." Stiles to Zubly, 25 April 1767, Stiles Papers.

Anglican churchmen and Zubly. Zubly recoiled from what he considered extravagant demands of distant ecclesiastical powers for fees and deference to authorities whom he did not acknowledge. To his dismay, however, few dissenters recognized the danger. In fact, he warned that the dissenters' indifference to their own principles was the gravest peril to religious liberty and dissent in the colony. Too many dissenters sought preferment and distinction and so readily fell in with the Anglicans on the contested issues. Zubly labored hard to awaken them to their true interest.[17]

Zubly's suspicions regarding Anglicanism, although ill-founded, reflected his stubborn independence and his Calvinism, but a more fundamental and immediate cause was the bitter dispute he waged with Samuel Frink, the pugnacious Anglican rector of Christ's Church Parish in Savannah. Frink slighted Zubly on several occasions, and he once refused to conduct the funeral service for one of Zubly's children. Zubly was especially nettled by Frink's insistence that dissenters pay him fees for burial rites and bell tolling charges, even though a dissenting minister performed the services. Frink sued Zubly to recover such fees in one instance. The action so outraged Zubly that he blasted him in a scathing rebuke, *Letter to the Reverend Samuel Frink* (1770). Zubly dredged up images of Star Chamber horrors from the Stuart period and quite uncharitably accused Frink of a malicious design to crush the free Protestant clergy in Georgia by arbitrary and onerous taxes. Borrowing a tactic from his Massachusetts friends, Zubly further charged his rival with lobbying secretly for an American episcopate. According to Zubly, an American bishop would grab for his own share of the dissenters' purse. Frink's petitions to London on the Zubly case were doubly damnable to Zubly's mind because they violated the principle of local rule. In the context of the growing rift between crown and colonies, Zubly's *Letter to the Reverend Samuel Frink*, like his political pamphlets, exposed his deeply ingrained abhorrence of distant authority interfering in local affairs—a fear nurtured in his native St. Gall, his Calvinist tradition, and his adopted home in Georgia. The pamphlet also reveals

---

[17]"Letter of Rev. John J. Zubly, of Savannah, Georgia, 1773," in *Proceedings* of the Massachusetts Historical Society 8 (1864-1865): 214-19. On Anglican dislike for Zubly see, for example, James Habersham to the Countess of Huntingdon, 5 April 1773, in Georgia Historical Society *Collections*, 6:225.

his potential inclination to view events in conspiratorial terms. Many other Americans shared this world view.[18]

A churchman and a close student of theology, Zubly could not escape his religious matrix. All his political pamphlets embodied the theme of America as the new Canaan and the Americans as the chosen people of God. This metaphor was carried most directly in his popular sermon, *Stamp-Act Repealed*, in which he cast America in the likeness of the twelve tribes of Israel. The Puritans first advanced this theme in America, but it reappeared in secular form in the colonial promotional literature extolling the abundance of this virgin land.[19] Zubly thus fused the two traditions. Citing Scripture freely in his writing, he saw the Providential hand working to preserve a saving remnant in America, and he further maintained that America's prosperity and liberty signalled divine favor. But this favor implied duty, as he reminded readers in his *Stamp-Act Repealed*. That duty, of course, was to glorify God and to safeguard liberty. While he rarely cloaked himself in the mantle of a Jeremiah during the troubled years of the American Revolution, Zubly's profound sense of stewardship quickened his political and religious interest.[20]

[18]For Frink's description of his difficulties in Georgia see Frink to Rev. Burton, 4 August 1768, 29 June 1769, 6 July 1770, "Georgia Letters, 1760-1782," Series C, Package 7, Part 3, Society for the Propagation of the Gospel in Foreign Parts Papers (microfilm, Library of Congress facsimiles). For Zubly's side of the Frink affair see Zubly to Benjamin Franklin, 9 July 1771, in William B. Willcox, ed., *The Papers of Benjamin Franklin*, 19 vols. to date (New Haven, 1959-), 18: 170-72; and the citations in ibid., p. 54n.

On the Americans' conspiratorial mind-set see Bailyn, *Ideological Origins,* pp. 95-99, 144-59. For another Zubly reference to narrow Anglicanism see his funeral sermon on the death of George Whitefield, *The Wise Shining as the Brightness of the Firmament* (Savannah, 1770), p. 23. That Zubly was aware of the New England controversy over an American bishop is evident in his correspondence with Ezra Stiles. See Stiles to Zubly, 29 June 1767 and 6 June 1768; and Zubly to Stiles, 10 October 1768, wherein he discounts support for the idea of an Anglican bishop in Georgia, and 19 April 1769, Stiles Papers.

[19]For this theme applied to Georgia see Trevor R. Reese, ed., *The Most Delightful Country in the Universe: Promotional Literature of the Colony of Georgia, 1717-1734* (Savannah, 1972).

[20]Perry Miller, "From Covenant to Revival," in James W. Smith and A. Leland Jamison, *The Shaping of American Religion.* Volume 1 of *Religion in American Life,* 3 vols. (Princeton, 1961), pp. 331-32, includes Zubly's *Law of Liberty* in the New England jeremiad tradition, arguing that Zubly's pamphlet reproduced the New England style of argumentation—calling on congregations and readers to avoid the wrath of God by resisting British tyranny. Miller does concede, however, that Zubly accomplished this with "somewhat less provincial egotism" than the New England divines.

More than a generous adaptation of Scripture, Zubly ransacked histories and legal commentaries to substantiate his political and constitutional preachments. For him, the clashes between Parliament and the colonies were fundamentally constitutional in nature, and it would be in constitutional discussions that Zubly made his major contributions to American thought and the Revolutionary movement in Georgia. Typical of his contemporaries, he laced his political pamphlets with citations and references to Coke, Blackstone, Rapin, Montesquieu, and English history, particularly the history of the great constitutional struggles of the seventeenth century. He further fortified his arguments with an amalgam of American Whig commonplaces—the contractual basis of government, Enlightenment principles, natural law, and the English common law. A true eclectic, he also borrowed willy-nilly from the classics. But he placed custom and legal precedent in the front rank of authority, and in this he steadfastly maintained that the Americans, not Parliament or its votaries, hewed to the correct constitutional interpretation. There existed, however, a curious irony in his marriage to custom and precedent, for his arguments pushed forward an American theory of government decidedly out-of-joint with British Whig assertions of Parliamentary supremacy in all matters. Much to Zubly's later discomfort, many of his ideas proved novel, even radical, and when embraced by men of a more violent, revolutionary stripe than Zubly, they would sweep the Revolution in Georgia over and past him.

The frontier of the constitutional debate was the question of representation, which first appeared during the Stamp Act crisis. While other American pamphleteers moved on to grapple with more complex constitutional problems, Zubly always retained a lively interest in the representation issue. Like most Americans, he rejected the facile argument of "virtual representation" propounded by the British ministry. According to devotees of this concept, Americans enjoyed representation in Parliament because Parliament represented interests, not men or specific geographic areas. Thus a merchant from London or a Middlesex farmer quite nicely represented the interests of the Savannah merchants and the backcountry Georgia cultivators, since merchant and farming interests were everywhere the same.

Obliquely in *The Stamp-Act Repealed*, and more directly and cogently in his *Humble Enquiry* (1769) and his *Calm and Respectful Thoughts* (1772), Zubly tore away at the British argument. Virtual representation ignored local conditions and effectively denied colonists any voice in government, for they elected not a single member of Parliament to represent colonial interests. Zubly favored "actual representation" whereby men stood for office by place and each place chose its own representatives. Out of this widely held belief in America developed the doctrine of government "by" as well as "for" the people.

Zubly was not, however, a democrat or even a friend of republics, for he once remarked that "a Republican Government is little better than Government of Devils."[21] *The Stamp-Act Repealed*, which he wrote partly to discourage political wrangling in Georgia, issued a stern warning that governments that became too popular were easy prey for demagogues and factionalism, the progenitors of mob rule and anarchy. But the people must have a place in government. For Zubly, the commons served both as the people's legitimate entrance to government and as a mirror of society. He consistently maintained that unless people participated directly in government, through the electoral process, of course, that government's laws had no binding effect upon them. While this logic repudiated virtual representation, it was so heavily laden with radical notions concerning an attorneyship status for representatives that revolutionaries employed it for democratic purposes. Zubly never saw this danger.

The crux of the constitutional debate centered on the location and containment of power. As heirs to the English commonwealthman tradition which characterized power as aggressive and liberty as passive, Americans believed that power and liberty could never safely commingle. The one devoured the other. In his trenchant *Law of Liberty* (1775), Zubly delineated the nature of the few peoples in history who had survived the great contests between power and liberty. Like his Swiss forbears, they were simple, rural folk, stubbornly proud of their freedom and suspicious of authority. History showed that men who relaxed their vigilance and became morally flabby and effeminate in their indulgence in luxury all fell into slavery. They deserved such a fate. The legacy of despotism and poverty left by, say, the Turks and the Spanish stood as stark reminders of failed virtue. Once lost, liberty could never be restored.

Some power was necessary, surely, to restrain man's passions and to

---

[21]Lyman H. Butterfield, ed., *The Diary and Autobiography of John Adams*, 4 vols. (Cambridge, Mass., 1961), 2:204. See also Benjamin Rush to David Ramsay, [March or April 1788], in Lyman H. Butterfield, ed., *The Letters of Benjamin Rush*, 2 vols. (Princeton, 1951), 1:454.

force him to serve the common weal. Man was by nature selfish and so required government. Government performed vital functions of ordering civil and commercial intercourse, securing men in their property, and defending freedom. Of itself, power counted for little; rather, Zubly and his generation feared power's intoxicating effects upon frail man. Man too easily succumbed to the blandishments of power. He trampled upon liberty. To control power's appeal and at the same time to harness its energy, so necessary to the corporate interest and social harmony, became the principal problems of eighteenth-century political science in America.

In time, with the formal break with England, American patriots would embark upon the task of drafting frames of government which specifically marked off the boundaries of power. Because of his opposition to independence and his open disdain for republican government, Zubly played no part in drawing up Georgia's first state constitution. Before that time, however, his definition of constitution fit well the prevailing American beliefs on the subject, and ironically furnished the Georgia patriots with a sophisticated, respectable justification for independence.

Simply put, Zubly argued that the constitution for the English speaking peoples was the sum of natural rights, law, custom, and history. The constitution created government and constricted power by dividing it through function into several overlapping spheres. No governmental body could supersede fundamental law because all were creatures of it. Here he departed from conventional British wisdom on sovereignty and constitutions which held that Parliament, as the embodiment of society—king, aristocracy, and people—was the fundamental law beyond which there could be no appeal. The Declaratory Act of 1766 following the repeal of the Stamp Act made the British position explicit. It also raised hackles on the back of Zubly's neck. By declaring that Parliament alone had the right to legislate for the colonies "in all cases whatsoever," the act scrapped the claims of the colonial assemblies to sole control over internal, distinctly local affairs, and it seemingly left the colonists unrepresented anywhere in the empire.

Zubly's logic drove him to raise some troubling questions about the colonies' place in the empire. Unable to confine the debate to a discussion of representation, Zubly faced up to the real issue separating American and English constitutional theorists—sovereignty. Each asked where ultimate political power lay. For the British, it resided in Parliament. The

Americans were not so tidy. Like his counterparts in the other American colonies, Zubly sought to shave and join the cherished American tradition of local semi-autonomy and the aspirations of the rising commons with the new imperial demands and British Whig theory.[22]

In his most original and enduring contribution to American political thought, *An Humble Enquiry* (1769), Zubly marshalled the authorities of English history and law to prove that Parliament's claim to complete sovereignty over the colonies was dubious and unhistorical at best. Carefully distinguishing between "empire" and "kingdom," he conceded that Parliament's authority encompassed matters of trade and the preservation of Englishmen's rights within the empire and in the kingdom of England. But in the empire Parliament's rule had always been uneven, sometimes nonexistent. Scotland and Ireland, for example, retained varying degrees of legislative independence, despite their union with England. In the case of the British settlements in North America, the crown rather than Parliament had established them, and local, indigenous institutions had fostered and sustained them. Indeed, most, if not all, of the substance of everyday life in the British North American colonies had been carried on by local government. While the Declaratory Act of 1766 correctly defined Parliament's role in the kingdom of England, it grossly inflated Parliament's legislative power in the empire, where, according to Zubly, Parliament was supreme only in matters of trade. In all else, local governments, properly invested with authority by the crown and the continued participation of the people and guaranteed by charter at the time of settlement, remained supreme in their respective spheres.

Zubly thus raised the colonial lower houses of assembly to coequal status with Parliament and fenced off their legislative preserves from Parliamentary or crown encroachments. For this reason, he roundly criticized his friend, Governor Wright, for dissolving the Georgia assembly in 1771 after that body elected a speaker of the commons contrary to Wright's royal instructions. When the assembly was

---

[22]In fairness to Zubly and his generation, it should be noted that the question of sovereignty was so troublesome that it took the Revolutionary period as well as the Confederation period for Americans to reach some kind of suitable, if fluid, formulation of the concept of sovereignty. On this point see Gordon S. Wood, *The Creation of the American Republic, 1776-1787* (Chapel Hill, 1969), who also makes good use of the Zubly pamphlets.

dissolved a second time in 1772 for the same reason and articles appeared in the *Georgia Gazette* defending the crown's right to control the assembly, Zubly attacked the crown prerogative in his *Calm and Respectful Thoughts* (1772). Zubly argued that the speaker was the servant of the house, and therefore of the people. To allow the election of the speaker to be annulled or monitored by the crown's agent negated and confounded the meaning of free choice. Linked with the commons' quest for other Parliamentary rights and immunities, the speaker contretemps measured the distance traveled apart by the commons and the governor during the Revolutionary period. Zubly—religious dissenter, rising planter, and American Whig—cast his lot with the assembly.

But Zubly's reliance on the commons, however radical in its constitutional implications, should not obscure his basic conservatism. By promoting the cause of the lower house of assembly, still in the hands of men of property, he hoped to arrest the radical "out-of-doors" activity of Georgia's patriots—mobs, rallies, parades—which shook the social and political order at home.

Ever a friend of order and property, Zubly neither counselled nor countenanced independence. In *The Stamp-Act Repealed* he condemned men whose excesses "might tend towards a separation or an alienation of affections," and ten years later, in his sermon on the *Law of Liberty*, he remained cemented in that conviction. As separation grew imminent and violence increased in Georgia, Zubly's alarm grew. His love of order always balanced his concern for the constitutional rights of Americans. He trembled at the talk of independence which, to his mind, would only hasten anarchy at home. Consequently, he vowed to "pray & fight against it" with unflagging purpose. While he beseeched Parliament to heed American petitions for redress, he lobbied "in every Company" in America "to Contradict & oppose every hint of a desire of Independency."[23] He hoped to control events which were beyond control. He served in the Second Continental Congress in the hope that a union of American Whigs could find the means both to "secure the rights of America" and to achieve "reconciliation with G. Britain."[24] The military campaigns of 1775 notwithstanding, Zubly, like John Dickinson of Pennsylvania, refused to recognize the incompatibility of these dual objectives.

[23]Journal of Rev. J. J. Zubly, 24 October and 16 September 1775, typescript, pp. 36 and 33, Zubly Papers.

[24]See Zubly's remarks in Worthington C. Ford, ed., *Journals of the Continental Congress, 1774-1789*, 34 vols. (Washington, 1904-1937), 3:482.

In assaying the future of liberty among English speaking peoples, Zubly assured his readers that the outstanding differences between crown and colonies were not irreconcilable. In his *Law of Liberty* and again in a petition to the king that he drew up for the Georgia Provincial Congress in 1775, he blamed ministerial inflexibility and ignorance rather than governmental corruption or kingly tyranny for the strained relations and bloodletting. The king needed only to stand for the constitution and recall his troops to save the empire. As late as September, 1775, Zubly informed the Earl of Dartmouth, the Secretary of State for the American Department, that a Parliamentary pledge to honor American constitutional rights would "instantly" calm the storm. Failure to do so, however, meant further carnage and even separation. Americans were "no idiots" and were "determined not to be slaves."[25]

Zubly knew whereof he spoke, for events in Georgia confirmed his most dire predictions. By the winter of 1775, after Governor Wright prevented the Georgia assembly from sending delegates to the First Continental Congress in Philadelphia, the disparate elements of the Georgia resistance came together. To protest the Coercive Acts against Massachusetts, the Continental Congress adopted an Association to boycott trade with the British and any colony which refused to cooperate with it, and thereby forced the revolutionary issue in Georgia. Still smarting from earlier defeats at the hands of Wright, the Georgia patriots attempted to erect a counter government in the form of a Provincial Congress. Members of the Georgia assembly, however, dominated the first Georgia Provincial Congress. Many of them remained friendly with Wright and wanted to go slow in challenging British authority. Disgusted, the more radical Calvinist population of St. John's Parish moved to secede from the colony altogether and to join the Continental Association. South Carolina's patriots warmly reviled Georgia for lying down before Wright. Such pressures prodded the Georgia patriots to bold action. They seized the colony's powder magazine and thus ended Wright's recourse to military force.[26]

---

[25]Zubly to William Legge, Earl of Dartmouth, 3 September 1775, is published in the preface to his *Law of Liberty*.

[26]The revolutionary transformation in Georgia is ably detailed in Coleman, *Revolution in Georgia*, pp. 55-75. On the dynamics of the "patriot" emergence in Georgia and the decline of conservative Christ Church Parish influence in the colony see Harvey H. Jackson, "Consensus and Conflict: Factional Politics in Revolutionary Georgia, 1774-1777," *Georgia Historical Quarterly* 59 (Winter 1975): 388-401.

Assembling at Tondee's tavern in Savannah on 13 June 1775, the patriots issued a call for another Provincial Congress. More important, the Tondee meeting called upon Georgians to obey the Association. Many of the planters and merchants who attended the Tondee session, Zubly among them, regathered later that day to foreswear any thought of independence and, indicative of their apprehensions of disorder in Georgia, to discuss methods of restraining violence in the city.

For all practical purposes, the Second Provincial Congress, which convened at Tondee's tavern in July, 1775, had assumed the legislative power in the colony. Every parish sent representatives to the Congress, although a significant number of them were conservatives who worked with the patriots in an effort to temper their radicalism. Zubly attended as one of the twenty-five delegates from Christ Church Parish. After choosing officers, the Congress retired to Zubly's church to hear him preach a sermon from the twelfth verse of the second chapter of James. He published this sermon as *The Law of Liberty*. The Congress set aside a day for fasting and prayer in the colony, drafted petitions to the king, addressed Wright on American rights, and elected delegates to the Second Continental Congress. Zubly had a hand in all of this, although he watched the unraveling of British authority with dismay.[27]

In appreciation of Zubly's labors and his pamphleteering, the Georgia Provincial Congress added him to the Georgia delegation to the Continental Congress. He reluctantly agreed to serve.[28] After a month's tour of New Jersey and New York, where he preached on several occasions, Zubly arrived in Philadelphia in September, 1775.[29] Initially at least, he cooperated fully with the Congress. In Philadelphia he mixed with Benjamin Rush, John Adams, and other learned men of science and law. John Adams, always parsimonious with praise, found the Georgia

[27]On Zubly's desire for a cautious policy see Zubly to Noble Wimberly Jones, [July ? 1775], Zubly Papers. On Loyalism in Georgia see Wallace Brown, *The King's Friends: The Composition and Motives of the American Loyalist Claimants* (Providence, R.I., 1965), pp. 231-46. The best treatment of American Loyalism is Robert M. Calhoon, *The Loyalists in Revolutionary America, 1760-1781* (New York, 1973).

[28]Zubly sought and received the consent of his congregation before he agreed to serve in the Congress. Allen D. Candler, comp., *The Revolutionary Records of the State of Georgia*, 3 vols. (Atlanta, 1908), 1:241, 248.

[29]On his northern trip see his Journal, 11 August to 7 September 1775, typescript, pp. 29-33, Zubly Papers.

minister to be a "warm and zealous Spirit,"[30] and Zubly doubtless earned the respect of other members of Congress by his erudition and compelling speaking style. Sensitive to the needs of Georgia's colonial economy and fearful of an Indian uprising if presents were not forthcoming, Zubly asked the Congress to exempt Georgia from the Association, particularly the non-importation agreement. He reminded the Congress that Georgia's patriots required powder and intelligence from abroad and could not carry on war without them. Otherwise, Zubly did not take an obstructionist stance at the Congress. Despite his avowed "hope for Reconciliation," he endorsed defensive military operations. The aggressive military program of the radicals, which included an invasion of Canada, was, however, farther than he was prepared to go. He chided the radicals for their martial ardor, but he continued to vote for military preparations.[31]

The radical drift of the Congress placed Zubly in a quandary. By supporting military resistance to safeguard American constitutional rights, he helped to push the colonies toward a break with the mother country. He equivocated; he hoped—to no avail. The dictates of supplying the Continental Army and the logic of the American Whig constitutional position demanded independence. When the drive for independence in the Congress gathered momentum in the late fall, Zubly openly swung over to the conservative side. Radicals attempted to drive him from the Congress. Samuel Chase of Maryland, with whom Zubly had quarreled earlier over Georgia's exemption request, excoriated Zubly and his Georgia colleagues as the ruin of America. In October Chase accused Zubly of maintaining a secret correspondence with Governor Wright. Zubly denied the charge, whereupon Chase produced a Zubly letter which the radicals had intercepted en route to Wright. Although the missive divulged nothing of consequence about the proceedings in Philadelphia, Zubly's false denial and his opposition to the radicals sealed his fate in the Congress.[32]

---

[30]Butterfield, ed., *Diary*, 2:172. Adams later recanted and took a jibe at Zubly for his antirepublicanism. Adams to Archibald Bulloch, 1 July 1776, in Edmund C. Burnett, ed., *Letters of Members of the Continental Congress*, 8 vols. (Washington, D.C., 1921-1936), 1:521.

[31]*Journals of the Continental Congress*, 3:482, 488, 491-92, 499-500.

[32]Ibid., 3:493-94.

"Greatly indisposed," he "abruptly" left Philadelphia for Georgia, which to his misfortune was under the control of his enemies. The Congress dispatched one of the Georgia delegates to Georgia to counteract Zubly's potential "to do mischief" there. Zubly promised not to address the government except in the presence of his fellow delegates, but this was a transparent attempt to prevent their testimony from going unchallenged.[33]

Contrary to the denigrations of his enemies, Zubly did not at first espouse the British cause in Savannah. He persisted in his preference for reconciliation, but he contributed nothing substantive to the British side. Intellectually a cosmopolitan, he remained, however, a political provincial and refused to take an oath of allegiance to the Continental Congress, the acid test of patriotism in 1776. The Georgia Council of Safety ordered him arrested. The chief justice of the state dismissed Zubly, but the Council had him arrested a second time lest his "going at large. . .endanger the public safety." After a perfunctory hearing in 1777, the Council declared him an enemy of the state. The Revolutionary government in Georgia, which was strapped for funds and eager to force obedience from lukewarm "patriots," chose to make an example of the harried minister by confiscating his estate and banishing him from Georgia.[34]

These actions occasioned Zubly's final excursion into constitutional theory, an appeal *To the Grand Jury*, published as a broadside in 1777. Zubly was convinced that he was but the "first victim" of a new tyranny rising in America. To meet this danger, he repositioned his constitutional weaponry to face the Revolutionary government in Georgia. In terms that anticipated the conservative criticism of legislative dominance and democracy during the 1780s, he blasted away at majority oppression, which was administered unchecked by a few self-appointed agents of the people who violated natural and constitutional rights with greater impunity than the British. Zubly warned Georgians that any government

---

[33]F. B. Dexter, ed., *The Literary Diary of Ezra Stiles*, 3 vols. (New York, 1901), 2:10; Zubly to Archibald Bulloch and John Houstoun, [November 1775?], and same to same, [November 1775?], Zubly Papers.

[34]Candler, comp., *Revolutionary Records*, 1:147-48, 326ff. For a reference to Zubly's quarrels with other Georgia Whigs after his flight from Philadelphia see P. Le Conte to J. LeConte, 1 January 1776, Sir Henry Clinton Papers (William L. Clements Library, University of Michigan, Ann Arbor).

that arbitrarily altered or ignored its constitution, however slightly, put constitutional, legitimate government "at an end."[35]

His appeal fell on deaf ears. Bitter and disillusioned, Zubly fled to South Carolina's Black Swamp in 1778, accompanied by his son David. While he worked his indigo plantation on Buck Island, he brooded over past injustices. One contemporary found Zubly "extremely agitated" and nursing a "strong indignation at the ingratitude and harshness" of the Georgia patriots. Still, he trusted that God would "vindicate the rectitude of his intentions" in the end.[36]

When the British recaptured Savannah in 1779, Zubly returned home. He resumed his demanding ministerial duties and generally tried to avoid political involvement.[37] He expressed ambivalent feelings about the British as masters,[38] but he cordially detested his personal enemies. Zubly spilled forth his venom in letters asking for compensation for property lost to the "late usurpers" who razed his home and threw his library into the Savannah River. He boasted that he had been "a thorn in their side." He also pressed his claims for damages due him by the British, who occupied his church and parsonage during the siege and employed his slaves in the army. Until his death in 1781, however, Zubly largely confined his political opinions and hatreds to the privacy of his diary and correspondence.[39]

---

[35]*To the Grand Jury of the County of Chatham, . . .October 8, 1777* (Savannah, 1777).

[36]Winslow C. Watson, ed., *Men and Times of the Revolution; or, Memoirs of Elkanah Watson* (New York, 1856), 49-50.

[37]According to Alexander A. Lawrence, *Storm over Savannah: The Story of Count d' Estaing and the Siege of the Town in 1779* (Athens, 1951), 39-40, Zubly served as chaplain to the provincial troops and turned his meeting house into a hospital for Hessian troops. Even if true, these actions hardly constitute active support for the British cause. Earlier, Zubly had not responded to an appeal by General Augustine Prevost, acting governor, inviting Zubly to return to Georgia. In fact, Zubly endorsed Prevost's letter and sent it to Benjamin Lincoln, the American general nearby, suggesting that Zubly was not yet ready to be identified with the British side alone. See Prevost to Zubly, 28 January 1779, and Zubly to Lincoln 29 January 1779, Keith Read Manuscript Collection (University of Georgia).

[38]Zubly to Mary Lambol Thomas, 29 March 1779, Misc. MSS—bMS Am 1649.5 [374]—(Houghton Library, Harvard University, Cambridge, Mass.).

[39]For Zubly's account of the "barbarous" destruction of his library and the confiscation of his estate see "Extracts of Letters, &c Found among the Papers of Rev. John J. Zubly, D.D.," pp. 1-4; and his Journal, 28 January, 15 March, 3, 7 April 1779, typescript, pp. 51a,

Zubly did not become a "Loyalist" because he was an Anglophile or an obstructionist. Rather, like other "Whig-Loyalists," he loved America and so sought to avoid her destruction in a civil war. Zubly believed that reconciliation and reform were possible within the empire. For him, as for other Whig-Loyalists, war meant mob rule, human suffering, and severing ties with England, actions that threatened liberty on both sides of the Atlantic. The problem Zubly faced was that circumstances afforded no chance for equivocation. The Declaration of Independence changed the legal status of "doubters" by changing the definition of treason. As Catherine Crary has observed, the Declaration made neutrality difficult, at best, and "signaled the beginning of proscription, confiscation, and more serious and widespread persecution."[40] Zubly understood all this,

---

52, 53-54, Zubly Papers. For his requests for compensation from the British see Zubly to [Sir James Wright], 30 November 1779; to ?, 9 April 1780; and to Capt. Moore, 10 August 1780, Zubly Papers.

[40]Catherine S. Crary, ed., *The Price of Loyalty: Tory Writings From the Revolutionary Era* (New York, 1973), p. 7. The term "Whig-Loyalist" is somewhat elusive. William H. Nelson, in *The American Tory* (Oxford, England, 1961), pp. 116-34, introduced the concept without precisely defining it. William A. Benton, in *Whig-Loyalism: An Aspect of Political Ideology in the American Revolutionary Era* (Rutherford, N.J., 1969), described Whig-Loyalists as men who came from the upper and upper-middle classes of colonial society and who "adhered to conservative Whig principles." (p. 14). They wanted to uphold the oligarchic pattern of American colonial politics, which they believed the Revolution threatened. Benton relies on the political writings of "nine prominent Whig leaders who later changed their affiliation" (p. 13) to prove that such men shared a common repugnance for harsh words, a predilection for personal autonomy, and a commitment to quiet reflection and rational discourse. They were patricians out of tune with the times. As Robert M. Calhoon notes (*The Loyalists in Revolutionary America*, p. 563), political writings (external evidence, if you will) do not necessarily reveal the springs of individual decisions to stay with the British in the hard days of the Revolution.

In each colony/state a small number of conservative Whigs, imbued with English Whig political ideology and active in criticizing British Parliamentary policy regarding the colonies, feared the American movement toward independence. They believed that war would unhinge the delicately balanced social and political order in America and that independence would invite civil war and foreign intrigue to America. Such men came over to the "Tory" side for reasons of principle, pride, and personal interest. More than anything else, ambivalence marked their character and caution their temperament. The Revolution did not permit much political vacillation or ambiguity. People had to choose sides. Zubly was one of those ambivalent men who was forced into the Loyalist camp by the uncompromising stance of the Georgia "patriots," who demanded, through loyalty oaths, full public endorsement of their policies. For reasons of principle, and some petulance, Zubly refused to do this. Because of his abhorrence of war generally, he was

but he could not escape the forces of revolution swirling about him. Once a victim of the Whigs' policies of proscription, confiscation, and persecution, he had only his bitterness and outrage to guide his political feelings. He became an implacable foe of the "patriots," an unforgiving minister fighting in this worldly Armageddon.

Zubly did vent his rage in one final series of essays, published in the *Royal Georgia Gazette* in 1780. In his essays Zubly revealed again the classic Whig-Loyalist argument that tied him to those other American Loyalists who had defended colonial liberty before 1775 but recoiled from independence and its attendant violence. Writing under the pseudonym "Helvetius," the Swiss-born minister scored the patriots for their desperation—manifested in their confiscation of Loyalist property, violence, and injustice in courts prosecuting those unsympathetic to the patriot cause. Zubly argued that rebellion inexorably propelled the rebels into more desperate actions to insure the success of their enterprise, for a failed rebellion meant ruin and sure death. Rebels blinded themselves to perversions of truth. In rebellion, Zubly wrote, men "must place perjury in the room of a lawful oath, to murder must be no crime; rapine and violence hold the place of equity and justice; nor can any design be too dark, or any action too villainous, for men that expect to succeed in wickedness." Success, however, "will sanctify all the measures they have made use of to obtain it." But at what price to law and liberty, asked Zubly. Zubly believed that Whig-Loyalists alone subscribed to discipline and restraint. Drawing on the history of the Swiss, again, he pointed out the virtue of patience rather than rebellion, because the Swiss achieved their "independence" without civil war and, so, without the threat of tyranny that follows civil war. Because war encouraged injustice, it could never be the instrument of justice. Zubly offered no solution to the dilemma of an

---

unable to stomach a protracted military contest. He knew that war left much misery, but little progress. It also led to an unthinking conformity as "proof" of loyalty. In that sense, Zubly's Whiggism limited his ability to adapt easily to the revolutionary conditions and, in the end, drew him toward the Tories. Under a less vigorous and vengeful "Whig" government in Georgia, Zubly might have drifted the other way, toward the American cause he had supported before 1776.

Typing Whigs and Loyalists is a ticklish business given the diverse personal and political spurs to thought and action. To get a sense of the diversity of Loyalist thought alone see Crary, ed., *The Price of Loyalty*; Calhoon, *The Loyalists in Revolutionary America*; and Timothy M. Barnes, "The Loyalist Press in the American Revolution, 1765-1781" (Ph.D. dissertation, University of New Mexico, 1970).

encroaching Parliament and the loss of American "liberty"—a dilemma he described in his earlier writings. In the end, he retreated to Scripture to find assurance that tyrants would suffer punishment and that good men would preserve their liberty.

For Zubly, the Revolution represented a moral crisis. The patriots' extremism, their willingness to unleash violence and social chaos in order to win their objective, threatened the harmony of the moral order God expected of the Americans, His chosen people. Zubly closed his Revolutionary writing with a stern warning: "the penalty due to obstinate rebellion in this life is a trifle not to be mentioned with what you must expect when all the ghosts of the slain, every drop of innocent blood you spilt, every act of violence and injustice which you concurred in or committed, all the confederates of your crime whom you have forced or seduced, every injured widow's groans, and every orphan's tear, whom you have ruined, the spoils of the honest and innocent whom you have robbed, every friendly warning which you rejected, will at once arise in judgment against you, and render you as compleatly miserable as you have rendered yourselves distinguishingly wicked."[41]

The war exhausted Zubly's emotional and physical resources and shattered his fortune and family. After his banishment, he was disowned by his brother and forsaken by his son John, who enlisted in the South Carolina militia. Zubly's older son David served on the British side. Like his father, he suffered humiliation and banishment in 1777.[42]

Zubly's family fragmentation only magnified his personal tragedy. History labeled him as the archetypal Loyalist. Much truth obtains in the charge. He did, after all, resist independence, and his Revolutionary pamphleteering aside, he did retain his political and social kinship with Governor Wright. But it is too easy to dismiss Zubly merely as a Tory trimmer, for he was a tangle of contradictions. A vigorous opponent of the established church, he displayed a veneration of authority rooted in custom and law. Comfortable with conservatives and himself of the

---

[41]*Royal Georgia Gazette*, 27 July, 3 August, 31 August, 7 September, 28 September, 12 October 1780. On Zubly as the archetypal Whig-Loyalist see Calhoon, *The Loyalists in Revolutionary America*, pp. 180-82; and especially the seminal investigation of Zubly's "Helvetius" essays, Janice Potter and Robert M. Calhoon, "The Character and Coherence of the Loyalist Press," in Bernard Bailyn and John B. Hench, eds., *The Press & the American Revolution* (Worcester, Mass., 1980), pp. 270-72.

[42]Cordle, ed., "Will of Dr. John Joachim Zubly," pp. 384-85n, 386-87n.

propertied class, he espoused a radical Whig constitutional interpretation and voted for military bills in the Continental Congress. Zubly's crime was rather one of excessive caution. His ambivalent relationship with the Revolutionary movement in Georgia mirrored the agonizing dilemma confronting his class, indeed his generation, which sought both liberty and order but feared extreme remedies to secure them. Zubly's life thus serves as an object lesson in the vulnerability of men of fixed beliefs and conservative temperament in the midst of revolutionary ferment. Death cut short his torment. On 23 July 1781, John Joachim Zubly, broken in body and spirit, passed away quietly in Savannah, the unacknowledged intellectual father of the Georgia revolution he did not want, and that no longer wanted him.

Editorial Method

The pamphlets and newspaper essays reproduced in this volume represent Zubly's principal contributions to the constitutional and ideological debates of the Revolutionary period. The pamphlets and essays are reprinted as found in the originals with the exceptions that superscripts have been lowered to the line, ligatures have been broken into their separate characters, and eighteenth-century tailed characters have been modernized. Also, the editor has silently corrected minor typographical errors in the originals, generally spelled out abbreviations of books and references to Scripture, and rendered dates and biblical citations in arabic numerals. More important, the editor has set the names of people, places, and nations in roman face rather than in italics or in small capitals, as they are in the originals—except where altering the original italics or small capitals impaired Zubly's emphasis or meaning. Because of the poor condition of the originals of these rare documents, it was often necessary to reconstruct Zubly's words from more than one copy of each pamphlet or newspaper essay, or by referring to a manuscript copy when available. If, as in a few cases, a word or line in the original is torn or illegible, this fact is so indicated: [Ed. torn] or [Ed. illegible]. Editorial additions and emendations are set in brackets. A source note for each document indicates the location of the best original copy of the work.

PAMPHLETS

Pamphlet 1

THE STAMP-ACT REPEALED

1766

The Stamp Act crisis of 1765 bred a large pamphlet literature in the American colonies. The Americans' response to Parliament's attempt to impose an internal tax on the colonies was the first truly "national" political event in the colonies. It was also the first Anglo-American controversy in which Georgians fully participated. Although Georgia's "patriots" did not refuse the stamps, or join the Stamp Act Congress, or honor the boycott of British goods, or engage in much violence—as did patriots in other colonies—they did begin to sort out their political beliefs and to discover common ideological bonds with American Whigs elsewhere. More than anything else, the pamphlet literature of the day introduced Georgians to political thinking in the other colonies.

Americans greeted Parliament's repeal of the Stamp Act in 1766 with relief and celebration. John J. Zubly captured the feelings of other prominent Georgians in 1766 who had recoiled from the strong words and threats of the Stamp Act crisis but also who had resented Parliament's encroachment on American rights. His sermon, *The Stamp-Act Repealed*, stressed obedience to law and the reciprocal obligations of both Christian rulers and subjects to honor law and order. Printed and reprinted at the behest of hearers and readers, Zubly's first political pamphlet enjoyed wide currency in the colonies, probably because it reflected general American political and constitutional attitudes at the time.

The pamphlet was first published in Savannah in 1766 by James Johnston. A second edition appeared in 1766, published in Savannah by James Johnston, in Charleston by Peter Timothy, and in Philadelphia by Henry Miller.

Source: Rare Books Room, University of Georgia Library

A
S E R M O N,

Preached in the Meeting at Savannah
in Georgia, June 25th, 1766.

By J. J. Zubly, V. D. M.

Published at the Request and Expence of the Hearers.

*Brethren, ye have been called unto liberty; only
use not liberty as an occasion to the flesh.
But if ye bite and devour one another, take heed
that ye be not consumed one of another.*
Galatians 5:13, 15.

Savannah: Printed by James Johnston.
1766.

The STAMP-ACT REPEALED, & c.

TEXT. Zechariah 8:10, 11, 12.

For before these days there was no hire for man, nor any hire for beast; neither was there any peace to him that went out, or came in, because of the affliction: for I set all men everyone against his neighbour. But now I will not be unto the residue of this people as in the former days, saith the Lord of hosts. For the seed shall be prosperous: the vine shall give her fruit, and the ground shall give her increase, and the heavens shall give their dew: and I will cause the remnant of this people to possess all these things.

It is remarkable that after Israel had conquered all their enemies, and taken possession of the land promised unto their fathers, they were very near breaking out into a civil war among themselves, and no sooner were they freed of any apprehension from powerful and troublesome neighbours, but the spirit of discord had well nigh succeeded in transferring the seat of war into their own bowels. We have an account of this important event in the 22d chapter of the Book of Joshua, and the sum of it amounts to this: The tribes of Reuben, Gad, and half the tribe of Manasseh, being settled on one, and all the rest of the tribes on the other side of the waters of Jordan, the former thought it necessary to erect an altar on the borders of their frontier, thereby to testify that tho' Jordan was their boundary, yet they were the same people, united by the same ties, natural, religious & political, and that they meant by this altar to inculcate and impress with these sentiments the minds of their latest posterity. The rest of the nation however took the alarm at their proceedings, looked upon this as a step towards independency, and separation from the rest of their brethren, and as they considered the matter in this view, it could not appear otherwise to them but exceeding alarming. Accordingly we are told, when the children of Israel heard of it, the whole congregation gathered themselves to go up to war against them; Joshua 22:12. Their minds were thoroughly enflamed, and every thing ready for blood and slaughter. Among all this enraged multitude it seems there were yet some men of moderation, and their lenient and healing counsels were the saving of the people. These tribes were but lately returned from acting the part of faithful auxiliaries to their brethren; it was not at all probable that those meant to separate their interests from that of the whole stock, who had given such signal proofs of their attachment to the rest; before things are carried to the last extremity, a solemn message is sent to the suspected tribes, and when they came rightly to understand one another, the fidelity of the three distinct tribes fully appeared, and, instead of looking upon them as offenders, we are told their answer pleased those sent among them,

> *And Phinehas the son of Eleazar the priest said unto the children of Reuben, and to the children of Gad, and to the children of Manasseh, This day we perceive that the Lord is among us, because ye have not committed this trespass against the Lord: now ye have delivered the children of Israel out of the hand of the Lord. And Phinehas the Son of Eleazar the priest, and the princes, returned from the children of Reuben, and from the children of Gad, out of the land of Gilead, unto the land of Canaan, to the children of Israel, and brought them word again. And the thing pleased the children of Israel; and the children of Israel blessed God, and did not intend to go up against them in battle, to destroy the land wherein the children of Reuben and Gad dwelt;* Joshua 22:31, 32, 33.

The spark which had like to kindle so great a fire was reasonably extinguished, a good understanding and mutual harmony restored, every man returned to his home and lived quietly under his vine and fig-tree in the land which God had so lately given unto them.

Methinks whoever peruses this account with attention may perceive some parallel between the case of Israel and what was lately our own. You all know that for some time past the situation between us and our brethren on the other side of the water has been exceeding alarming. Complaints ran high, and it was even talked of that the ten tribes intended to go to war against their brethren, and that notwithstanding during a very late war these had given every possible token of loyalty and attachment. An unhappy ill-advised act of the British legislature laid the foundation of our griefs, and it seemed as tho' the continuance of that act and an universal alienation of minds must go hand in hand, the consequences of which might easily be foreseen, they are not to be expressed, because they cannot be thought of without horror.

There were not wanting in Britain, nor yet in America, some of the descendants of the young counsellors of Rehoboam who would have convinced us of the justice of that act by deadly arguments, and would not have been unwilling to see America ruled with a rod of iron, but blessed be God who defeated their counsels, who placed a king on the British throne as tender of the liberty of the subject as jealous of the glory of his own government; blessed be God in whose hands are the hearts of all men, that he inclined the British parliament to hear the cries of the innocent, and, by a just, noble, and generous repeal of that ill-concerted measure, to dissipate our fears, remove our difficulties, restore our confidence, to give us a pleasing opportunity to offer our publick thanks unto Britain's God, and, like on the jubilee of old, to proclaim liberty throughout all the land to all the inhabitants thereof.

I do not know any event ever happened to British-America more deserving of a publick day of thanksgiving throughout all that wide extended empire, and I would in the most serious manner call upon my congregation to offer thanks unto the Most High, because he has been favourable unto our land, and also to make a proper return to our most gracious king, and the British legislature, for the removing of our shoulders from the burden, and delivering our hands from the pots:

> My heart is toward the governors of Israel that offered themselves willingly among the people. Bless ye the Lord. They that were delivered from the noise of archers in the places of drawing water; there shall they rehearse the righteous acts of the Lord, even the righteous acts towards the inhabitants of his villages in Israel: then shall the people of the Lord go down to the gates. Judges 5:9, 11.

The words which I have read unto you will afford us ample matter for suitable meditation on this happy event; they are words of God himself, and in their first intention are designed to put Israel in mind of the pleasing change of their publick affairs from the time they had begun to lay the foundation of the temple: Before that time we are told there was no hire for man nor beast, no peace in all their border, and the hand of God against them to visit them with severe afflictions; and after that God declares, that he will be no longer to them as in days past, that now they may expect every kind of blessing, and that the remnant of the nation should henceforth possess and enjoy all these things.

As these words are expressive of the gloomy state of the nation before that period, and the pleasing prospect now offered, they will want but very little accommodation to our present purpose.

My business therefore, under divine assistance, will be to

Take some notice of the day of Jacob's trouble, and the melancholy state of the remnant of Judah while the hand of the Lord was against them. I would, in the next place, make a few remarks on the great and precious promises given unto the penitent remnant of the Jewish nation. And, lastly, endeavour to make some improvement on the whole suitable to the design of our present meeting.

May I be enabled to speak on these things in a becoming manner, and may we not dare to put God off with a little outward shew, or the empty formality of this meeting, but may we offer up soul and body unto our sovereign benefactor and preserver; may this be the tribute of our gratitude and our reasonable service!

Mercies received appear the greater when they come after a long and painful want; the return of the light is the more acceptable for the preceeding darkness; and so God here puts them in mind of the distress under which they laboured till now, that the promise of peace and plenty might be the more welcome. If we consider the words in their full extent they may lead us back to the state of the nation at and during the invasion of the Chaldeans, and before Judah was carried into captivity; then indeed there was no hire for man nor beast, no peace to him that came in nor went out: Besides the scourge of war, Judah also suffered by drought and famine: "Judah mourneth, and the gates thereof languish: they are black unto the ground; because the ground was chapt, for there was no rain in the earth, the plowmen were ashamed, they covered their heads." Jeremiah 14:2, 4. All this calamity increased in proportion as the Chaldeans got the country in their possession, and laid a close siege to the holy city and to their sanctuary. This mournful description was more than once applicable to the land of Judah, and it is mentioned as one of their usual afflictions when they departed from God; *In those times there was no peace to him that went out, nor to him that came in, but great vexations were upon all the inhabitants of the countries,* 2 Chronicles 15:5. It is true indeed by this time the days of captivity were accomplished, a number of them returned to the land of their fathers, but even on their return their situation was still deplorable, and their difficulties exceeding great; Jerusalem was a heap of stones, and all the country around a mere desolation; they met with opposition from the Samaritans, and all their afflictions had not yet made them wise enough to agree among themselves; their neglect also in building the house of God had brought on them very severe judgments; they looked for much and it came to little, and when they brought even that little home God did blow upon it; when a man came to an heap of twenty measures there were but ten, and when one came to the wine press to draw out fifty vessels there were but twenty, and all this because the house of the Lord lay waste, and every man ran to his own house; Haggai 1:9; 2:16. Such was their wretched state at the time of this prophecy, and how wretched must a people be where there is no hire for man nor beast, no peace in coming in and going out, and where the judgments of God set every man against his neighbour in the greatness of the affliction.

When there is no hire for man or beast, it is a plain sign that business is at a stand, and every stagnation of this kind threatens the very vitals of a country. This calamity falls heaviest upon the lower and middling class of people, who make up the body and the most useful part of every nation. When the fields lie waste, the husbandman mourneth, the necessaries of life are with difficulty procured by the rich, and hunger and want seem unavoidable to the poor; sometimes when the multitude of inhabitants is greater than the land can bear, even the industrious cannot long find employ, and for want of that are reduced to distress; sometimes when by war and other devastations countries are so drained that labourers are not to be had, a man is more precious than fine gold, yea than the golden wedge of ophir; Isaiah 13:12. Though these cases be opposite yet the effect is the same; neither does it affect those only who are more immediate sufferers; the rich cannot live without the poor, and he that hires cannot do without some one to hire. Trade may indeed supply the wants of a nation, but trade is only an artificial supply; a country that has room for the spreading of its inhabitants, and has ground for tillage proportionable to their increase, must have greatly the advantage over a mere trading nation; the former can find those resources within itself for which the latter must be indebted to trade with its colonies and other nations. The gains of trade may possibly be larger than those by cultivation, but a country well cultivated will always nourish and maintain its inhabitants, a country blessed with natural advantages will easily procure the conveniencies and even superfluities of life, either within itself, or at least by the exports of its natural produce; *The profit of the earth is for all, even the king himself is served by the field;* Ecclesiastes 5:9. but when there is no hire neither for man nor beast, it is a sure sign that cultivation and trade is languishing, and it is with bodies politick as it is with the natural body when once they begin to languish, if a remedy is not speedily found out and adhibited, it must affect every part of the whole, and the whole gradually fall into decay and consumption.

This was the case of the small remnant left in Canaan; they were only some of the meanest of the people, husbandmen and dressers of vineyards, and it seems probable that even these were rather slaves than subjects to the king of Babylon; hence they complain that they are servants in their own land, Nehemiah 9:36. *Our inheritance is turned to strangers, our houses to aliens. Our necks are under persecution: we labour, and have no rest;* Lamentations 5:2, 5.

During all these disasters, it was doubtless an additional and severe affliction, that there was no peace to him that came in nor went out; those that were already captives in Babylon could not with any safety return into their own land, and they that were left in it, and fain wanted to retire into Egypt, or any other place of security, could not go out; and even among themselves there was no peace, no unanimity, but continual jarrings and discords. Some very remarkable instances of the kind are mentioned in the forty-first chapter of Jeremiah; even after their return all things were so unsettled, that, notwithstanding the hopeful appearance of their being once more restored to their own land, there was no peace to him that came in nor to him that went out; this was little better than war, and war in its best light is as destruction of the human species, but war among brethren, intestine feuds and civil wars as they are called, of the worst evil are the worst species; when the right hand is lifted up against the left, when the members of the same body seek each other's destruction, the whole body must needs feel, and if they continue, be destroyed by it. And here I cannot but remember the address made by some general to an Abyssinian monarch, who could imagine it worth his while to go to war with his own subjects, in order to make them submit to some religious rites and ceremonies, which he thought himself in conscience bound to impose upon them, and which they thought themselves in conscience bound to suffer any hardship rather than submit unto; a battle was fought, the prince was victorious, the field covered with the slain, when the general thus addressed the conquering monarch, pointing at the heaps of the slaughtered; "These were your own subjects, and in every other cause willing to shed their blood and lay down their lives for you—they were our brethren, our own flesh and blood, and every victory of the kind you gain over them is a step towards the entire ruin of your own nation." Methinks the warrior that spoke so, spoke like a sensible man and good patriot. The king gained the battle and gave up the point, wisely considering, that the gaining the affection of loyal subjects would be a greater security to his reign and kingdom than any submission he could force them unto by any act of mere power.

Union of minds and interests is the real strength of any nation, a kingdom divided against itself cannot stand; Israel fell indeed by the sword of the Chaldeans, but their own internal divisions gave the finishing stroke; the distress which they had brought upon themselves was great exceedingly, the hand of the Lord was stretched out against them, and the people returned not to him who did smite them; their affliction, instead of humbling them before God, only served to heighten their animosities against one another; their affliction is expressly mentioned as the cause of their disturbances, they hated, mistrusted, supplanted one another, and therefore there was no peace to him that came in, nor yet to him that went out.

There was no peace to him that came in, nor to him that went out, *because of the affliction.* When people think they have nothing more to hope they are apt to conclude they have also nothing to fear. When tyranny and oppression once arrive at a certain height, they become intolerable even to loyalty, and must recoil upon their authors. It is dangerous for sovereigns to make the experiment, how much their subjects may be able and willing to bear. Oppression makes even a wise man mad, and when any kingdom is all in confusion within itself, when violence beareth rule, and the good of the community ceases to be the supreme law, when unreasonable burdens are laid upon some to procure ease unto others, when jarring interests and different factions divide the state and impose upon the sovereign, such a nation not only ceases to be formidable to its neighbours and enemies, but it is also in very great danger of falling into the condition within itself which is here described, no peace to him that goes out nor to him that comes in.

Neither do all these things spring up out of the dust, or come upon a people by chance, or in the common course of things: *Shall there be evil in the city, and the Lord hath not done it?* Amos 3:6. God indeed *is not the author of confusion but of peace,* 1 Corinthians 14:33. He does not love iniquity but he also hateth oppression. Sometimes the sins of the subject are punished by arbitrary sovereigns, and oppression and arbitrary power are sometimes visited (and overset too) by the violence of unruly subjects.

There is a very remarkable instance of this in the reign of the son of Salomon. He came to the throne by hereditary right, unhappily for him he and his council probably thought that right indefeasible, his father had made his yoke heavy upon the land, at his accession to the throne, the subjects modestly represent their grievance, the sons of violence reject the moderate request of the sons of just and decent freedom, a tax, till then unheard of it would seem, is imposed, an officer is sent to gather the odious tribute, but the officer, by the verdict of all Israel, is stoned with stones, the king himself retires with precipitation, a war is resolved on, one hundred fourscore thousand men take up arms against Israel, and appear ready to fall on; but the word of God came unto Shemaiah, the man of God, saying, Speak unto Rehoboam, the son of Salomon king of Judah, and unto all the house of Judah and Benjamin, and to the remnant of the people, saying, Thus saith the Lord, ye shall not go up, nor fight against your brethren the children of Israel; return every man to his house, for this thing is of me, saith the Lord. And we are further told, they hearkened therefore to the word of the Lord, and returned to depart according to the word of the Lord; thus the shedding of blood was at that time prevented, and a stop put to a cruel and intestine war by an immediate interposition of divine providence, and that at the expence of Rehoboam, who was never able to bring back the ten tribes, but they continued a separate kingdom till they fell into the hands of their common enemy.

I do not mention all this to justify or approve in every respect the conduct of the ten tribes, but to observe that if Rehoboam had taken the salutary advice of his old prudent counsellors, the defection and ensuing division would not have happened. (1 Kings 12. *throughout*.)

God cannot delight in, bless, or approve any thing that is wicked: *Though hand join in hand, the wicked shall not be unpunished,* Proverbs 11:21. Oppression and rebellion are both wicked, and may become by a righteous judgment of God a scourge to one another. God abhors sin and evil, but even sin and evil is not committed without his knowledge and sufferance; he forms the light and creates darkness, he makes peace and creates evil, he the Lord does all these things; Isaiah 45:7. His wisdom and justice in some cases may permit the peace and tranquility of a sinful nation to be interrupted or taken away, by suffering the rulers to be intoxicated with too high notions of power, or by suffering the subjects to go beyond the just bounds, in asserting and maintaining their just rights, and confusion and disorders are the natural effects of all this, and it is as natural a consequence that in those days there is no hire for man nor beast, no peace to him that goes out nor comes in, and that every man is against his neighbour on account of the affliction.

Thus far the gloomy part; let us next take notice of the pleasing prospect that opens by the change of the scene and the divine promise.

What God himself marks out as a very signal divine blessing, men certainly should receive as a precious mark of his favour. To remove so great an affliction, and to change their mournful condition into peace, plenty, and liberty, must be unto them an irresistible proof that God was again returned unto them in mercy; and this indeed he assures them of in express words:

> *I will not be unto the residue of my people as in former days, saith the Lord of hosts; for the seed shall be prosperous, the vine shall give her fruit, and the ground shall give her increase, and the heavens shall give their dew, and I will make the remnant of my people to possess all these things.*

Here is a general promise that God would not deal with them as he had of late. God changeth not neither in his nature or purposes; there is no shadow with him of variableness or turning; but there is a connection between man's carriage towards God and the way of God towards man: *The Lord is with you, if ye be with him; and if ye seek him, he will be found of you; but if ye forsake him, he will forsake you;* 2 Chronicles 15:2. With the pure he shews himself pure; and in this sense it is said, that with the froward he will shew himself froward; Psalm 18:26. National sins bring on national calamities, and national reformation a national blessing; the same God that threatens to pluck up, pull down, and destroy a rebellious kingdom, will also turn from the evil he has threatened when they return from the evil which they have committed; and that this was the case at this time in Israel appears plain from the prayers of Daniel, Ezra, Nehemiah, and many others; while they continued rebellious, the hand of the Lord should continue to be heavy upon them, but now they returned unto God, he would return unto them in mercy.

The labourer and husbandman should now be employed, the fields should be cultivated, and in the land that lay desolate, and almost uninhabited, in the land that was without man or beast, fields should be bought again for money, and there should be hire for man and beast; *Jerusalem should be inhabited as towns without walls, for the multitude of men and cattle therein,* Zechariah 2:4.

Their coming in and their going out should be in peace, he should strengthen the bars of their gates, and give peace unto their borders.

They should no longer be a disunited nation, but unite like the heart of one man; *I will* (saith God) *give them one heart and one way, that they may fear me for ever, for the good of them and of their children after them,* Jeremiah 32:39.

Neither does God only promise a removal of those evils under which in former days they groaned, but there is life also in his favour; God in his very nature is kind unto all, and his tender mercies are over all the works of his hands. Nothing but mercy would always attend man, had not man turned away from the love of his maker. Sin only makes a separation between us and our God, and when the cause of his displeasure is removed, the streams of his kindness follow their natural course, and flow down upon man. The order and economy of the whole creation speaks aloud the kind designs of God to man; fury is not in him; punishing is his strange and the doing kindness is his natural work: Accordingly on their being turned unto him, and he unto them, he promises them the very reverse of the evils under which they had hitherto laboured; plenty instead of famine, the dew of heaven and rain in due season instead of drought, and every kind of temporal prosperity and abundance in the land to which they were now restored; the heavens should not be of brass, nor the earth of iron; God would no longer forbid the clouds to rain upon them, but he would hear the heavens, and they should hear the earth, and the earth should hear corn, wine, and oil, and these should hear Jezreel, Hoseah 2:21, 22. Neither should these blessings be only transitory but durable, the days of their mourning should be at an end, and the remnant of the nation now returned unto the Lord and to his sanctuary should rejoice in the possession of all these blessings; they should no longer hang up their harps by the willows, but again sing the songs of Sion in their own land, and give thanks unto the Lord, who had brought them again from the heathen, and turned their captivity like the streams in the south: *O Lord, I will praise thee; though thou wast angry with me, thine anger is turned away, and thou comfortedst me. Cry out and shout, thou inhabitant of Zion; for great is the holy one of Israel in the midst of thee;* Isaiah 12:1, 6.

And this naturally leads me, which was the last thing proposed, to endeavour an improvement of what has been said suitable to the design of our present meeting.

Some among us possibly may be ready to ask, what meaneth this service, it is neither Sabbath nor new moon. To them I would answer: We are met to-day to offer our thanks unto the great ruler of all things, that he has averted from us a very great evil, which in part indeed was come upon us already, and which, considered as a punishment of our sins, we but too justly deserve.

We are met to offer thanks unto God, that our invaluable privileges are preserved, that our land is not become a land of slaves, nor our fields a scene of blood. We are met to give thanks unto God, that our gloomy apprehensions are removed, that the British parliament has seen the justice of our complaints, that our superiors, by this act of justice and moderation, have shewn themselves superior to themselves. We rejoice that affection and confidence is restored between us and our mother country. We are met to give thanks unto the Most High, that, by the repeal of this act, there is hire again for man and beast, that our ports are open, our trade unmolested, that we may go to and fro in safety, that men are no more set every man against his neighbour, that Manasseh is not against Ephraim, nor Ephraim against Manasseh; and we are also met to pray, that our posterity may enjoy all these things, that mercy and truth may be the blessing of our days, and of our whole nation, and that our civil and religious liberties may be preserved inviolable till time shall be no more.

I suppose there are few or none hearing me that think we have not now any particular cause to be thankful; if any should think so, I should despair of convincing them that we really have; it is generally observed, that we best know to value our mercies from the want of them, but I sincerely wish there may never be any conviction of this kind in all the British dominions.

Come then, my friends, let us make mention of the mercies of the Lord according to all his goodness, and according to the multitude of his loving-kindnesses which he has shewn unto the British nation. Your own minds will too easily suggest unto you what must have been our case if this unhappy act had not been repealed; and should not our gratitude bear some proportion to the greatness of our escape? Should we not thankfully review every circumstance that brought about this pleasing event, and offer our humble and sincere thanks to the kind providence of God, that gave success to the noble and unwearied endeavours of our friends for that purpose? I think the almost unanimous, steady, and prudent union of the Americans, does honour to their present generation, and as it was very providential, and to many I suppose very unexpected, so I look upon it as a real matter of gratitude. I would not be understood to vindicate every thing that a confused multitude or a few individuals may have done in a time of publick confusion, but the manly, nervous, and constitutional representations made by the representatives of the people, may be looked upon as one of the means which providence has made use of to set the justice of the American complaints in its true light, and to excite us able and worthy friends to stand up as noble champions for our cause. Had a whole people, who looked upon themselves as oppressed and dealt with contrary to their natural privileges, been disregarded, there is no saying what might have been the consequence; and the consequence must have been felt on each side of the water; we must sink or swim together. That all our fears have subsided, that all this jealousy has been removed, that the dark night which seemed to hang over our heads is turned into the light of a hopeful morning, surely calls for our loudest and sincerest thanksgiving: Offer therefore unto God thanks, give unto the Lord glory and strength, let those that cried unto the Lord in trouble, and he saved them out of their distresses, give thanks unto his name. *He brought them out of darkness, and the shadow of death, and brake their bands in sunder. Oh, that men would praise the Lord for his goodness, and for his wonderful works to the children of men!* Psalm 107:14, 15.

And, in the next place, let our thanks be given to our great and good King, the friend of mankind, and the father of his people. He glories to reign in the hearts of his subjects; and no king can have a better title to the hearts of those over whom he rules. If it is a *pleasure to him* to repeal an act that gives pain unto his subjects, may all his servants copy after him, and act worthy of the principles of so great a king, and so good a master; and may every possible demonstration of loyalty and affection be ever paid him by all, but especially by his American subjects. The Americans, who, I believe I may justly say to a man, have been friends to the succession in his illustrious house, if possible, must now shew a still greater degree of attachment in return for this royal condescension and favour.

> Bless, O God, the king; long let the crown flourish on his head. Give him the desires of his soul; may he ever be a king after thine own heart; give him wise counsellors and faithful subjects; let his reign be long, peaceable, and glorious; may the

wicked never stand before his throne, and so his throne be ever established in righteousness; and may our posterity in some distant generation pay him the mournful tear, when he is taken up into a kingdom that cannot be shaken.

Let me further beseech you, my hearers, to remember the rock from which you were hewn; by descent or incorporation we are now all Britons; let Britain's interests be ever dear to us all. Pray for the prosperity of the nation, for in her prosperity you shall prosper. We have seen our mother-country act the part of a tender parent; let us never fail to act the part of truly dutiful children. May Britons have a love for one another which many waters cannot quench. May eastern and western Britons ever be more firmly united than Joseph and Ephraim, which were made like one stick in the hands of the prophet. If God abhors him who soweth discord among brethren, let us abhor them who would do any thing that might tend towards a separation of interests or an alienation of affections. Let Britain and British America ever be like one heart and one soul; he that would divide them, *anathema sit,* let him be held accursed by both.

It is a remark of the wisest king, *Evil men understand not judgment, but they that fear the Lord understand* (take notice of, observe, and improve) *all things,* Proverbs 28:5. Let us remember then, and let our posterity know it, that if a prudent, proper remonstrance had not been made and received, the year 1765 must have been the fatal year from which the loss of American liberty must have been dated. Let us also remember, that the year following was remarkable for the repeal of an act that give so universal uneasiness, and had like to be so destructive to Britain on each side of the great waters.*

If we record these remarkable interesting events, it may not be improper to subjoin: Fear God, honour the king, stand fast in your liberty, and be not entangled with the yoke of bondage.

Let us forgive our enemies and honour our friends, the more so because some of them (which is a pleasing honourable circumstance)

---

*The Stamp-Act was to have taken place Nov. 1, 1765, and it took place in all provinces conquered from the French and Spaniards in the last war, also in most of the islands, the military government of Nova Scotia; and in Georgia stamps were for shipping only. The said act was repealed in the house of commons by a majority of 108, and a majority of 34 in the house of Lords; and the repealing act received the royal assent March 18, 1766.

have at all times signally distinguished themselves in the cause of liberty, and deserved greatly of the British nation. Let every injury received be written in sand, and all kindness be preserved in marble, and every friend of liberty and his country be held in everlasting remembrance.

The design of the repeal was to remove inconveniencies and consequences detrimental to the British kingdoms; let us then do nothing which might continue those inconveniencies which that wise and salutary act means to prevent.

Especially let us never give any handle to any to call in question our loyalty to the king, and our sincere and firm attachment to our mother-country; let us ever be zealous for its prosperity, and promote it to the utmost of our power; let each one of us say upon this occasion:

> *Pray for the peace of Britain; they shall prosper that love thee.*
> *Peace be within thy walls, and prosperity within thy palaces.*
> *For my brethren and companions sakes I will now say, Peace*
> *unto thee. Because of the house of the Lord our God I will seek*
> *thy good;* Psalm 122:6, 7, 8, 9.

Let us pay a chearful obedience to the laws of the realm, and on all occasions approve ourselves worthy subjects of the best of kings. Let us always return a filial respect to the indulgence and tenderness of an affectionate parent. Let us convince even those who have taken upon them to vilify and misrepresent the Americans how greatly they have been mistaken, and how very unjust have been their inflammatory reflections. Let the mean tools of faction be put to shame, (if they are capable of that) by a conduct the very reverse of that which they would have laid to our charge. Let us by well-doing put to silence the ignorance or malice of foolish or wicked men. Let every distinction of names and parties, every national prejudice, be buried in everlasting oblivion. Let the good man whoever he be be the object of universal love and esteem, and the bad man the only object of aversion and abhorrence. Let there be no other emulation but who shall best promote the good of the whole. Render to every one his due, tribute to whom tribute, custom to whom custom, fear to whom fear, honour to whom honour.

> *Submit yourselves to every ordinance of man for the Lord's*
> *sake, whether it be to the king as supreme; Or unto governors,*
> *as unto them that are sent by him for the punishment of evil-*
> *doers, and for the praise of them that do well: As free, and not*
> *using your liberty for a cloke of maliciousness, but as the*
> *servants of God;* 1 Peter 2:13, 14, 16.

There is a very essential difference between liberty and licentiousness, and it is highly criminal under pretence of the one to indulge the other. If any excess of this kind has been committed, may it be sincerely repented of and carefully avoided for the future, *so speak and so act as they that shall be judged by the law of liberty*, James 2:13.

Above all, let us ever remember, that *righteousness exalteth a nation, but sin is a reproach to any people*, Proverbs 14:34. Our temporal happiness cannot be more surely promoted, nor our civil and religious liberties be better secured, than by a life suitable to the dignity of our christian profession. Christianity is a benevolent institution, that bears a friendly aspect to civil government, and does not in the least diminish the natural or civil rights of the subject. It teaches superiors to rule in the fear of God, and to look upon their subjects as their fellow creatures and brethren, whose happiness to promote is the very design of their office; it engages subjects to obey for the Lord's sake, not only to the gentle but also to the froward. We cannot be good christians unless we are also good subjects and good members of the community; let every one then depart from iniquity that is named after Christ. By promoting our eternal we also shall secure our temporal welfare; nothing that has a tendency to make us unhappy hereafter can have any tendency to make us happy here. If ever (which God forbid) we should be cursed with a tyrannical oppressive government, our sins must be the cause of it. O! let us not sin away our mercies, neither let us sin any more lest something worse befal us. We can never be said to be free while we are the servants of sin, neither can any bondage equal that of being led captive by Satan according to his will; and yet this is the case of every graceless sinner, *While they promise them liberty, they themselves are the servants of corruption: for of whom a man is overcome, of the same is he brought into bondage*, 2 Peter 2:19. How insignificant will our struggle for liberty appear, while we deliberately give up ourselves to be slaves unto lust; if we abhor bondage, O! let us at least take care that our bondage may not be eternal; chains of eternal darkness are the portion of every impenitent sinner; and *Know ye not that to whom ye yield yourselves to obey, his servants ye are to whom ye obey, whether of sin unto death, or of obedience unto righteousness?* Romans 6:16. When will the poor captive begin to feel his fetters and groan for liberty? Where the spirit of the Lord is there is liberty, and where the spirit of the world and sin reigns there is slavery and bondage. Every deliberate sin helps to rivet the chain, and the longer vicious habits are indulged the more difficult it is to shake off their dominion. Man was made free, but he also was made good; the sinner has lost his original goodness, and liberty departed from him, when he hearkened to the voice of the tempter; one cannot be recovered without the other; if we will be truly free we must become truly good; we must be renewed in the spirit of our mind, and be created after God in righteousness and true holiness, Ephesians 4:24. This, my hearers, is the true idea of liberty, to be freed from every hurtful constraint, and to be able to do all that tends to make us truly happy, or else to be free indeed is neither more nor less than to be heartily engaged for him whose service is perfect freedom.

O! My hearers, with what pleasure did we lately receive the news which makes the subject of our thanksgiving to-day, how did joy sparkle in every countenance, how warmly did we shake hands and congratulate one another upon the occasion; we seemed like people that had been apprehensive of being shipwrecked and happily made a harbour; we seemed almost like animals in the air pump to whom breath and life is restored by the return of that element; never before have I seen any news received with equal and so universal satisfaction; and all that was right; there were reasons more than sufficient for great fear, and when they subsided it was meet they should be succeeded by joy as great: But with what woeful coldness and indifference have too many carried themselves towards the best news that was ever sent from heaven upon earth; how little we have been affected with the glad tidings of great joy, that unto us is a saviour born. Jesus Christ himself came to preach deliverance to the captives, to set at liberty them that were bruised, to preach the acceptable year of the Lord; he was in bonds that he might break our chains, he laid down his life as a ransom for those that were in bondage of Satan and sin, he died that we might eternally live. Our king is also our saviour, his subjects are the purchase of his blood, and he invites strangers to come and kiss his sceptre, with no other view but that he may have the pleasure of making them eternally happy. Behold how much has he loved us, and shall we now escape if we neglect his great salvation? How ungrateful are we to him, and how unjust to ourselves, if we chuse to continue in that slavery which he has been at such amazing pains to redeem us from.

Come then, my friends, let us embrace this opportunity and become his real subjects; let us chearfully forsake the service of vanity and sin, and unreservedly give ourselves up to the Lord that bought us. How happy would it be, if from this pleasing event we might also date our sincere and hearty endeavours at least, to become his freemen, that, being delivered from the fear of our enemies, we might serve him *in holiness and righteousness all the days of our life,* Luke 1:75. then, and not till then, shall we be a people really free and truly happy; then will the son make us free, and we shall be free indeed; then shall we have a most indisputable right to the glorious liberty of the sons of God.

When shall the kingdom of Christ extend over all the earth, and homage be paid him by those who sit now in darkness and in the shadow of death? When shall his gentle reign be the bless of every nation, ignorance, slavery, and superstition, be altogether banished from the earth, and the blessings of peace, liberty, and the gospel, be scattered over the whole wide creation?

For these things, my brethren, let us pray, thy kingdom come, and seeing we look for a kingdom that cannot be shaken, let us by faith and holiness be daily preparing for the same; there the wicked cease from troubling and the weary are at rest.

Now to the King invisible, immortal, and eternal, to him who is able to keep us, and to present us before God with exceeding great joy, to the only wise God our saviour, be glory and majesty, dominion and power, both now and ever. Amen.

AN HUMBLE ENQUIRY

1769

From the enactment of the Declaratory Act in 1766 to the Boston Massacre in 1770 a series of Parliamentary acts and British administrative policies sorely taxed the colonies. Parliament's attempts to force New York to obey the Quartering Act, its passage of the Townshend duties, the abuses of corrupt customs commissioners in the colonies, Lord Hillsborough's Circular Letter, and the presence of British troops in Boston, among other events, combined to persuade many Americans that the English ministry regarded the colonies with contempt, at best, and as the first projected victims of an evil design to destroy British liberty, at worst. American political and constitutional thinkers began to take a closer look at the implications of the Declaratory Act in which Parliament asserted its claim to legislate for and bind the American colonies and people to its authority "in all cases whatsoever." Such a naked assertion of Parliamentary power aroused American fears of legislative tyranny, and the unlucky and ill-considered British policies fueled such apprehensions. From 1766 through 1770 Americans matured rapidly in their constitutional theory. They began to question Parliament's role to legislate for the empire at all and to posit a theory of divided sovereignty.

Zubly participated in this restructuring of American constitutional thought. His pamphlet, *An Humble Enquiry*, was not a response to any particular incident in Georgia; rather, it grew out of his interest in the external, abstract issues of American and British affairs. Sometimes rambling and confused, it was Zubly's most original contribution to the American Whig definition of constitutions and of Parliament's role in the empire.

Zubly disposed of the artificial distinction some British writers drew between indirect and direct taxes by arguing that no citizen was bound by any law, including tax legislation, to which he had not consented. Zubly almost took the short step to suggest that Parliament had no authority to legislate for America, but like so many other Americans faced with the implications of their arguments about Parliament's limited legislative powers in the empire, Zubly retreated from his own logic.

Zubly's references to natural law and the social contract attested to his knowledge of the social theories of the Enlightenment. More important, his equation of natural law and the British constitution demonstrated that he had embraced the then still forming concept of natural law constitutionalism. Zubly retained his faith in the British constitution as the chief bastion of social and political stability and liberty, and he was confident that within the constitutional framework Americans and the British government could work out their differences, provided that the crown presented its requests in a manner consistent with the natural rights of men and with the civil and constitutional liberty of the British. The British constitution was supreme over all things British, including Parliament and the crown. Parliament could not enact laws contrary to the constitution. In that light, the Declaratory Act was unconstitutional for it violated the natural rights of the Americans, still British subjects, and so the constitution.

The pamphlet was published in Charleston in 1769. Extracts of the pamphlet appeared in the *Georgia Gazette* from 28 June through 5 July 1769, and the entire pamphlet was reprinted in London in 1774, with a few minor changes, under the title, *Great Britain's Right to Tax Her Colonies, Placed in the Clearest Light by a Swiss.*
Source: Rare Books Room, University of Georgia Library

AN
HUMBLE ENQUIRY

Into

The Nature of the Dependency of
the American Colonies upon
the Parliament of Great-Britain,

And

The Right of Parliament to lay Taxes
on the said Colonies.

By a Freeholder of South-Carolina.

A House divided against itself cannot stand.

When people heard ship money demanded *as a right*, and found it by
sworn judges of the law adjudged so, upon such grounds and reasons as
every stander-by was able to swear was not law, and so had lost the
pleasure and delight of being kind and dutiful to the King, and, instead of
GIVING, were required to PAY, and by a logick that left no man any
thing that he might call his own, they no more looked upon it as the case
of one man, but the case of the kingdom, nor as an imposition laid upon
them by the King, but by the judges, which they thought themselves
bound in publick justice not to submit to. It was an observation long ago
of *Thucydides*, "That men are much more passionate for injustice than
for violence, because (saith he) the one proceeding as from an equal
seems rapine, when the other proceeding from a stranger is but the effect
of necessity." —When they saw reason of state urged as elements of law,
judges as sharp-sighted as secretaries of state, judgment of law grounded
upon matter of fact of which there was neither enquiry nor proof, and no
reason given for the payment but what included all the estates of the

standers-by, they had no reason to hope that doctrine, or the promoters of it, would be contained within any bounds; and it is no wonder that they who had so little reason to be pleased with their own condition were no less solicitous for, or apprehensive of the inconveniences that might attend any alteration.—*History of the long Rebellion*, vol. 1, p. 70, 71.

Printed in the Year 1769
[Price Twelve Shillings and Sixpence]
AN HUMBLE ENQUIRY, &C.

Though few or none claim infallibility in express terms, yet it is very difficult ever to persuade some men they are mistaken. We generally have so good an opinion of our own understanding, that insensibly we take it for granted those that do not think as we do must needs be in the wrong. When disputes are once heightened by personal prejudice, or the bitterness of party, it becomes so much the more difficult to the disputants themselves to see their mistakes, and even to bystanders the truth appears wrapped up in a cloud, and through the fog and dust of argument becomes almost imperceptible.

These remarks I believe will particularly hold good in the subject now in agitation between Great-Britain and her colonies, a subject however of too serious a nature to be given up to prejudice, or to be decided by the rage of party. Every argument pro or con deserves to be most carefully weighed, and he that sets the whole in the clearest light does the publick no inconsiderable service, and that whether it be by pointing out the justice of the American claims to Great-Britain, or setting such constitutional arguments before the Americans as must either leave obstinacy inexcusable, or will dispose loyal and reasonable men to a chearful acquiescence.

The argument on which the Americans seem to lay the greatest stress is, they say that it is a principle of the British constitution, that no Englishman ought to be taxed but by his own consent, given either by himself or his representative. I find it admitted by such as disapprove the American claims, that no man is bound by any law to which he hath not given his consent either in person or by a representative. Perhaps these two propositions are not perfectly equivalent; however it seems clear, that he that holds that no man is bound BY ANY LAW to which he has not personally or by a representative consented, must also admit, that no man is bound by any law that lays a tax on him without his consent given by himself or representative. What is true of ALL laws in general must also hold true of EVERY law in particular. If no law can operate upon any man that hath not in the above manner given his assent to it, certainly no such law can be binding upon whole communities, or any considerable part of the whole nation. In the spirit of the above principle, it seems essential to law, that it be assented to by such on whom it is afterwards to operate. To suppose, therefore, that a law is binding upon such as have not given their assent, is to suppose (I argue upon that principle) a law may be valid and binding at the same time it is confessedly destitute of the very essential point to make it so; and if the assent of those that are to be governed by the law is not necessary or essential to the making of it, then representation is a mere superfluous thing, no better than an excrescence in the legislative power, which therefore at any convenient time may be lopped off at pleasure, and without the least danger to the constitution; the governed then have no part in the legislation at all, the will of those in power, whoever they be, is the supreme and sole law, and what have been above asserted to be a constitutional principle seems to me to fall to the ground without remedy to all intents and purposes.

Supposing, on the other hand, that principle, as is asserted to be constitutional, then to me, as is further asserted, it seems to be of the very nature of it, that it be general and hold in all cases. This it does not only clearly imply, but also fully and strongly express; but yet if so, it would also seem that no man, or no people, in no case, or by no power whatever, can be bound to pay a tax to which they have not consented either personally or by their representatives. Every constitutional principle must be general and hold in all cases, and I may add in all places too, for it is usually said that the liberties of an Englishman follow him to the end of the world, much more then must they follow him over all the British dominions; this is so true, that by an express law, the children of British parents, though born in a foreign dominion, are just as much entitled to all British liberties as those who have been born within the realm.

An inference may possibly hence be drawn, that if so, the British colonies are subject to none of the acts of the British Parliament, (*scil.* because they never assented to them neither in person nor by representative) and therefore must be considered as independent of the legal or parliamentary power of Great Britain. I confess I should be sorry to see America independent of Great Britain, and if any of the arguments the Americans make use of imply an independency on the mother state, I should shrewdly suspect there must be some fallacy couched under an otherwise specious appearance. The sum and strength of this inference I conceive lies thus: The British legislature must be the supreme power in all the British dominions, and if so, all the British dominions ought to pay obedience in all cases to all the laws in which they are mentioned that may be enacted by the British Parliament, and to refuse obedience in any such case is to declare themselves an independent people.

I freely own I have not heard any thing stronger said in favour of taxation by the British Parliament, and I think this argument is highly deserving the most serious consideration. Every good man would wish to hear the voice of dispassionate reason before he forms his judgment in any debate. Vulgar prejudices may sway vulgar minds, but a wise man is neither carried away by the torrent of power, nor the blast of popularity. I would endeavour therefore to consider this argument with all the candour and impartiality I am capable of; I would do it with a mind open to conviction, and with steadiness sufficient to follow truth wherever she may lead me.

To have a clear view how far this argument may affect the present question between Great Britain and her colonies, it will be necessary carefully to state the relation which they bear to one another; without this we shall never have a precise and determinate idea of the matter. The argument I think is made up of two propositions, *viz.*

> The Parliament of Great Britain is the supreme legislature in all the British empire.
>
> All the British dominions therefore ought to pay obedience thereto in all cases and to all the laws in which they are mentioned, and to refuse obedience to any such is to declare themselves an independent people.

Before I proceed to take a distinct view of each of these propositions, I repeat, that they are said to be built upon a constitutional principle, and that this principle must be general and hold in all cases; this must undoubtedly be admitted, for what enters into the very essence of the constitution must doubtless operate as far as the constitution itself. Let us now proceed to consider every part of these two propositions distinctly, and this must infallibly lead us to form a sound judgment of the whole.

The kingdom of Great Britain consists of two parts, north and south, or England and Scotland, united since 1707 into one kingdom, under the name of Great Britain. This union hath not been so full and absolute, as to put both kingdoms in all respects upon a perfect equality; but tho' the legislature is the same, yet the laws and the administration of justice are not the same in every instance. The same legislature making laws that affect only the one or the other of these kingdoms, and even laws made to be binding upon both, do not affect both alike, of which the difference in raising the supplies by land tax is a very full and striking proof, this could not be the case if the union between the two kingdoms was so entire and absolute, as for instance between England and the principality of Wales.

The British Empire is a more extensive word, and should not be confounded with the kingdom of Great Britain; it consists of England, Scotland, Ireland, the Islands of Man, Jersey, Guernsey, Gibraltar, and Minorca, &c. in the Mediterranean; Senegal, &c. in Africa; Bombay, &c. in the East-Indies; and the Islands and Colonies in North America, &c. As England, strictly so called, is at the head of this great body, it is called the mother country; all the settled inhabitants of this vast empire are called Englishmen, but individuals, from the place of their nativity or residence, are called English, Scotch, Irish, Welch, Americans, &c.

Scotland and Ireland were originally distinct kingdoms and nations, but the colonies in America, being settled upon lands discovered by the English, under charters from the crown of England, were always considered as a part of the English nation, and of the British empire, and looked upon as dependent upon England; I mean, that before the union of the two kingdoms, (and very few colonies have been settled since) they depended on England only, and even now I suppose are rather considered as a dependance upon England than of the two kingdoms united under the name of Great Britain. Were it not for the union, which incorporates the two kingdoms, the colonies never would have depended on that part of Britain called Scotland, and by the terms of the union I apprehend England has not given up or brought her colonies under the dominion of Scotland, but tho' dependent on Great Britain, they still remain what they always were, English colonies.

All the inhabitants of the British empire together form the British nation, and that the British Parliament is the supreme power and legislature in the British nation I never heard doubted.

By the English constitution, which is that which prevails over the whole empire, all Englishmen, or all that make up the British empire, are entitled to certain privileges, indefeasible, unalienable, and of which they can never be deprived, but by the taking away of that constitution which gives them these privileges. I have observed that the British empire is made up of different kingdoms and nations, but it is not the original constitution of Scotland or Ireland, but of England, which extends and communicates its privileges to the whole empire. This is an undeniable principle, and ought never to be lost out of sight, if we would form a sound judgment on the question now to be considered.

From the consideration above admitted, that the British Parliament is the supreme legislative power in the whole British empire, the following conclusion has been drawn; the colonies (and the same I suppose is meant of all the British empire, of which the colonies are a part) are bound by and subject to all the laws of the British Parliament in which they are mentioned, or are subject to none of any kind whatsoever.

Before this can be properly discussed, it must be observed, that Great Britain has not only a Parliament, which is the supreme legislature, but also a constitution, and that the now Parliament derives its authority and power from the constitution, and not the constitution from the Parliament. It may also be very fairly inferred hence, that the liberties of Englishmen arise from and depend on the English constitution, which is permanent and ever the same, whereas the individuals which compose the Parliament are changed at least once every seven years, and always at the demise of a king.

The Parliament of Great-Britain is the supreme legislature in the British empire. It must be so either absolutely or agreeable to the constitution; if absolutely, it can alter the constitution whenever it sees fit; if absolutely, it is not bound by the constitution, nor any thing else; if agreeable to the constitution, then it can no more make laws, which are against the constitution, or the unalterable privileges of British subjects, than it can alter the constitution itself. Supposing a Parliament, under some of the arbitrary reigns of the last century, should have made a law, that for the future the king's warrant should be sufficient to lay a tax on the subject, or to oblige him to pay ship money, it would have been an act of the supreme legislature, but it may safely be doubted, whether the nation would have thought it constitutional. I conclude therefore, that the power of Parliament, and of every branch of it, has its bounds assigned by the constitution.

If the power of the Parliament is limited by the constitution, it may not be improper next to enquire, whether the power of the British Parliament affects all the subjects of the British empire in the same manner.

If the power of the British Parliament affects all the subjects of the British empire in the same manner, it follows, that all the laws made by the British Parliament are binding alike upon all those over whom this power extends, or in other words, that all the subjects of the British empire are bound not only by those laws in which they are expressly mentioned, but every law by the Parliament made, for what need is there to mention every individual of those for whom the law is made in general, every subject therefore of the British empire, upon this supposition, must be bound by every law of the British Parliament, unless expressly excepted.

Those that hold the subjects of Great-Britain, living without England or Scotland, are bound by every law in which they are mentioned, seem also clearly to hold, that the same persons are not bound by such laws in which they are not mentioned. Thus the alternative, that the subjects of the British empire must be subject to all or none of the laws of the British Parliament, is limited even by those who plead for an universal submission. He that is only bound to obey some laws, cannot be said to be bound by all laws, as, on the contrary, he that is bound to obey all laws, is excused in none.

I suppose, before the union with Scotland, none would have scrupled to call the English Parliament the supreme legislature of all the British empire, though Scotland was still an independent kingdom, and by the union Scotland and its Parliament was not swallowed up and absorbed by England and its Parliament, but united with the kingdom, and the Parliaments also of the two kingdoms united in one general legislature. The ecclesiastical laws and constitution also of each kingdom remains as it was before, i. e. entirely different from each other.

Perhaps it may not be amiss to conceive, that the authority of the British Parliament extends over the whole British nation, though the different respective subjects are not altogether alike affected by its laws: That, with regard to national trade, the power of making it most beneficial to the head and every branch of the empire is vested in the British Parliament, as the supreme power in the nation, and that all the British subjects every where have a right to be ruled by the known principles of their common constitution.

Next, it may be proper to take a nearer view of how far, and in what manner, the acts of Parliament operate upon the different subjects of the British empire.

England doubtless is the first and primary object of the British Parliament, and therefore all laws immediately affect every resident in England; and of the king himself it has been said, *Rex Anglia in regno suo non habet superiorem nisi Deum & legem.* Proceedings at law I take to be the same in England and England's dependencies.

Scotland is united with England, and therefore there is a different operation of the laws that subsisted before and those that have been made since the union, and even these do not affect Scotland as of themselves; but in consequence of and in the terms of the union between the two nations, the union makes no alteration in proceedings at law, nor does it take away any private property.

Ireland is a distinct kingdom, and hath been conquered from the native Irish two or three times by the English; it hath nevertheless a Parliament of its own, and is a part of the British empire. It will best appear how far the British Parliament think Ireland dependent upon Great-Britain, by inserting, *A Bill for the better securing of the Dependency of Ireland.* The act was as follows:

> Whereas attempts have lately been made to shake off the subjection of Ireland unto, and dependence upon the imperial crown of this realm, which will be of dangerous consequence to Great-Britain and Ireland. And whereas the House of Lords in Ireland, in order thereto, have, of late, against law, assumed to themselves a power and jurisdiction to examine, correct and amend, the judgment and decrees of the courts of justice in the kingdom of Ireland; therefore, for the better securing of the dependency of Ireland upon the crown of Great-Britain, may it please your Majesty, that it may be enacted, and it is hereby declared and enacted, by the King's most excellent Majesty, by and with the advice and consent of the Lords Spiritual and Temporal, and Commons, in this present Parliament assembled, and by the authority of the same, That the said kingdom of Ireland hath been, is, and of right ought to be, subordinate unto, and dependent upon the imperial crown of Great-Britain, as being inseparably united and annexed thereunto, and that the King's Majesty, by and with the advice and consent of the Lords Spiritual and Temporal, and Commons of Great-Britain, in Parliament assembled, had, hath, and of right ought to have, full power and authority to

make laws and statutes of sufficient force and validity to bind the people and kingdom of Ireland.

And be it farther enacted, by the authority aforesaid, That the House of Lords of Ireland have not, nor of right ought to have, any jurisdiction to judge of, affirm, or reverse any judgment, sentence, or decree, given or made in any court within the said kingdom, and that all proceedings before the House of Lords upon any such judgment, sentence, or decree, are, and are hereby declared to be utterly null and void to all intents and purposes whatsoever.

The occasion of this bill was an appeal brought 1719 from the House of Peers in Ireland to the House of Peers in England. A Pitt was the first that spoke against it in the House of Commons, because, as he said, in his opinion it seemed calculated for no other purpose than to encrease the power of the British House of Peers, which in his opinion was already but too great. The Duke of Leeds protested against it in the House of Lords, and gave fifteen reasons to support the claim of the House of Peers in Ireland. The bill however passed, though Mr. Hungerford, Lord Molesworth, Lord Tyrconel, and other members, endeavoured to shew, that Ireland was ever independent with respect to courts of judicature. Some proposals have several years ago been made to incorporate Ireland with Great-Britain, but without any effect.

The Islands of Guernsey and Jersey, though in ecclesiastical matters considered as a part of Hampshire, are under the direction of an Assembly called the Convention of the States of Jersey, &c. The Isle of Man hath lately been annexed to the crown, but their own Manks laws still obtain in the island.

The British colonies and islands in America are not the least important part of the British empire; that these owe a constitutional dependence to the British Parliament I never heard they denied; though of late they have frequently been charged with it, these charges have not been grounded upon any declaration of theirs of the kind, their very petitioning, petitions and resolutions, manifestly speaking the very reverse; but their aversion to certain new duties, laid upon them for the sole purpose of raising a revenue, have been made a handle of against them, and they have as good as been charged, that they declare themselves an independent people. These insinuations the Americans are apt to look upon as being neither very fair nor very friendly; however at present I would only consider what kind of dependence is expected from the American colonies. An act of Parliament has fixed that of Ireland; a later act of the same power hath also fixed that of America, though, as will appear from the comparison, not altogether on the same footing. The act is entitled, *An Act for the better securing the Dependency of his Majesty's Dominions in America upon the Crown and Parliament of Great-Britain*, and runs thus:

Whereas several of the Houses of Representatives in his Majesty's colonies and plantations in America have of late, against law, claimed to themselves, or to the General Assemblies of the same, the sole and exclusive right of imposing duties and taxes upon his Majesty's subjects in the said colonies and plantations, and, in pursuance of such claim, passed certain votes, resolutions and orders, derogatory to the legislative authority of Parliament, and inconsistent with the dependency of the said colonies and plantations upon the crown of Great-Britain, may it therefore please your most excellent Majesty, that it may be declared, and be it declared, by the King's most excellent Majesty, by and with the advice and consent of the Lords Spiritual and Temporal, and Commons, in the present Parliament assembled, and by the authority of the same, That the said colonies and plantations in America have been, are, and of right ought to be, subordinate unto and dependent upon the imperial crown and Parliament of Great-Britain, and that the King's Majesty, by and with the advice and consent of the Lord's Spiritual and Temporal, and Commons, of Great-Britain, in Parliament assembled, had, hath, and of right ought to have, full power and authority to make laws and statutes of sufficient force and validity to bind the colonies and people of America, subjects of the crown of Great-Britain, in all cases whatsoever.

And be if further declared and enacted, by the authority aforesaid, That all resolutions, votes, orders and proceedings, in any of the said colonies or plantations, whereby the power and authority of the Parliament of Great-Britain to make laws and statutes as aforesaid is denied, or drawn into question, are, and are hereby declared to be utterly null and void to all intents and purposes whatsoever.

This is the standard of dependence which the Parliament of Great-Britain hath fixed for the British colonies on the 18th of March, 1766. The Stamp Act was repealed the same day, and the opinion of several noblemen who protested against that repeal was,

> that this declaratory bill cannot possibly obviate the growing mischiefs in America, where it may seem calculated only to deceive the people of Great-Britain, by holding forth a delusive and nugatory affirmance of the legislative right of Great-Britain, whilst the enacting part of it does no more than abrogate the resolutions of the House of Representatives in the North-American colonies, which have not in themselves the least colour of authority, and declares that which is apparently and certainly criminal only null and void.

I presume I may venture to affirm, that in and by this act, the Parliament did not mean to set aside the constitution, infringe the liberties of British subjects, or to vindicate unto themselves an authority which it had not before, was known to have, and would always have had, though this act had never been made. I also find, that, in order to overset any act, law, resolution, or proceeding, of the colony Assemblies, nothing seems necessary, but that the Parliament should declare it null and void to all intents and purposes whatsoever. And it seems pretty clear, that the same power that can disannul any act by a simple declaration, with one single stroke more, can also annihilate the body that made it.

The remark already made, that though all the different parts of the British empire are in a state of dependence upon the Parliament of Great-Britain, yet that the nature and degree of dependence is not exactly alike in the respective different parts of the same, will receive new strength and light, if we compare the act for better securing the dependency of Ireland with that for better securing the dependency of the colonies. Both acts, though at different times, have been made by the same authority, and for a similar purpose, and none can better tell us what kind and degree of dependency the Parliament expects and requires of its dependents than the Parliament itself.

The Irish is entitled in very general words, for the better securing the dependency of Ireland.

The title of the American law is more explicit; Ireland's dependency is mentioned, but the dependency of the Americans is more clearly expressed, and said to be upon the crown and Parliament of Great-

Britain. America seems to owe two dependencies, one to the crown, and one to the Parliament.

The preamble of the Irish bill brings no less a charge than an attempt to shake off subjection unto and dependence upon the imperial crown of Great-Britain.

The preamble of the American bill brings no such accusation, but only, that the Americans have claimed an exclusive right to lay on taxes on his Majesty's subjects within the colonies, and passed votes and resolutions derogatory to the legislative power of Parliament, and inconsistent with the dependency of the said colonies and plantations upon the crown (the word and Parliament is not made use of in this place) of Great-Britain. The principal differences between these bills seems to me to lie in this, that Ireland is said to be subject to and dependent only on the crown of Great-Britain, whereas America throughout is declared subject, at least dependent and subordinate, not only to the crown, but also to the Parliament of Great Britain, and then Ireland is only declared dependent upon, and subordinate to, in very gentle terms, whereas the right of making laws to bind the Americans is expressed in these very strong, most extensive terms, IN ALL CASES WHATSOEVER.

Time was when the dependency of the colonies upon England was spoke of exactly in the terms made use of for Ireland; the charter of this province saith, "our pleasure is, that the tenants and inhabitants of the said province be subject IMMEDIATELY to the crown of England, as depending thereof forever;" but by the late law all America is said to be dependent on crown and Parliament. This alteration seems to me by no means immaterial, but to imply a change both in the subjection expected from the colony and in the authority to which the colony owes dependency and subordination. In Parliament, King, Lords, and Commons, constitute the supreme power; but as each of these has its own distinct unalienable right, and incommunicable prerogatives, rights, or privileges, so I cannot but conceive dependency upon the crown and dependency upon crown and Parliament are things not exactly alike. If (as asserted in the charter) the colonies at some time or other were only dependent on the crown, and now are subordinate unto and dependent upon crown and Parliament, it should seem both the authority on which they depend, and the nature of their dependency, hath undergone some alteration; neither doth this appear to me a trifling alteration, and it seems to me at least if so it must needs make some alteration in the system of government and obedience.

Hitherto all appeals from the colonies, after passing thro' chancery in America, have been made to the King in council; this I conceive must have been in consequence of the dependency of the colonies immediately upon the crown; but perhaps for the future appeals will not be carried to the King in council, but to the King and Parliament.

The crown has hitherto had a right of a negative upon all American laws, and they were obliged to be passed in America with a saving clause; but if, as is asserted in the declaratory bill, the King has a right and power to make laws to bind the Americans, by and with the advice and consent of the Lords Spiritual and Temporal, and Commons of Great-Britain, assembled in Parliament, then probably the same authority must also concur to repeal the laws made in America whereas the crown hitherto repealed any law made in America without asking or waiting for the consent of Lords and Commons.

It appears also, by a late act suspending the Assembly of New-York, that the parliamentary authority also extends to suspend, which is but another word for proroguing or dissolving (or annihilating) Assemblies; all which has hitherto been done by the crown without the interfering of the Parliament: But that the crown hath a right of proroguing or dissolving the Parliament itself by its own authority I suppose will not be denied. I cannot dismiss this subject without observing, that even the declaratory bill speaks of the Assemblies in America as Houses of Representatives. If it is allowed that they are represented in America, unless they are represented doubly, they cannot be represented any where else; this strikes at the root of virtual representation, and if representation is the basis of taxation, they cannot be taxed but where they are represented, unless they are doubly taxed, as well as doubly represented.

It is evident upon the whole, that a much greater degree of dependency and subordination is expected of America than of Ireland though, by the way, Ireland, in the preamble of their bill, is charged with much greater guilt than America; nay, the words in ALL CASES WHATSOEVER are so exceeding extensive, that, in process of time, even hewing of wood, and drawing of water, might be argued to be included in them.

It was necessary to state the authority claimed by Parliament over America as clearly and fully as possible; with regard to the Americans it must be owned, when they profess to owe dependency and subordination to the British Parliament, they do not mean so extensive and absolute a dependency as here seems to be claimed, but that they think themselves in a constitutional manner dependent upon and in subordination to the crown and Parliament of Great-Britain, even those votes, resolutions, and proceedings, which are disannulled by the House of Commons and the declaratory bill, most fully and chearfully declare.

It has indeed been said, that unless they are subject to all the British acts in which they are mentioned, they are subject to none of any kind whatsoever, and consequently to be considered as independent of the legal and parliamentary power of Great-Britain; but I should think it might be as fairly and safely concluded, that while the Americans declare themselves subject to any one law of the British legislature, it cannot be said they declare themselves independent, or not subject to any law whatsoever.

In so delicate and important a matter, may I be permitted to observe, that the measure of power and of obedience in every country must be determined by the standard of its constitution. The dispute seems to lie between the Parliament and colonies; the Parliament will certainly be the fitting judges; I will not take upon me to say that the Americans may not look upon Parliament as judge and party; however, it is very possible for a judge to give a most righteous sentence, even where he himself is deeply interested, but they that are sufferers by the sentence will ever be apt to wish that he had not been party as well as judge.

From what hath been said hitherto, the due and constitutional authority of the British Parliament appears clear, and it does not less so I hope, that the subordination to and dependency on the British Parliament is not exactly the same in all the respective parts of that extensive empire; perhaps this will appear with still greater evidence by taking a particular view of the subject of taxation.

Any unlimited power and authority may lay on the subjects any tax it pleaseth; the subjects in that case themselves are mere property, and doubtless their substance and labour must be at their disposal who have the disposal of their persons. This is the case in arbitrary governments; but the British empire is an empire of freemen, no power is absolute but that of the laws, and, as hath been asserted, of such laws to which they that are bound by them have themselves consented.

Did the power and authority of the British Parliament in point of taxation extend in the same manner over all its dependencies, e.g. the same over Scotland as over England, over Ireland in the same manner as over Scotland, over Guernsey and Jersey as over Ireland, &c. then the very same act which lays a general tax would lay it also at the same time upon all over whom that authority extends. The laws of every legislature are supposed to extend to and be made over all within their jurisdiction, unless they are expressly excepted. Thus an excise law extends to all the British kingdom, because it is a publick law; but acts have frequently been made to lay on a penny Scots on beer, which, being for a local purpose, cannot operate on the whole kingdom. The same I believe may be said with regard to the method of recovering small debts; it seems absurd to say, that any supreme legislature makes an unlimited law which at the same time is designed not to be binding upon the greatest part of the subjects within that empire. Was it ever known that the land tax being laid on the whole united kingdom, the bishoprick of Durham, and the manor of East-Greenwich, were not also supposed to be included? and if any part within the immediate jurisdiction, and equally dependent on the same legislature, should be designed to be excused from, or not liable to pay a general tax, would it not be absolutely necessary that such a place should be expressly excepted? If, because America is a part of the British empire, it is as much so, or in the same manner is a part of it, as is the bishoprick of Durham, or the manor of East-Greenwich, nothing can be plainer than that it must be affected by every tax that is laid just in the same manner and proportion as is the bishoprick of Durham, or manor of East-Greenwich. This hath not been the case, nor thought to be the case hitherto. Ireland and America have not been called upon to pay the British land tax, malt tax, nor indeed any tax in which they have not been expressly mentioned; the reason of which I presume must be, either that the British Parliament did not look upon them as any part of the kingdom of Great-Britain, or else did not think them liable to any tax in which they were not expressly mentioned. If any subjects of the British empire are not liable to any or every tax laid on by the British Parliament, it must be either because they are not liable by the constitution, (as not being represented) or because they are excused by the favour of Parliament; if they are not liable by the privileges of the constitution, their not being compelled to pay is no favour, the contrary would be oppression and an anticonstitutional act; if they have been hitherto excused by the lenity of the British Parliament, it must be owned the Parliament bore harder on those who were made to pay those taxes than on those who by their lenity only were excused.

The noble Lords who protested against the repeal of the Stamp Act observe,

> it appears to us, that a most essential part of that authority, (*sc.* the whole legislative authority of Great-Britain, without any distinction or reserve whatsoever) the power of legislation, cannot be properly, equitably, or impartially exercised, if it does not extend itself to all the members of the state in proportion to their respective abilities, but suffers a part to be exempt from a due share of those burdens which the publick exigencies require to be imposed upon the whole: A partiality which is directly and manifestly repugnant to the trust reposed by the people in every legislature, and destructive of that confidence on which all government is founded.

If in the opinion of these Noblemen, therefore, it is partiality to suffer any part of the state to be exempt from a due share of those burdens which the publick exigencies require should be imposed upon the WHOLE, it would also seem to be a species of partiality, to lay a burden on ANY PART of the state which the other parts of the same state are not equally bound to bear. Partial burdens, or partial exemptions, would doubtless affect those that are burdened or exempted in a very different manner; but if not extending alike to the whole, must still be looked upon as partial. And if this partiality is inconsistent with the trust reposed BY THE PEOPLE in every legislature, it would also seem that the legislature could not lay any burdens but as entrusted by the people who chose them to be their representatives and a part of the legislature. We may hence also learn what is to be expected, if every other part of the British empire, England and Scotland only excepted, have hitherto been exempted from the taxes paid in England, which it must be owned are very heavy, by mere favour; or, as some seem to express it, *"flagrant partiality and injustice;"* their being indulged time immemorial will not be deemed a sufficient plea to excuse them always, but with an impartial hand the very same taxes that now obtain in Great-Britain will be laid upon Ireland, America, Jersey, Guernsey, the Mediterranean, African and East-India settlements, and, in short, on every individual part of the British empire. Whether a design to do this be not ripening apace I will not take upon me to say, but whenever it does, it must make some alteration in the policy of the mother and infant state, nay in the system of the whole British empire.

There are several parts of the British empire that pay no tax at all; this I take to be the case of Gibraltar, Minorca, Newfoundland, East-Florida, and all the African and East-India settlements, &c. The reason is, that all these places have no legislature of their own, and consequently none to give or dispose of their property; had these places been taxed by Parliament, there might however this reason been given, that having no representatives within themselves, and having never contributed any thing to the publick burdens, though they all receive protection, perhaps greater than the American colonies, the Parliament supplied that defect; but this cannot be urged against the colonies, who both have legislatures, and also contributed to the publick burdens, and that so liberally, that even the crown and Parliament thought they had exerted themselves beyond their abilities, and for several years gave them some compensation. I may mention those parts of the British empire as striking instances, that where there is no representation, taxation hath not been thought of, and yet Newfoundland, which is not taxed at all, is certainly as much represented in Parliament as all the colonies, which are designed to be doubly taxed.

By the constitution taxes are in the nature of a free gift of the subjects to the crown; regulations of trade are measures to secure and improve the trade of the whole nation. There is no doubt but regulations may be made to ruin as well as to improve trade; yet without regulations trade cannot subsist, but must suffer and sink; and it seems no where more proper to lodge the power of making these regulations than in the highest court of the empire; yet a man may trade or not, he may buy or let it alone; if merchandizes are rated so high that they will not suit him to purchase, though it may be an inconvenience, yet there is no law to compel him to buy; to rate the necessaries of life, without which a man cannot well do, beyond their real value, and hinder him at the same time from purchasing them reasonably of others, is scarce consistent with freedom; but when duties are laid on merchandizes not to regulate trade, but for the express and sole purpose of raising a revenue, they are to all intents and purposes equal to any tax, but they can by no means be called the free gift of those who never helped to make the law, but, as far as in them lay, ever looked upon it as an unconstitutional grievance.

If taxes are a free GIFT of the people to the crown, then the crown hath no right to them but what is derived from the GIVERS. It may be absolutely necessary that the subject should give, but still he that is to give must be supposed the judge both of that necessity, and how much he may be able and ought to give upon every necessary occasion. No man can give what is not his own, and therefore the constitution hath placed this right to judge of the necessity, and of what is to be given, in the Commons as the representatives of all those who are to give, in vesting a right in them to give publick supplies to the crown; it did not, could not mean to invest them with any power to give what neither belongs to them, nor those whom they represent; and therefore, as no man constitutionally "owes obedience to any law to which he has not assented either in person or by his representative;" much less doth the constitution oblige any man to part with his property, but freely and by his own consent; what those who are representatives are not willing to give, no power in Great-Britain have any right violently to take, and for a man to have his property took from him under pretence of a law that is not constitutional, would not be much better than to have it took from him against the express consent of those whom he constitutionally made his representatives.

It is held a maxim, that in government a proportion ought to be observed between the share in the legislature and the burden to be borne. The Americans pretend to no share in the legislature of Great-Britain at all, but they hope they have never forfeited their share in the constitution.

Every government supposes rule and protection from the governors, support and obedience from those that are governed; from these duly tempered arises the prerogative of the crown and the liberty of the subject; but he that has not a right to his own hath no property, and he that must part with his property by laws against his consent, or the consent of the majority of the people, has no liberty. The British constitution is made to secure liberty and property; whatever takes away these takes away the constitution itself, and cannot be constitutional.

To form a clear judgment on the power of taxation, it must be enquired on what right that power is grounded. It is a fundamental maxim of English law, that there is a contract between the crown and subjects; if so, the crown cannot lay on any tax, or any other burden, on the subject, but agreeable to the original contract by authority of Parliament; neither can the Lords properly concur, or the Commons frame a tax bill for any other purpose but the support of the crown and government, consistent with the original contract between that and the people.

All subjects are dependent on and subordinate to the government under which they live. An Englishman in France must observe the laws of

France; but it cannot be said that the dependency and subordination in England is the same as dependency and subordination in France. In governments where the will of the sovereign is the supreme law, the subjects have nothing to give, their ALL is in the disposal of the government; there subjects pay, but having nothing of their own cannot give; but in England the Commons GIVE and GRANT. This implies both a free and voluntary act, and that they give nothing but their own property.

Though every part of the British empire is bound to support and promote the advantage of the whole, it is by no means necessary that this should be done by a tax indiscriminately laid on the whole; it seems sufficient that every part should contribute to the support of the whole as it may be best able, and as may best suit with the common constitution.

I have before observed the different degree of dependency on the mother state; I shall now review the same again, with a particular regard to imposing or paying taxes, and if a material difference hath always obtained in this respect, it will confirm my assertion, that every branch of the British empire is not affected by the tax laws of Great-Britain in the self same manner.

The Parliament has a right to tax, but this right is not inherent in the members of it as men; I mean, the members of Parliament are not (like the Senate of Venice) so many rulers who have each of them a native and inherent right to be the rulers of the people of England, or even their representatives; they do not meet together as a court of proprietors to consider their common interest, and agree with one another what tax they will lay on those over whom they bear rule, or whom they represent, but they only exercise that right which nature hath placed in the people in general, and which, as it cannot conveniently be exercised by the whole people, these have lodged in some of their body chosen from among themselves, and by themselves, for that purpose, and empowered for a time only to transact the affairs of the whole, and to agree in their behalf on such supplies as it may be necessary to furnish unto the crown for the support of its dignity, and the necessities and protection of the people.

It would be absurd to say, that the crown hath a right to lay on a tax, for as taxes are granted to the crown, so in this case the crown would make a grant to itself, and hence the bill of rights expressly asserts, that *the levying of money for or to the use of the crown, by pretence of prerogative, without grant of Parliament, for a longer time or in any other manner than the same is or shall be granted, is illegal;* hence also there is a material difference between money bills and all other laws. The King and Lords cannot make any amendment in money bills as the House of Lords frequently doth in all others, but must accept or refuse them such as they are offered by the Commons, the constitutional reason of which is very obvious, it is the people only that give, and therefore giving must be the sole act of those by whom the givers are represented. The crown cannot take till it is given, and they that give cannot give but on their own behalf, and of those whom they represent; nay even then they cannot give but in a constitutional manner; they cannot give the property of those they represent without giving their own also exactly in the same proportion; every bill must be equally binding upon ALL whom they represent, and upon every one that is a representative.

Every representative in Parliament is not a representative for the whole nation, but only for the particular place for which he hath been chosen. If any are chosen for a plurality of places, they can make their election only for one of them. The electors of Middlesex cannot chuse a representative but for Middlesex, and as the right of sitting depends entirely upon the election, it seems clear to demonstration, that no member can represent any but those by whom he hath been elected; if not elected he cannot represent them, and of course not consent to any thing in their behalf. While Great-Britain's representatives do not sit assembled in Parliament, no tax whatever can be laid by any power on Great-Britain's inhabitants; it is plain therefore, that without representation there can be no taxation. If representation arises entirely from the free election of the people, it is plain that the elected are not representatives in their own right, but by virtue of their election; and it is not less so, that the electors cannot confer any right on those whom they elect but what is inherent in themselves; the electors of London cannot confer or give any right to their members to lay a tax on Westminster, but the election made of them doubtless empowers them to agree to or differ from any measures they think agreeable or disagreeable to their constituents, or the kingdom in general. If the representatives have no right but what they derive from their electors and election, and if the electors have no right to elect any representatives but for themselves, and if the right of sitting in the House of Commons arises only from the election of those designed to be representatives, it is undeniable, that the power of taxation in the House of Commons cannot extend any further than to those who have delegated them for that purpose; and if none of the electors in England could give a power to those whom they elected to represent or tax any other part of his Majesty's dominions except themselves, it must follow, that when the Commons are met, they represent no other place or part of his Majesty's dominions, and cannot give away the property but of those who have given them a power so to do by choosing them their representatives.

The Parliament hath the sole right to lay on taxes, and, as hath been observed in Parliament, 'tis not the King and Lords that GIVE and GRANT, but this is the sole act of the Commons. The Commons have the right to do so either from the crown or people, or it is a right inherent in themselves. It cannot be inherent in themselves, for they are not born representatives, but are so by election, and that not for life, but only for a certain time; neither can they derive it from the crown, else the liberty and property of the subject must be entirely in the disposal and possession of the crown; but if they hold it entirely from the people, they cannot hold it from any other people but those who have chosen them to be their representatives, and it should seem they cannot extend their power of taxing beyond the limits of time and place, nor indeed for any other purpose but that for which they have been chosen. As the Commons in Parliament cannot lay any tax but what they must pay themselves, and falls equally on the whole kingdom of England, so, by a fundamental law, they cannot lay but such a part of the general tax on some part of the united kingdom. The principality of Wales was never taxed by Parliament till it was incorporated and represented, and, poor as it is, it pays now considerably larger than Scotland, which is as big again. When England is taxed two millions in the land tax, no more is paid in Scotland than 48,000*l.* and yet to lay a higher land tax on North-Britain the British Parliament cannot, it cannot without breaking the union, that is, a fundamental law of the kingdom. All the right it hath to tax Scotland arises from and must be executed in the terms of the union.*

*While Scotland was yet a separate kingdom, it was once debated in Parliament, whether a subsidy should first be granted, or overtures for liberty first be considered; when the Queen's Ministry insisted on the former, a member urged, that it was now plain the nation was to expect no return for their expence and toil, but to be put to the charge of a subsidy, and to lay down their necks under the yoke of slavery, &c. Another member said, that he insisted for having a vote upon the question which had been put: That he found as the liberties of the nation were suppressed, so the privileges of Parliament were like to be torn from them, but that he would rather venture his life than that it should be so, and should chuse rather *to die a freeman* than *live a slave*. Some pressed for the vote, adding, that if there was no other way of obtaining so natural and undeniable a privilege of the Parliament, *they would demand it with their swords in their hands*.

See Annals of Queen Anne for 1703, page 76. These were no American speakers.

The Islands of Guernsey, &c. are not taxed by the British Parliament at all, they still have their own States, and I never heard that the British Parliament ever offered to hinder them to lay on their own taxes, or to lay on additional ones, where they are not represented.

Ireland is a conquered kingdom, the greater part of its inhabitants Papists, who in England pay double tax. The Romans always made a difference between their colonies and their conquests, and as reasonable, allowed greater and indeed all common liberties to the former. Ireland hath been conquered twice again upon the natives since its first conquest, nevertheless it hitherto had its own legislature; if the Parliament of Great-Britain claims a right to tax them, they never yet have made use of that right, and seeing for ages past they enjoyed the privilege of having their own property disposed of by representatives in a Parliament of their own, it is very natural to suppose, that they think themselves entitled to these things, and the more so, because, in the very bill that determines their dependency, they are not said to be dependent on the British Parliament, nor yet on crown and Parliament, but only on the crown of Great-Britain.

I would now proceed to take a distinct view of the point in debate between Great-Britain and her colonies.

It seems to be a prevailing opinion in Great-Britain, that the Parliament hath a right to tax the Americans, and that, unless they have so, America would be independent of Great-Britain.

And it seems to be a prevailing opinion in America, that to be taxed without their consent, and where they are not and cannot be represented, would deprive them of the rights of Englishmen, nay, in time, with the loss of the constitution, would deprive them of liberty and property altogether.

It is easily seen, that this is a very interesting subject, the consequences in each case very important, though in neither so alarming and dangerous to Britain as to America. With regard to Great-Britain, if it should not prove so as is claimed, the consequence can only be this, that then no tax can be laid, or revenue be raised, on the Americans, but where they are represented, and in a manner which they think consistent with their natural rights as men, and with their civil and constitutional liberties as Britons. The dependency of America upon Great-Britain will be as full and firm as ever, and they will chearfully comply with the requisitions of the crown in a constitutional manner. The question is not, whether the Americans will withdraw their subordination, or refuse their assistance, but, whether they themselves shall give their own property, where they are legally represented, or, whether the Parliament of Great-Britain, which does not represent them, shall take their property, and dispose of it in the same manner as they do theirs whom in Parliament they actually represent. The Americans do not plead for a right to withhold, but freely and chearfully to give. If 100,000*l.* are to be raised, the question is not, shall they be raised or no? but shall the Parliament levy so much upon the Americans, and order them to pay it, as a gift and grant of the Commons of Great-Britain to the King? or, shall the Americans also have an opportunity to shew their loyalty and readiness to serve the King by freely granting it to the King themselves? It is not to be denied the Americans apprehend, that if any power, no matter what the name, where they are not represented, hath a right to lay a tax on them at pleasure, all their liberty and property is at an end, and they are upon a level with the meanest slaves.

England will not lose a shilling in point of property; the rights and privileges of the good people of Britain will not be in the least affected, supposing the claim of the Americans just and to take place; whereas every thing dreadful appears in view to the Americans if it should turn out otherwise. The crown cannot lose; the Americans are as willing to comply with every constitutional requisition as the British Parliament itself can possibly be. The Parliament cannot lose, it will still have all the power and authority it hitherto had, and ought to have had, and when every branch of the legislature, and every member of the British empire, has a true regard to reciprocal duty, prerogative and privilege, the happiness of the whole is best likely to be secured and promoted.

The Americans most solemnly disclaim every thought, and the very idea of independency; they are sometimes afraid they are charged with a desire of it, not because this appears to be the real case, but to set their arguments in an invidious light, and to make them appear odious in the sight of their mother country. This is not a dispute about a punctilio, the difference in the consequence is amazingly great; supposing America is not taxed where not represented, and supposing things are left upon the same footing in which with manifest advantage to Britain and America they have been ever since Britain had colonies, neither the trade nor authority of Britain suffers the least diminution, but the mischief to the colonies is beyond all expression, if the contrary should take place. If they are not to raise their own taxes, all their Assemblies become useless in a moment, all their respective legislatures are annihilated at a stroke; an act passed by persons, most of whom probably never saw, nor cared much for America, may destroy all the acts they ever passed, may lay every burden upon them under which they are not expected immediately to sink, and all their civil and religious liberties, for which their forefathers went into this wilderness, and, under the smiles of Heaven, turned it into a garden, and of immense consequence to the mother country, will, or may be at an end at once. Probably the present Parliament or generation would never carry matters to this length, but who knows what might be done in the next? The first settlers of the American wilds never expected that would come to pass what we have seen already. It seems as if some evil genius had prevailed of late; had these new duties been laid on payable in England, at least the expence of a Board of Commissioners, and of the swarms of new officers, might have been prevented; but it looks as though some men wished that America might not only be borne hard upon, but also be made to know and feel that their liberty and property lay at the mercy of others, and that they must not flatter themselves to enjoy them any longer than the good pleasure of some who would willingly take away what *they* never did give. I have endeavoured candidly to state the question, let us now endeavour to view the claim made on each side as calmly and impartially as possible.

'Tis said the British Parliament hath a right to tax the Americans. If this proposition is incontrovertible, it must certainly be built on such a basis and such clear principles as will be sufficient to dispose loyal and reasonable men chearfully to acquiesce in it. There are some points in government which perhaps are best never touched upon, but when any question once becomes the subject of publick debate, strength of reason is the sole authority that with men of reason can determine the matter.

If the Parliament of Great-Britain have a right to tax the Americans, it must either be the same right in virtue of which they have a right to tax Great-Britain, and be vested in them by the same power, or it must be a distinct right either inherent in themselves, or vested in them by some other power.

The right of the Commons of Great-Britain to lay on taxes arises, as I conceive, from their having been chosen by the people who are to pay these taxes to act in their behalf and as their representatives. There may be other qualifications necessary, that a man be a Briton born, subject of the King, possessed of a certain estate, &c. but none is so absolutely necessary as election. He that hath been a representative had a right to refuse or concur in any tax bill whilst a member, but if he is not chosen again in a following Parliament, he hath no right whatever to meddle in the matter: this proves that the power is originally in the people, and the legislative capacity of the whole House, and of every member, depends upon their free election, and is of force no longer than for the time for which they have been elected; this being elapsed, the trust reposed in them entirely ceases, it absolutely returns to the body of the people; in that interval during which the people are unrepresented, any power their representatives might have is entirely and solely in the people themselves, no tax can be laid on, nor any law to bind the people be formed, for this plain reason, because there are no persons qualified for that purpose. The people have not representatives assigned, but chuse them, and being so chosen, the rights of the people reside now in them, and they may, but not before, act in their behalf. Now, when the crown issues writs of election, it is not to empower the electors to chuse representatives for America, nor yet for all Great-Britain, but only for some certain place specified in the writ; and when the electors of Great-Britain chuse representatives, their meaning also is not to chuse representatives for their fellow subjects in America, or any where else, but for themselves. In Great-Britain English electors cannot elect in behalf of Scotland, and Scotch electors cannot in behalf of England; and for the same reason neither Scotch nor English can elect any for America. These electors do not represent the Americans, nor are they their proxies to vote in members in their behalf; neither can British electors give any instructions to British representatives, or invest them with any power to dispose of the rights and property of any of their fellow subjects without the kingdom of Great-Britain. It seems not unreasonable then to conclude, that the right which the elected acquire by their election to pass tax laws binding upon their electors does not at the same time give them a right to represent and lay on taxes on those who never invested them with any such power, and by whom they neither were nor could be elected. If the Americans themselves are not received as voters in the bishoprick of Durham, manor of East-Greenwich, or any place mentioned in their charters, and the same liberty and privileges with those places therein secured unto them, if they are not allowed to chuse any representatives for themselves in the House of Commons, it seems natural, that what they have no right to do themselves, none can have a right to do for them, and so no body can chuse or send a representative for them to any place where they are not allowed to sit or be represented. If so, the electors of Great-Britain never in fact elected representatives for

America, nor could these electors possibly convey any power to give away property where they have no property themselves. The electors do not represent America, neither their representatives by them elected; the electors cannot dispose of the property of America, therefore they cannot give a power so to do unto others. In England there can be no taxation without representation, and no representation without election; but it is undeniable that the representatives of Great-Britain are not elected by nor for the Americans, and therefore cannot represent them; and so, if the Parliament of Great Britain has a right to tax America, that right cannot possibly be grounded on the consideration that the people of Great-Britain have chosen them their representatives, without which choice they would be no Parliament at all.

If the Parliament of Great-Britain has a right to tax the Americans distinct from the right which they derive from their electors, and which they exercise as the representatives of the people of Great-Britain, then this right they must hold either from the crown, or from the Americans, or else it must be a native inherent right in themselves, at least a consequence of their being representatives of the people of Great-Britain.

It is plain that the colonies have been settled by authority and under the sanction of the crown, but as the crown did not reserve unto itself a right to rule over them without their own Assemblies, but on the contrary established legislatures among them, as it did not reserve a right to lay taxes on them in a manner which, were the experiment made in England, might be thought unconstitutional, so neither do I find that a reserve of that kind was made by the crown in favour of the Parliament, on the contrary, by the charters all the inhabitants were promised the enjoyment of the same and all privileges of his Majesty's liege subjects in England, of which doubtless not to be taxed where they are not represented is one of the principal. As to any right that might accrue to Parliament from any act or surrender of the Americans, I believe it hath never been thought of; they have a profound veneration for the British Parliament, they look upon it as the great palladium of the British liberties, but still they are not there represented, they have had their own legislatures and representatives for ages past, and as a body cannot be more than in one place at once, they think they cannot be legally represented in more than one legislative body, but also think, that by the laws of England *Protestants* ought not to be doubly taxed, or, what they think worse, taxed in two places.

If therefore this right of taxing the Americans resides in the Commons of Great-Britain at all, it must be an inherent right in themselves, or at least in consequence of their being representatives of the people of Great-Britain. The act for better securing the dependency of the colonies, which I have inserted at large, evidently seems to tend this way. That the colonies were thought at the disposal of Parliament one might be led to think, because by that act, from the simple authority of the crown, which they were till then subject to by their charters, they were now declared to be subordinate to and dependent (on the joint authority) of crown and Parliament. Yet, concerning this act, I would only observe, that however it may determine the case from that day, it cannot be the ground on which the subordination of the colonies originally was or now can be built; for it declares not only, that the colonies are and ought to be, but also that they always have been, subject to crown and Parliament. A law binds after it is made, it cannot bind before it exists, and so surely it cannot be said, that the colonies have *always* been bound by a law which is above a hundred years posterior to them in point of existence. It is also a little difficult to reconcile this law with prior charters; our Carolina charter makes our province subject immediately to the crown, and near a hundred years after a law is made to declare, that this was not and must not be the case, but that the Americans always were and ought to be subject to crown and Parliament. Perhaps this hath not been so seriously considered as it may hereafter, but neither this nor any law can be supposed to be binding *ex post facto*, or contrary to our fundamental constitution. Montesquieu observes, that the British constitution (which God preserve) will be lost, whenever the legislative power shall be more corrupted than the executive part of the legislature.

And after all, in this very law, the Americans are allowed to be represented in their own Assemblies, and to lay on duties and taxes, though not exclusively; but whether America, or any part of the British empire, should be liable to have taxes imposed on them by different legislatures, and whether these would not frequently clash with one another to the detriment of crown and subjects, I leave others duly to consider.

It is said, if America cannot be taxed by the British Parliament, then it would be independent of Great-Britain. This is now a very popular cry, and it is well if many join in it only because they know no better. This is not, will not, cannot be the case. America confessedly hath not been thus taxed since it was settled; but no body in Britain or America ever dreamed that America was independent. In England the people cannot be taxed when the Parliament does not sit, or when it is dissolved; are they then therefore independent. Scotland cannot be taxed in the same degree as England; is it therefore independent? Ireland and Jersey have their own legislatures, and so tax themselves; will you call them independent? All those parts of the British empire that have no Assemblies pay no taxes at all, neither among themselves, nor to Great-Britain; but it will not therefore be said, that they are independent. The Parliament itself claims a right to refuse supplies till their grievances are heard and redressed, this is looked upon as a constitutional remedy against any encroachments by the crown, and hath very often been made use of in former reigns, and yet the Parliament neither claimed nor were charged with a desire of independency. Those who so freely charge with a desire of independency, and even treason and rebellion, would do well to consider, that this charge, heinous as it is, reflects greater disgrace on those who unjustly make it, than on those on whom it is unjustly made. A man of honour would not easily forgive himself whenever he should discover that he made so rash a charge against two millions of people, as innocent, loyal and well affected to their King and country, as any of his fellow subjects or himself possibly can be. There never was an American Jacobite, the very air of America is death to such monsters, never any grew there, and if any are transported, or import themselves, loss of speech always attends them. The loyalty of the Americans to their King hath not only been ever untainted, it hath never been as much as suspected. There is a difference between independency and uneasiness. In the late reign, the people in England were uneasy at the Jew Bill, and it was rapidly repealed; in the present, the Cyder Act was an odious measure, and immediately altered, and that without any disgrace or diminution of parliamentary authority. If there hath been any appearance of riot in America, perhaps it may hereafter appear at whose instigation, the law was ever open, and even overbearing odious Custom-House Officers might have been redressed, if they had thought fit to apply for a legal rather than a military remedy. In England it is possible Majesty itself hath met with indignities which have not been shewn in America even to those men to whom the nation in general is indebted for the present uneasiness, and it is not improbable, that, after all that hath been said and done, the Americans will be found an exception to the general rule, that oppression makes even a wise man mad: An ancient rule, the truth of which hath been experienced in England oftener than in America. The opinion of the Americans is, that to be taxed where they are not represented would deprive them of the rights of Englishmen, nay, in time, with the loss of the constitution, might and must deprive them of liberty and property altogether. These it must be owned are gloomy apprehensions; two millions of people are so thoroughly prepossessed with them, that even their children unborn may feel the parents impressions; should there be any real ground for them, the Americans can hardly be blamed; they sit uneasy under them; they can no more help their uneasiness, than deny the blood which glows in their veins, or be angry with the milk that was their first nourishment. This is not a dark abstruse point, but seems plain and essential to the very being of liberty. The sole question is, Is it, or is it not, the right of an Englishman not to be taxed where he is not represented? Can you be tired of being represented, O Britons! Is it consistent with the constitution you so justly boast of to be thus taxed? Then representation is not essential to your constitution, and sooner or later you will either give it up or be deprived of it. A borough that does not exist shall send two representatives, a single county, neither the largest nor richest, shall send forty-four members, and two millions of souls, and an extent of land of eighteen hundred miles in length, shall have taxes laid on them by such as never were nearer to them than one thousand leagues, and whose interest it may be to lay heavy burdens on them in order to lighten their own. And are these, who are thus taxed, unrepresented, unheard and unknown, Englishmen, and taxed by Englishmen? Do these enjoy what the charters most solemnly ensure them, the same and all the privileges of the subjects born and resident within the realm? I must doubt it.

Let those who make light of American grievances give a plain answer to this plain question, Are the colonies to be taxed by Parliament represented in Parliament? if they are, by whom, or since when? if not, once more, Is it, or is it not, the right of Britons not to be taxed where not represented? Here the whole matter hinges, and surely the question is not so impertinent but a civil answer might be given before a mother sends fire and sword into her own bowels. When constitutional liberty is once lost, the transit is very short to the loss of property; the same power that may deprive of the one may also deprive of the other, and with equal justice, those that have not liberty enough to keep their property in reality have no property to keep. Some that look no further build right upon power, and insist the Parliament can do so. If power is all that is meant very like it may, so it may alter the constitution. If a stately tree should take umbrage at some diminutive shrubs, it can fall upon and crush them, but it cannot fall upon them without tearing up its own roots; it can crush those within reach, but its own branches will take off the weight of the impression, permit the shrubs to send forth new shoots, while there is no great probability that the envious oak will return to its former stand and vigour. *C'est une chose a bien considerer,* (this ought to be well considered first) said *Moliere's Malade imaginaire,* when his quack proposed to him to have one of his arms cut off, because it took some of the nourishment which in that case would center in the other, and make it so much the stronger. If every Assembly in America is suspended, the consequence must be, that the people are without their usual legislature, and in that case nothing short of a miracle seems capable to prevent an anarchy and general confusion. No power can alter the nature of things, that which is wrong cannot be right, and oppression will never be productive of the love and smiles of those that feel it.

The Parliament can crush the Americans, but it can also, and with infinitely greater certainty and ease, conciliate their affections, have the ultimate gain of all their labours, and by only continuing them the privileges of Britons, that is, by only doing as they would be done by, diffuse the blessings of love and concord throughout the whole empire, and to the latest posterity; and which of these two is the most eligible, it is NOW for you, O Britons! to consider, and in considering it, *majores vestros cogitate & posteros,* think on your ancestors and your posterity.

Those whom God hath joined together, (Great-Britain and America, Liberty and Loyalty) *let no man put asunder: And may peace and prosperity ever attend this happy union.*   Feb. 1, 1769.

Pamphlet 3

LETTER TO THE REVEREND SAMUEL FRINK

1770

Throughout the Revolutionary crisis Zubly retained a consuming interest in Anglican and Protestant dissenters' relations in Georgia, and America. Like many American Whig thinkers, Zubly linked the established church with British political authority, believing that its action prefigured or reflected British political and imperial policy. The religious diversity in the American colonies made religious toleration an accepted fact of life by the mid-eighteenth century, however much various religious groups despised and feared one another and however much the Great Awakening inflamed inter- and intradenominational feuds. In some ways, the experience of religious toleration encouraged religious dissent by removing political penalties for leaving an established church. It also facilitated political toleration in America, for a people who tolerated differences in matters of faith were receptive to differences in matters of government—to a point. American Whigs drew on the tradition of religious dissent in the Anglo-American world to guard political dissent. In the wake of the Great Awakening, which still throbbed in Georgia in the 1760s, and in the vortex of the political disputes of that period, it was easy for men like Zubly to see disturbing parallels between the Anglican church hierarchy's efforts to collect fees from dissenters and to exert a greater direct control over the colonial religious establishment, by appointing an Anglican bishop for the colonies, for example, and Parliament's desire to raise a revenue in the American colonies and to acquire greater direct political control there by redesigning imperial administration and reviewing colonial political activity closely.

Against this background of concern, even distrust, Zubly's personal problems with Samuel Frink, the rector of Christ's Church Parish in Savannah, took on larger meaning for the Revolution. Savannah apparently was not large enough to contain two such strong personalities as Zubly and Frink. They clashed over a host of petty issues, but divided mainly over the question of the dissenters' relationship with the established church and the payment of fees for religious duties. Their personal rivalry ended in the courts and in the press, where it assumed a political character. In 1770 Zubly published his side of the argument as *A Letter to the Reverend Samuel Frink*. The pamphlet showed Zubly at his most petulant self, but it also scored points for the American Whig connection between Anglican authoritarianism and politican despotism. The pamphlet followed others, principally written in New York and New England, that warned against Anglican efforts to restrict dissenters' rights or to tax them with unfair fees.

The pamphlet was published in 1770, most likely in Savannah by James Johnston. In 1775 Henry Miller of Philadelphia brought out a new edition.

Source: Henry E. Huntington Library and Massachusetts Historical Society copies

A
LETTER

To The

Reverend Samuel Frink,
A. M. Rector of Christ Church Parish in Georgia,

Relating To

Some Fees demanded of
some of his Dissenting Parishioners.

1 Corinthians 13:1. *Though I speak with the tongues of men, and of angels, and have not charity, I am become as sounding brass, or a tinkling cymbal.* Mark 9:51. *Have salt among yourselves, and peace with one another.*

Reverend Sir,

To follow peace with all men is the duty of every Christian, but Ministers of the Gospel, by their office, are more particularly bound to study the things which make for peace. The servant of the Lord must not strive, but be gentle unto all men; a wrangling disposition is utterly unbecoming his character, and, to charge that disposition on any that are not guilty of it, though it may not give a right to recriminate, yet surely it leaves them very excusable that speak or write only in their own defence; even in the opinion of the Apostle it is not always possible to be at peace with *all* men; that we should do so as far as in us lies is all that is expected; and even, when we are willing to bear and forbear what may only affect our persons, and sit still under grievous aspersions, in hopes of appearing with better advantage in some future day, there may be circumstances in which to be altogether silent may hurt a good cause, nay truth itself may be wounded through our sides, while we do not give its friends a fair opportunity to judge of its merit.

I hope I am not mistaken, Reverend Sir, when I assert there is no private or personal difference between you and me; if there should, I freely own I should be the more sorry for it, because I always maintained honourable thoughts of your kind and benevolent temper. I am sorry if you (and perhaps others with you) cannot return me the same compliment, but I can truly say I made it my study to gain your good-will ever since you became my neighbour. When you first settled in your parish you did me the honour to accept of an invitation, and I then had an opportunity of making you a very sincere offer of my respects and services, but there has been very little intercourse between us since that time; I never had the pleasure of a single visit in return for some which, I am now afraid, I obtruded on you; and when you were lately sick, and I waited on you, I had not the happiness of being admitted; you sent your compliments by your servant to the door, and informed me you were much better. I hope I may appeal to such in this place as have known me in a ministerial character upwards of five and twenty years, that I never was a bigot. Your worthy predecessor sometimes did not think it beneath him to accept of my services, and what his opinion was of me and my conduct on his dying-bed (which often makes us view things in a truer light) some worthy gentlemen still living may possibly remember. You will excuse, Reverend Sir, my addressing you in this publick manner, when you consider you as good as forbid me to write to you on the subject in private. You write me, "Mr. Frink is very sorry that Mr. Zubly is so troublesome to him, and is always seeking occasion to quarrel and make a disturbance in his parish." This is a heavy accusation; if it is grounded on the letter I took the liberty to write to you, the effect has been the very reverse from the intention, I meant to prevent a law-suit in which I expected you as party, and in which I thought to appear in behalf of a widow, my hearer. You know, Sir, such an action you have brought against us before, and it seemed to me that it could not be very honourable to ourselves, nor edifying to the generality of our hearers, that we should appear in Court against one another for the sum of three and sixpence *Sterling*, claimed by one without any express law, and refused by the other because he would not suffer a precedent to be established to require wages where no work had been done or desired.

You indeed now tell me, "Mr. Frink once for all tells Mr. Zubly that he does not dictate the parish sexton in those dues that belong to the sexton; the sexton has a right to take care of what belongs to himself;" but you will recollect, Sir, that though now the blame is thrown upon the sexton, in the action formerly brought you yourself appeared in Court as plaintiff, the account for tolling the bell is made out as due to you, and you had men after your own heart, a proselyted Catechist, a Vestryman, (who served upon that jury and not before nor since) and your own Clerk, to determine the matter. I may possibly have expressed myself in your opinion too strongly against that trial, but this you take no further notice of than by calling me troublesome and contentious; a single good argument to prove the justice of such a demand would have silenced me for ever. Is it not strange, Sir, that in a free Protestant country the ringing of a bell should prove a bone of contention. I do not know which would be the greatest hardship, the depriving us of the conveniency of a bell, which it seems is the strong inclination of the Justice that gave his charge to the jury, or the making us pay for a bell we do not desire to make any use of, and which formerly we were denied to have the use of when we would have been glad to pay for it.* When we had no bell, nor place of worship, of our own, we sometimes could hardly obtain the use of the parish bell for love or money, and now we have one of our own, it seems we are not to make use of it unless we pay a fine of three shillings and sixpence for the non-usage of your's; on what principle of reason, justice, or natural equity, this can be grounded, I am entirely ignorant, and if this claim, for which we have already been prosecuted three several times, has any foundation in reason, justice, or equity, it must be just and reasonable to make you also pay for services never performed or required; I dare say you would think this an entire alteration of the case, perhaps none but a young Star-Chamber would fix such an imposition on Protestants, and no

---

*Some time ago a parishioner was executed for murder; the Provost Marshal, (as usual) in my hearing, ordered the bell to toll, but the bell was not tolled; it was judged the reason of this must be because the unhappy man, originally a Papist, being visited during his long confinement by nobody but a Dissenter, chose that the same should also attend him to the last; though it must be owned he expected the Rector of the parish would also attend at least that day, and expressed his uneasiness that the passing knell should be denied him as he passed by the church to the gallows.

Court of Justice ever could decree a man a reward for doing nothing.

You observe, "that Mr. Frink does not dictate to the Parish Clerk," but it is not long since my sexton received a message as from you not to toll our bell without first giving you notice, and I must do your sexton the justice, that, in an account brought me a very few days ago, he very readily dropt the demand for tolling the bell; no sexton before him made such a demand, and the present did not make it till he first had the sanction of a precedent under his Rector.

Upon the whole, I would willingly hope for the future you will leave people to themselves who are very unwilling to give you any disturbance. I have always been happy in a good correspondence with the gentlemen of the established Church; there never was the shadow of any uneasiness between me and the Rectors of those parishes in Carolina where I officiated. A good understanding between Ministers has usually a very happy effect upon hearers; it cannot be for the interest of religion to widen our differences, or "to inculcate that Jews should have no dealings with Samaritans." It is an easy matter to say harsh things of any particular man or set of people; but as praises cannot make us better, so reproach undeserved cannot make us worse than we really are. You have once been a Dissenter yourself, and, for your nearest relation's sake, will not scruple to allow that men not inferior to you in any thing may be among them still. To condemn them by wholesale, and to insinuate "that it is an equal crime to transgress the laws of the Church or the laws of the Land," "that the man that will be his own God will also be his own King," can give no great idea of the Preacher's notions of candour, charity, and Christian liberty. I should think it possible to maintain every right, and yet also to maintain a friendly intercourse with those of a different opinion. It is a pity any thing should be called a right which is an injury to another, or that any present or future incumbent of any parish should follow the precedent which so much pains are now taken to establish as a rule for the whole province. This is very different from the spirit of moderation so strongly breathing in the writings of our Episcopalian brethren in the North in favour of an American Bishop, for which purpose I heard it whispered a petition has been sent home from this province, and if one should come and demand all his fees with equal rigour as his inferior Clergy, it is obvious what is to expected; neither do I know any place besides this where differences are carried even to the grave, and one set of Christian Ministers have refused every invitation to assist at the funerals of their Dissenting Christian brethren, or think themselves disgraced to walk in the company of a Dissenting Minister.

I should not have addressed myself to you in this publick manner if you had thought proper to pay the least regard to my private request, but while I am apprehensive that the same measures are intended against my Dissenting friends all over the province, I could not but think it necessary to inform them of the steps taken *pro & con.* in this place. I will not trouble you with a vindication of my character; we must go through evil reports as well as good reports; if we may but meet with the approbation of the only Judge that can save and condemn all will be well at last. That you may be very useful in his service now, and meet with his plaudit hereafter, is the sincere prayer of, Reverend Sir, your very humble servant.

Some Letters between Mr. Frink and Zubly now follow.

To the Reverend Mr. Frink.

Reverend Sir,   Jan. 10, 1770.

My sexton informs me that Battoon, brought him a message as from you not to ring our bell in case of any death without giving you previous information; if you think, Sir, you have any authority over our bell or sexton, I will take it kind in you if you will let me know by a few lines on what that authority is grounded. Unless I receive a written answer from you signifying the contrary, I shall consider the whole matter as a piece of impertinence of Battoon, (of which indeed I think him very capable) and treat it accordingly. I am respectfully, &c.

The Answer.

Mr. Frink's compliments wait on Mr. Zubly; he is sure that he never gave any direction to Battoon with regard to what is mentioned per letter. Mr. Frink is sorry to find so many in his parish busy in breeding differences, which is contrary to his nature and inclinations. He wishes Mr. Zubly and his family well.   Jan. 10, 1770.

Mr. Zubly to Mr. Frink.

Mr. Zubly's compliments wait on Mr. Frink; he is very happy in Mr. Frink's kind answer; Mr. Frink must now see "who is breeding differences in the parish so contrary to Mr. Frink's nature and inclination," and will doubtless think his honour engaged to shew a proper resentment against the man who made bold with his name to carry an impertinent, and, as it now appears, false message.

Perhaps an execution now said to be issued about the very thing in question is also issued without Mr. Frink's knowledge, and contrary to his inclination.

Mr. Z. observes, that on funerals Mr. Frink has no scruple to walk with Dr.-----; he therefore must have been ashamed of Mr. Z. only when he bid the Doctor and him walk alone at the funeral of the Rev. Mr. Matthews. Mr. Z. owns he was never used so before by any gentleman.

He is greatly obliged to Mr. Frink for his good wishes, and begs leave to make him a sincere tender of his respects, and of any services he may be capable of upon any occasion.   Jan. 11, 1770.

This produced the following ANSWER.

Mr. Frink's compliments to Mr. Zubly, and wishes that he might have an opportunity of conversing with him, as he is not perfectly acquainted with what Mr. Zubly drives at in the literary way.

Mr. Frink will be at leisure Saturday morning.   Jan. 11, 1770.

Mr. Z. waited on Mr. Frink twice that Saturday morning, but had not the pleasure of finding him at home.

Mr. Z. to Mr. Frink

Reverend Sir,   April 2, 1770.

One of my hearers, the Widow H. informs me there is a summons out against her for the Church bell at her late husband's funeral, which you know was made no use of upon that occasion. I was really in hopes no such demand would ever be made any more, and though you carried the cause once, I should think a victory before such a Judge, such a jury, and in such a cause, more scandalous than a defeat. I am still in hopes you will think better of it, and not suffer it to come into Court, or ever to be mentioned hereafter; it is a claim which neither justice, law, nor equity, can support. Unless you favour me with assurances to the contrary, I must take it for granted you intend to go on, and wherever there is a plaintiff it is just there also should be a defendant, and this seems the greater a hardship as the fee in question is nowhere demanded neither in Britain nor America, but only in Christ-Church parish, Georgia. I am, &c.

Mr. Frink's ANSWER follows:

Mr. Frink is sorry that Mr. Zubly is so troublesome to him, and is always seeking occasion to quarrel and make a disturbance in his parish. Mr. Frink once for all tells Mr. Zubly that he does not dictate the parish sexton in those fees that belong to the sexton, the sexton has a right to take care of what belongs to himself; as for Mr. Frink's part, he can assure Mr. Zubly he will support his right as Rector of the parish of Christ-Church. Mr. Frink expects to hear no more on the subject from Mr. Zubly. Savannah, April 3, 1770.

To this no answer was made whatever.

But as it is now absolutely denied that the Dissenters were ever sued for or cast for a fee when the Church bell was not tolled, the following account and summons are subjoined:

1796. JOSEPH GIBBONS, Esquire, Dr.

To the Rev. Mr. Frink.

To tooling the bell, —   £. 036
To the ground, — — .036

_____

£. 070

GEORGIA, Christ-Church Parish. To any Constable of the said Parish.

Mr. Joseph Gibbons, You are hereby summoned to appear at the Court of Conscience, to be held at the Court-House in Savannah, on the first Thursday in May next ensuing, at ten of the clock in the forenoon, to answer a complaint entered against you by the Reverend Mr. Frink. And in case, &c.   *Signed J. Ottolenghe.   April 12, 1769.*

Mr. Frink accordingly appeared personally, and the proceedings on the said trial were published in the *Georgia* Gazette, May 10, 1769.

A REMARKABLE case having been tried last week before the Court of Conscience, which being designed as a precedent, and likely to affect numbers of people, it is thought proper to inform the publick of the issue.

Some months ago, a poor man died; the person who out of charity had taken care of him in his sickness intending to bury him without any charge to the parish, had him buried in the way of his profession as a Dissenter, the Meeting bell tolled, and the sexton of the Meeting attended.

Since that the Mate of a vessel died, who being a Presbyterian, his Captain also thought fit to have him buried in his own way.

Thereupon a suit was brought against the Captain and the other person for the following fees, being the account given in the first case:

To tolling the bell, — £.036
To the ground, — £.036

———

£. 070

A law being produced the fee for the breaking of the ground was not disputed, but as to tolling the bell, it was thought no man could be entitled to wages that had done no work, so the decision was left to a jury.

The Judge, who had declared his opinion upon the merits of the cause long before the trial, upon the trial observed, that the sexton had a legal right to a fee for any *burial,* within the parish, *whether* he was desired to attend or no, *and* though in a private plantation. He *also with his usual good manners declared, that the Dissenters had no right to the use of a bell at all, and that the Rector of the parish was to blame that he had it not pulled down.*

The Judge who gave the charge was Joseph Ottolenghe, Esq. some time Catechist at Savannah.

The Jurymen were, William Ewen, Esq. Mr. Thomas Lee, and Mr. Jonathan Peat.

Mr. Ewen being a Member of the late Assembly was never known to have served before upon a jury in the Court of Conscience, and being one of the Vestry, had also previously given his judgment against the defendant.

Mr. Thomas Lee is Clerk of the Church; and those two made the majority.

I need not say a verdict was given against the defendant.

It is however thought that many persons will still refuse paying people that do no work for them; and as no law obliges any person to have any bell rung at all, and Protestant Dissenters, bu the charter of this province, are allowed the free exercise of their religion, which I think means, that they should not be taxed for it, they must still think the liberty given them by a charter is not to be taken away by such a Judge and such a Jury. And if a parish sexton is entitled to a fee for every burial, it will be a double hardship upon such parishes as are chiefly inhabited by Dissenters, such as St. Matthew's, St. John's, and St. Andrew's, parishes. And if any Justice should have a right to pick a jury of whom he is more than morally sure that they concurred with him in prejudging the matter before it comes to a hearing, a trial in that case will be worse than a mere formality.

It is also thought, that to decide such a matter is above the jurisdiction of the lowest court in the province; for though a suit for three shillings and sixpence comes properly enough within the compass of small and mean causes, yet to establish a precedent of thie nature, that will be pleaded all over the province, it not a trifling matter.

It is a remark of the Earl of Clarendon, that to discountenance and suppress all bold enquirers and opposers, the Council-Table and Star-chamber enlarged their jurisdiction to a vast extent, "holding (as *Thucydides* said of the *Athenians*) for honourable that which pleased, and for just that which profited." An execution for the fee thus sued for is actually issued.

Sufficient vouchers are at hand, that the fee for breaking the ground was never refused, though it appears now that this also has been demanded without law, and that the fees demanded have been raised very considerably within these two years on persons buried of all denominations.

As a proof of what airs some persons can give themselves, the following advertisement, which in itself is a curiousity, is added; it was stuck up on a cottage where a Dissenter had preached for some time past occasionally, and an offer of a sermon once a month it is said has since been made provided no Dissenters ever preach in the same place.

> *"Enigma—A Riddle to be answered before*
> *any presume to hold forth in this place,*
> *Audeat nemo sine auctoritate Sanctae Ecclesiae Anglicanae &*
> *permissu Parochialis R D F hos intra muros suam Haeresin*
> *intonare, non, si dixeris Argisontem illum cujus Nomen Zeta*
> *incipit; & parte altera oublier Gallica Lingua Oblivisci denotat,*
> *Uzzae Judicium—aliter Deum celestesq. potestates precibus*
> *meis commovebo; ut Vox tandem faucibus illi haereat,*
> *parvumque fructum inde ferat, quia nunc secundo velit mihi*
> *hujus pauperis Tecti Clavum tenenti injurias afferre, nec bene*
> *vertat illis, ex audientibus me qui illum aut alium mihi &*
> *Ecclesiae legibus latae oppositum huc invitant non Religionis*
> *verae, sed dissentionis gratia. Vetat interdicat Numen Loci*
> *eorum Confilia prava, meaque defendat audiatque verba Pater*
> *Filius & SS.*   *Gymnasiarcha.*

A bill to allow Protestant Dissenters a burying-ground in the Commons of Savannah (where Negroes bury undisturbed and unmolested by any) lately passed the Lower and miscarried in the Upper House of Assembly. Upon that occasion it has been said that the question amounted to no less than, whether the Church or Meeting should be looked upon as established by law, as though a quiet grave to the dead in a place many had a property in while living could give a Church establishment to survivors. It has also been said the dispute was, whether the Rector or the Dissenting Minister should be entitled to the fee of three and sixpence, and that that fee accordingly has been paid to the latter; but as the Gentleman who asserted these things now acknowledges that he paid nobody but the sexton, and "it is no concern of his to what use the money is applied," it is hoped he must be sensible of his mistake: That Gentleman, though he seems rather a little angry, adds, "I have only to pray God, of his infinite mercy, to cleanse the thoughts of your heart, by the inspiration of his holy spirit, that you may live peaceably with all mankind." I thank him for this, look upon the prayer as charitable and excellent, and, if he had not confined it to a single person, perhaps it might be still better. If any man can prove that I ever required any fee for burying, I will give him ten shillings for every shilling he may prove the receipt of; and if any man asserts what he cannot prove, with a view to make his neighbour and well wisher appear odious, though he may not chuse to hear of it, he must allow the injured to think. People may think they are in authority to throw dirt, but no doubt every man has a right to scrape it off when it is thrown upon him.   J.J. ZUBLY

Pamphlet 4

CALM AND RESPECTFUL THOUGHTS

1772

The strained relations between Americans and the British government from the 1760s on increased American legislators' jealousy of their rights and privileges. Like other American colonial assemblies, the Georgia Assembly claimed the rights and immunities of Parliament for its members and in the 1760s sought a large degree of political autonomy. In 1770 Governor James Wright tangled with the Georgia Commons House over its right to determine its own representation and to control its members. The Commons House refused to enact a tax bill until Wright acknowledged its claims, whereupon the governor, whose instructions from the crown forbade him granting such powers to the assembly, dissolved the legislature. When the Commons House attempted to re-elect Noble Wimberly Jones speaker in 1771, Wright disapproved the choice, probably because he suspected Jones was a ringleader in the opposition to British measures. Wright went to England on leave in the summer of 1771, leaving Georgia political relations in a stir.

James Habersham, the acting governor in Wright's absence, inherited a difficult situation, which he promptly aggravated in early 1772 when he disapproved the Commons House's unanimous election of Jones as speaker. The House then elected Archibald Bulloch speaker, after Jones declined to serve, and Habersham accepted the decision. The acting governor, however, demanded that the House expunge the reference to Jones's 1772 election from its journal. The House refused to do so, and Habersham dissolved the assembly.

This impasse left Georgia without a tax bill, a militia bill, and other necessary legislation. Zubly joined other Whigs in criticizing Wright and Habersham for their actions, and his pamphlet, *Calm and Respectful*

Thoughts, summed up popular feeling in the colony. Although marred by Zubly's historical error regarding the crown's right to veto a speaker, the pamphlet was a strong statement about contemporary American conceptions of legislative rights and crown prerogatives. In essence, Zubly maintained that the representatives of the people must be free in their choices because they were the freely elected choices of the people.

Relations between the assembly and the governor improved after Wright returned to Georgia in February, 1773, but the clash over the speaker marked the political coming of age for the Georgia Commons House and a significant decline in the governor's popular support in the colony.

Calm and Respectful Thoughts appeared serially in the *Georgia Gazette* between May and June 1772. It was published in pamphlet form in 1772, probably by James Johnston of Savannah.

Source: Rare Books Room, Chapin Library, Williams College

CALM AND RESPECTFUL THOUGHTS

on the NEGATIVE
of the CROWN on a SPEAKER
chosen and presented by the
REPRESENTATIVES of the PEOPLE:

Occasioned by some PUBLICATIONS in the
GEORGIA GAZETTE, of *May* and *June* 1772,
wherein the late ASSEMBLY of that PROVINCE
is charged with encroaching on the RIGHTS of
the CROWN.

BY A FREEMAN.

Pro Rege & Patria semper. Buckingham's Epitaph.

It is a remark of a very considerable writer of our own,
*that it cannot be improper to canvass any constitutional
question when decency is observed, and nothing advanced but
on the credit of the best authorities,* because in a British
country every man ought to be acquainted with the laws by
which his liberty and property are insured.

Under the shelter of this observation some remarks have been ventured
abroad, which I humbly apprehend have been rather condemned with
severity, and replied to with personal reflections, than canvassed or
answered with calmness or strength of argument. As the subject however
has been formally dropt by one of the writers, I should not now take pen
in hand could the other have been satisfied to enjoy his victory, without
continuing to load the late Assembly with reflections, which I will not say
are designed, but appear to have a tendency to set this province in the
worst light at home, and to render the late Representatives as odious as
possible in this province. My design is to take off the odium which is cast

upon this province as though it meant to invade the Prerogative of the Crown. If the late Representatives have acted contrary to the sense of their Constituents they will doubtless be marked for it at a next election; if the majority of inhabitants should think the Crown has not a right of rejection, let their arguments be first considered before they are accused of a design of encroaching on the Prerogative.

I will own my obligations; the most light I received in this controversy has been from that very writer, and, upon the most mature consideration, I must own the right he contends for appears to me more problematical than ever. I will however still leave this right as I found it (I always wished it should remain unagitated) undetermined and undecided; but I hope I am not too sanguine to flatter myself that those that read what may make against it will be convinced they that hold the negative may still be honest men, and good and loyal subjects, whether in a private character, or as the Representatives of a free and loyal people. I design to mention some arguments which persuade me this negative is not clearly established, and I shall take so much notice of the arguments brought in support of it to examine whether they really prove what is intended.

It may not be improper first to lay down a few general principles which are universally allowed. It is agreed on all sides that the existence of a House of Commons is now as necessary and essential to our Constitution as the existence of a King and House of Lords. It is agreed that the Commons being the Representatives of the people the people ought to chuse them, the King and Lords must not interfere in the choice, and any one duly chosen, and not by law incapacitated, the election cannot be set aside. It is agreed that the Crown must call the House, issue writs of election, and may adjourn, prorogue, or dissolve the House, but to reign without Parliament is contrary to the Constitution; to dissolve wantonly, and without cause, is not against the Constitution, but it seems an improper use of a very legal power. The design of a House of Commons is to be a check on the Prerogative, and to watch over the rights of the people. Prerogative is placed in the Crown that the people may not encroach on the rights of the Crown. By the wisdom of the Constitution every branch of the Legislature forms a mutual check upon the other, the people are a check upon the Nobility, and the Nobility upon the people, while the King is a check upon both, and his executive power is again checked and kept within due bounds by the two Houses, through the privilege they have of enquiring into, impeaching, and punishing the conduct of the King's evil Counsellors. The House of Commons is to consult for the good of the nation, and all monies give to the King are given only by the Commons; whatever is necessary for this purpose is their undeniable privilege, for, unless they may freely consult, and do that for which they are called together and constituted a House, the very purposes of their meeting must be defeated. I suppose therefore it will not be denied, as the Crown calls the Commons together for national purposes, the Commons so met must have a right or privilege to every thing that appears necessary to answer the purposes for which they are called and met together. This I take the true idea of the privileges of the House, and as the House cannot subsist nor act properly without them, to deny or curtail these privileges is attempting the abolition of the House itself, and of course destroying the Constitution. The fairest way therefore to judge of any claim of either branch of the Legislature is to consider the effect it may have on the other branches, and whatever clasheth with any known right or privilege of either King or any of the two Houses cannot be constitutional, whatever would prevent the Crown in the execution of those laws made by the Legislative cannot be supported, and if the Crown has any power that may restrain freedom of debate, or abridge the liberty of giving and granting in the House of Commons, or impede them in business, otherwise than by adjournment, prorogation, or dissolution, I cannot see how the House may be conceived free and independent in their deliberations.

I believe few men will deny any of these principles; let them be kept in constant view when we enquire into the question whether the Crown has a right to reject a Speaker duly chosen and presented for approbation.

The House of Commons must have a Speaker. All Assemblies met for consultation have found it necessary to place one over themselves to keep up order and regulate their debates; if 500 men were all to speak at once, and none have authority to call them to order, the voice of wisdom must be lost in noise, and prudent counsel swallowed up in confusion. Formerly both Houses are said to have had but one Speaker between them, but as both Houses became more distinct, and the Commons more important, they of course had a Speaker of their own, who is so necessary that ordinarily they do no business without him.

This Speaker they must either chuse themselves, or he must be placed over them by the Crown. "The Speaker of the House of Lords is the Lord Chancellor or Keeper of the Great Seal, or any other Appointed by the King's Commission; and if none be so appointed, the House of Lords (it is said) may elect;" *Blackstone*, vol. 1. p. 181. The Speaker of the House of Commons is chosen by the House, but must be approved of by the King, ibid. "It is true the Commons are to chuse their Speaker," *Coke.* How far the King's approbation is necessary is the question in dispute, but all agree that the Commons must chuse their Speaker, and it seems the choice is of more importance than presentation or approbation, because without choice there can be no such thing as either.

The Speaker chosen ought to be a person properly qualified. If every Member of Parliament ought to be independent and uninfluenced by any views of honour or interest but the public good, the Speaker ought to be so much more. He ought to be equally well acquainted with the privileges of the House and the rights of Prerogative, and of sufficient fortitude to act consistent with both on every occasion, neither courting popularity by disputing the just rights of the Crown, nor have an eye to gain or promotion by betraying any right of the subject. *The election of any Member to be Speaker is a solemn declaration of the House that they judge him the man best qualified for that business.* I believe it seldom, if ever, happened, that a Member was chosen Speaker the first time of his serving as a Member. A person is usually pitched upon who, from long experience, is well acquainted with the privileges and proceedings of the House, and of whose abilities also the House have had long and sufficient experience. The Speaker has been called a servant of the House, and as the King has an undoubted right to chuse, and must be the best judge of his own servants, so the Commons are best acquainted with the character of every Member of their House, and thereby best able to judge who is the fittest for any particular business that may be assigned.

The Speaker sits in the House, not in the name or as a Commissioner of the King, but though his seat is a little raised *as a Member upon a par with the rest,* chosen and appointed by themselves; not to do any business for the King, but their business, to be their mouth, regulate their debates, and execute their orders; neither is he to have *"eyes to see, or ears to hear, but as directed by the House."*

It is not denied by any that the Commons must chuse, nor that their choice ought to be free, and it has been allowed that they are not obliged to chuse a person nominated or recommended by the Crown, supposing the Crown should think proper to recommend or make such a nomination, but as it has always been customary to present the Speaker so chosen to the King for approbation, it is hence concluded that the King may set aside the choice of his Commons, and reject a Speaker so presented. If the want of such a right of rejection had any apparent tendency to render some other absolute rights of the King more precarious, or to endanger his Crown or the Constitution, the King ought undoubtedly to have it, for he ought to have his right, and every thing that may legally secure it; if the exercise of that right, though not necessary to the King, might add to his greater dignity, and in no case whatever bring any danger to the subject, I would in mere decency make a compliment of it to the King; but if it should appear that the claim and exercise of that right had even a distant tendency to hurt the subject, and wound the Constitution, I would then wish that the King had and insisted to have all the just rights of his Royal Prerogative, and no more.

That I may treat the question in the most inoffensive manner, I declare that I mean not to write against the right claimed by the Crown; I only propose some doubts which I shall be glad to see cleared up, and with pleasure will I join all my fellow loyal subjects to acquiesce in any claim that may appear the constitutional right of the Crown.

As it is agreed on all hands the Commons must chuse their Speaker, in the very nature of things it seems implied that he whom they chose ought to be considered as Speaker. Whom are they to chuse? A Speaker. By whose authority are they to chuse him? By the King's command, and as the Representatives of the people; if, after having thus received the King's command, and sitting as the Representatives of the people, they have chosen a man to be Speaker, the person so chosen is not what they chose him, it will be equally difficult to assert what it seems just as difficult to deny, that they made a choice, or that they had not authority to make the choice they actually have made.

It has been allowed "that the Commons may freely chuse whom they please for their Speaker," but asserted, "that the Crown, for its own preservation, has a right to reject an improper person," (*Georgia Gazette*, June 10.) By an improper person here must be understood one whom the Commons thought proper, but who is thought improper by the Crown. Now let any one ask himself whether he should think he enjoyed the right of freely chusing whomsoever he pleased for his own servant if another had the right to put a negative on the servant he had actually chosen, under pretence of being improper for the service of him by whom chosen, and thereby deprive him of his service at pleasure. To talk of a free choice, which yet may be controuled and annulled by another, seems inconsistent with the very nature of choice, and at most it can only be called a freedom to chuse upon condition that another do not invalidate the choice; if the person chosen be equally acceptable to him that chuses and to him that must approve, it matters very little by whom such a choice is made; but if acceptable and necessary only to those by whom the choice was made, I cannot see what their choice avails if it may be set aside at pleasure by another, perhaps too it might be set aside for that very reason because the person chosen is suspected of being more in the interest of those by whom he is chosen than may be consistent with the designs of him by whom he is rejected.

Those that chuse a Speaker to do the business of the House have first been chosen themselves to do the business of the nation; they are not met by their own authority, nor to do their own business, nor the King's business, but the business of the nation; they cannot debate the concerns of the nation without a Speaker to direct and regulate their debates; but it is of infinite concern to the nation that no man mislead, restrain, or impede their debates; a Speaker might do all this, and were he to do it to serve the Crown, it would be in vain to look to the Crown for relief, he would be a dead weight to them, and they unable to help themselves; it seems therefore that the choice of a Speaker by the Representatives should be as free and final as the choice of the people of the Representatives who are to chuse the Speaker.

The sitting of the Commons, though called by the King's writ; the privileges of the House, though prayed for of the King; the freedom of debate; are all matter of right, and not of favour; the very design of the House of Commons is to prevent too extensive or an undue influence of the Crown; if any proceedings of the House become matters of favour of the Crown, what becomes of the intrinsick right and authority of the Commons? A Speaker was excepted against, because, "if the King always should accept a person pitched upon by the House, then it would be no great favour to be chosen a Speaker." Here the exception against a Speaker was however sweetened with a reason being given; but if the Speaker holds his place, not by the choice of the Representatives, but by the favour of the Crown, it is then evident that the principal man in the House of Commons holds his place under the favour and influence of that very power to prevent whose too powerful influence, and restrain it within its proper bounds, is, or ought to be, the principal object of the Representatives of a free people.

The whole of the law and custom of Parliament has its original from this one maxim, that whatever matter arises concerning either House of Parliament ought to be examined, discussed, and adjudged, in that House to which it relates, and not elsewhere, *Blackstone Com.* 1. 163.

In consequence of this the Commons may judge void the elections of Members already sitting, and declare those duly elected, who have not been returned so by the proper Officer; and it would seem strange if they, who have a right to judge of every election in the kingdom, should not have a right to chuse their own Speaker, if they were judges who is properly elected a Representative of the whole nation, and yet liable to have a negative put on a choice made by themselves of their own servant. The House of Commons have an undoubted right by their own act, and without any concurrence or interfering of the Crown, to expel any of their Members, the Speaker not excepted, for misbehaviour, the reason of which seems to be, as the Crown is not supposed to interfere in elections, neither ought it in expulsions; but if the Speaker holds his place by the King's favour and approbation, so as without that he is not Speaker *"pleno jure,"* it would seem strange that the Commons should have a right to drive a man by their sole authority from a post where they never could have placed him without the King's command and favour. To depose a man from a post which he could not hold, nor be chosen to, but with the King's approbation, seems to be a greater power than to chuse their Officer without the King's approbation.

If the King has a right to reject a Speaker chosen, he must hold that right either in virtue of some act of Parliament, or it must be a part of his Royal Prerogative; the former was never asserted, the latter is the subject in question.

Upon a supposition the King had a clear constitutional right to nominate, or even impose a Speaker, as soon as the House meets, that right seems clearly given up, by his ordering or giving the House leave to chuse a Speaker themselves. As it is said even the Lords may elect, unless the King appoints a Speaker for them, it seems clearly to follow that the King requiring the Commons to chuse, he means that the person by them chosen shall actually be Speaker, for they are not commanded to make choice of one or more persons of whom the King may chuse one, but simply and absolutely to chuse a Speaker for themselves. That the King does not interfere in the choice of a Prolocutor of the Law vocation, which has been called a Parliament in miniature, I conclude, because when Dr. Jane was preferred to Dr. Tillotson, King William did not reject, though certainly not as agreeable to the King's principles, as that excellent man

Dr. Tillotson; and as elections are to be made, according to Coke, *sine prece,* without prayer or gift, so he observes they ought also to be made *sine praecepto,* without the King's command by writ or otherwise, and he saith an act for that purpose was a close and prudent salve, not only for that sore, but for all other in like case, and is but an act declaratory of the ancient law and custom of Parliament.

If we would argue from facts, but one instance has been produced where the choice of the Commons was excepted against, and none whatever where the Commons submitted to a rejection; but the case of Sir Edward Seymour will come in more fully hereafter. It is difficult to conceive how the House may preserve freedom in debate if they are not at liberty to chuse the person by whom these debates are to be directed. That they may chuse any man whom the King shall approve is in reality saying they may chuse no man but whom the King approves, and that would seem perfectly equivalent to they have no right to chuse any man but whom the King chuseth; the King will not approve of any person but who he is morally sure will enter into all his measures; if by any means, whether by influence, nomination, choice, refusal of approbation of any other, the King gets a man of such a cast in the chair of the House of Commons, the King then has so far the direction, and a most powerful influence over the whole House.* It is only in behalf of such a Speaker that it can be the Crown's interest to contend. Such a Speaker, under pretence of calling to order, may interrupt the freedom of debate, and stop an enquiry into any mal practice or escape; by a sham sickness, or his absence from the House, an offender may escape; but, supposing the

---

*That a Speaker may impede the business of the House in favour of arbitrary measures of the Crown we have a striking instance in the Parliament 1673; the Commons remonstrated against the marriage of the Duke of York with a Papist, which has been productive of so much mischief to the nation. "To cut short these agreeable attacks, the King resolved to prorogue the Parliament, and with that intent came unexpectedly to the House of Peers, and sent the Usher to summon the Commons. It happened that the Speaker and the Usher nearly met at the door of the House, but the Speaker being within, some of the Members suddenly shut the door and cried, *To the chair, to the chair;* while others cried, The black rod is at the door. The Speaker was hurried to the chair, and the following motions were instantly made—The alliance with France is a grievance—Evil Counsellors about the King are a grievance.—There was a general cry, *To the question, to the question;* but (behold now the benefit of a Speaker agreeable to Charles II.) the Usher knocking violently at the door, *the Speaker leapt from the chair,* and the Parliament being prorogued gave the Duke leisure to consummate his marriage. *Rapin.*

Crown should reject a Speaker, on account of his being too popular, or having too great an influence in the House, it would not only be treating the body of Representatives as men that are not able to judge for themselves, but it is apparent that the power of rejecting a man because he is popular and disagreeable to the Crown is as dangerous a power in the hands of a bad ruler as can well be imagined.

When a Speaker is presented to a King for approbation the King must either be willing that all things should continue and proceed according to the known Laws and Constitution of the land, or he must have contrary views; in the former case he can hardly have any motive or cause to reject any person that is presented, the Speaker alone can make no alteration, and if the Commons should attempt any thing against the Crown a dissolution would legally ensue; but should a ruler intend to make any alteration in the laws, a Speaker might be a proper instrument in his hand for that purpose. The King it should seem can have no reason or motive to reject any Speaker, but on a suspicion of his having a stronger bias to the popular side than to the just Royal Prerogative; but besides, that the King, in case of rejecting such a one, must also harbour very hard thoughts of his Commons, it is easily seen what such a power might lead to. Of a wise and good Prince nothing is to be apprehended, but against wicked or weak Princes, or rather pernicious and evil Counsellors, the people can never be too much upon their guard.

It is not to be supposed, when a Speaker is presented, his character and principles can be unknown to the King's Ministers, but supposing they were, I cannot see how that should be any ground for rejection; if he is known to be a fit tool the right of rejection will be immaterial, he will be sure not to be rejected; if known to be a man zealous for the just rights and liberties of the nation, a patriot Prince can have no thought to reject such an one; and that an arbitrary Sovereign, who will not reject a man of a contrary stamp, should have a right to reject the only man that is fittest to oppose him and serve the nation, I think a very dangerous part of the Prerogative, and I am at a perfect loss how to reconcile such a power with the spirit and design of the Constitution of a free people.

These considerations I must own strongly influence me to doubt whether the Crown has a constitutional right to set aside and reject a Speaker chosen by the Representatives of the people. It is but fair, however, to hear what has been said in support of this right, and I do not mean that the arguments in favour of it should lose any of their force in my hands, I mean to represent them in all their weight, and as to these arguments and my remarks *valeant quantum valere possunt,* let them go as far as they may.

Two writers have appeared among us in favour of this claim of the Prerogative; what Neuter advanced, like his signature, is nothing neither here nor there; but, as he talks of a contagious political delirium, I am much afraid he has been in the neighborhood of the contagion, however I wish him well over.

I intend to consider every argument of G. B. *si pergama dextra defendi potuissent hac vice defensa suissent.* I dare say what books and arguments in this cause are not found with him will in vain be looked for any where else in this province.

Two passages have been quoted from Coke in support of this negative; Coke saith: *"The Commons shall present their Speaker in the Upper House to the King, who shall disable himself, and in most humble manner intreat the King to command them to chuse a more sufficient man."* From this passage it is said to appear that the new Speaker in the face of the whole House of Commons admits a power of rejection in the Crown; but is not this rather a large conclusion from small premises? Does not the Speaker's intreaty that the King would order a fitter man to be chosen favour as much of compliment as any thing else? Does it not at least look as much like compliment as like an acknowledgment of the right of rejection? However, if this proves any such right, the argument I conceive must stand thus: The Speaker is to disable himself (i.e. plead his inability) and intreat the King to command the Commons to chuse a fitter man; therefore (because he pleads his inability, and wisheth a fitter man may be chosen) the Crown has a clear right to put a negative on any man the Commons shall chuse as their Speaker. I despair to convince that man of any thing, except what he himself pleaseth, who can be convinced by such an argument. Coke also saith:

> It is true the Commons are to chuse, but seeing that after their choice the King may refuse him, for avoiding of expence and time, and contestation, the use is, (as in the congé d'eslier of a Bishop) that the King doth name a discreet and learned man, whom the Commons elect, but without their election no Speaker can be appointed for them.

The only expression in this passage that may be construed in support of this claim is, that the King *may* refuse. It has been observed that all this may mean no more than that the King may do it though he has no constitutional right so to do; and to this it has been answered, that Coke declares what he writes is grounded upon the authority and reason of books, rolls of Parliament, and judicial records, and that to make any objection against it is to make objections not against Coke, but (forsooth) against the Constitution itself; but as no book, authority, reason, parliamentary roll, or judicial record, has been produced older than this passage, I apprehend all this, notwithstanding what Coke saith with regard to the King's *may* may be bare narrative still, and no legal declaration of what the King may legally do; and I am the more inclined to doubt this matter, because I find Coke does not always speak like a Legislator, or one that declares the law; in this case, e. g. he saith every Member of the House being a Counsellor, he should have three properties of the elephant—that he has no gall—that he is inflexible and cannot bow—and that he is of ripe and most perfect memory. Now this seems a very good simile, but that any law declares a Member of Parliament should be like an elephant I still doubt, though I think all that write and act in publick ought to be without gall, and all Legislators inflexibly right. I don't know when Coke wrote, but should any writer now assert, while the Parliament sits, the King has as much authority in the choice of their Speaker as in the election of a Bishop by congé d'eslier, he would hardly be in any danger of receiving the thanks of the House; but perhaps these things may better suit the meridian of Georgia, and, great as the authority is, I presume it is no treason to say that the Constitution is now better understood than even a Coke explained it in the days of the Stuarts; and yet after all he expressly saith, though he seems to begin rather abruptly: True it is the Commons must chuse their own Speaker, and he cannot be appointed for them. All that was thought law in the days of Coke has not been thought so since.*

---

*Sir Edward Coke, the great oracle of the English law, had not only concurred with all other Lawyers in favour of this Prerogative of dispensing power, but seems even to believe it so inherent to the Crown that an act of Parliament itself could not abolish it, because from the law of nature the King has a right to the service of all his subjects. *Hume's Hist. of England,* vi. 394. On this principle Papists may be made Counsellors in Grenada, and why not in England? and men of known loyalty and approved abilities may be rejected as Speakers. I dare say, however contemptibly G. B. may speak of those that do not understand an ambiguous passage of Coke as he does, he will never set his name to any proposition that with Coke declares the dispensing power legal. The Revolution, as Hume justly observes, having put an end to these disputes, the acquisition of real liberty shewed the danger of the subsistance of such a Prerogative.

I am really surprised at the stress that has been laid on the case of Sir Edward Seymour, rejected by Charles II. in 1679. It has been said, "he was rejected," "the King never gave the matter up," "prorogued the House for a *few days*," "that the House dropt the matter, which it seems they had mistaken," "and proceeded to the choice of another person," (See *Georgia Gazette* for April 29, 1772:) And again, (*Georgia Gazette* for May 13) "that the King asserted the right of nomination," "rejected one Speaker and nominated another," and, N. B. because, "the House declined to chuse him prorogued them," "that the House did not assert their right but chused Gregory," "and did not shew a want of publick spirit by impeding publick business, had they done so it is supposed Charles would have dissolved them, lest they should serve him the same trick that had been served his father: And again, (*Georgia Gazette* May 29) "that in the next session they repaired their mistake, and chose a different person." Now, whoever puts all this together will naturally conclude, that the Commons chose a Speaker disagreeable to the King, whom the King rejected; that, on their not rescinding their choice, the King insisted on his having such a right, and never gave it up, but prorogued them for some days, and that then they dropt the matter, repaired their mistake, gave up their claim so far that now "it can't be said to be undecided," chose another person, and so all was well, the King's right established, and whoever now thinks and saith otherwise is a fiery Republican, and as bad (or nearly) as the Long Parliament. I do not mean to criticize upon this account given by an author of whom it has been said "that he writes unsoured by party, and with an apparent view to give candid information;" but I advise the reader next to peruse a different account given by two authors who have never been deemed partial, and who at least cannot be said to be influenced by our Georgia disputes.

Thus Rapin:

> The Parliament began with a warm dispute between the King and the Commons about the choice of a Speaker. The Commons having chosen Mr. Edward Seymour, the King, who knew Seymour was a particular enemy of the Earl of Danby, refused his approbation, and ordered the Commons to proceed to a new choice. The House was extremely displeased with this refusal, alledging, that it was never known that a person should be excepted against, and no reason given, and *that the thing itself of presenting a Speaker to the King was*

but a bare compliment. The King, on his side, insisted on the approbation or refusal of a Speaker when presented to him as a branch of his Prerogative. During a six days dispute, the Commons made several representations to the King, to which he gave very short answers. At last, as the Commons would not desist from what they thought their right, the King went to the Parliament, and prorogued it from the 13th to the 15th, that is, for one day's interval between the two sessions. The Parliament meeting the 15th, the King ordered the Commons to proceed to the choice of a Speaker; then, to avoid a revival of the dispute, they chose Mr. William Gregory, Serjeant at Law, who was approved by the King. *Rapin,* vol. 2 p. 703.

The account given in the Parliamentary Debates is still fuller:

The Chancellor, by the King's commands, ordered the House of Commons to proceed to the choice of a Speaker, who was to be presented to the King the next day, and being returned to their House, Colonel Birch did nominate and recommend the Right Honourable Edward Seymour, Knight of the Shire for the county of Devon, Treasurer of the Navy, one of his Majesty's most Honourable Privy-Council, and Speaker of the last Parliament: Being a person acceptable to the King, and one who for his great integrity, ability, and long experience in the employment, was the fittest person for so great a trust. And Mr. Seymour being unanimously called upon to the chair, was conducted thither by Sir Thomas Lee, Sir Thomas Whitmore, and divers other members, and being there placed, he made a gratulatory speech to the House for their great kindness and affection towards him, in their unanimous choice of him: But still he desired the House that they would proceed to a new election, "For the long sittings of the late Parliament had so impaired his health, that he doubted he should not be well able to undergo the service of the House as would be expected from him:" But the House not admitting of any excuse, confirmed their choice, upon which *he desired leave,* "That he might intercede with his Majesty, that he would be pleased to discharge him of the duty."

But it appears, that he need not have been so urgent; for the King and the Earl of Danby taking this choice to be an ill presage, that this

Parliament would begin where the last ended, were resolved not to approve of it: And as soon as he appeared to be presented, the Lord Chancellor stood up, and said,

> That if his Majesty should always accept a person pitcht upon by the House of Commons, then it would be no great favour to be chosen a Speaker; and therefore his Majesty, being the best judge of persons and things, thought fit to except against Mr. Seymour, as being fitly qualified for other services and imployments, without giving any reason to the persons chusing or the persons chosen.

And therefore he ordered them to fix upon some other person by to-morrow morning, to be presented to the King for his approbation. The Commons immediately returned back to their own House, where Sir John Ernly stood up and acquainted them, "He had orders from his Majesty to recommend Sir Thomas Meers to them to be their Speaker, as a person well known in the method and practice of Parliaments, and a person that he thought would be very acceptable and serviceable to them." But the House in a great heat cryed out, *No, no!* and fell into a warm debate. Mr. Sacheverell said,

> It was never known that a person should be excepted against, and no reason at all given, and therefore concluded, that it was done purposely to gratify some particular persons. Mr. Williams said for above a hundred years, it had not been known that a Speaker presented was ever excepted against; and the thing itself of presenting him to the King, as he humbly conceived, was but a bare compliment. Sir Thomas Clarges alledged, that there were Parliaments long before there were speakers chosen, and afterwards, for the ease of the House among themselves, they pitched upon a Speaker.—All our lives and liberties are preserved by this House, therefore we are to preserve the liberties of it. Mr. Garraway objected, if Mr. Seymour be rejected and no reason given, pray who must chuse a Speaker, the King or we? It is plain not we?—Sir Thomas Lee said, we address'd ourselves to his Majesty the last Parliament, as fearing his person to be in danger, but we received no answer at all in a whole week; we were immediately prorogued unexpectedly; and a little after dissolved, as unexpectedly; and I suppose, the same persons that gave that advice, gave this also.

Others concluded, that all this was only for a bone of contention, fearing they should agree, and so called to adjourn, which was soon agreed to.

These heats were so much the greater, because they reasonably supposed that it was all occasioned by the Earl of Danby; whose power was not wholly at an end; and between whom and Mr. Seymour there was a particular resentment. However, the first thing resolved on the next day, being Saturday, was,

> That an humble application be made to the King, to acquaint his Majesty, that the matter yesterday delivered by the Lord Chancellor, relating to the Speaker, is of so great importance, that this House cannot immediately come to a resolution therein: And therefore do humbly desire his Majesty, that he will graciously be pleased, to grant some further time for this House to take the matter into consideration.

And they ordered the Chancellor of the dutchy, the Lord Cavendish, the Lord Russel, and Sir Henry Capel, immediately to attend his Majesty with this vote. Being returned in a short time, the Lord Russel acquainted the House, That they had attended his Majesty, who was sitting in Council; and that his Majesty, as soon as he was informed they were to wait upon him from the House immediately came out, and received them with great chearfulness and kindness: And having delivered their message, his Majesty retired to the Council-Chamber, and coming out again, was pleased to return the following answer by word of mouth, which they had reduced to writing:

> Gentlemen,
>
> I have considered of your message, and do consent to a further time, which I appoint to be on Tuesday next, unless you shall find some expedient in the mean time; for as I would not have my *prerogative* intrenched upon, so I would not do any thing against the privileges of the House.

Upon the said Tuesday they drew up this humble Representation.

> We your Majesty's most dutiful and loyal subjects, the Commons in this present Parliament assembled, do with all obedience return your Majesty most hearty thanks for the favourable reception, and gracious answer your Majesty was pleased to return to our late message; wherein your Majesty was pleased, not only to *allow us longer time,* to deliberate of

what was delivered to us by the Lord Chancellor, relating to the choice of a Speaker, but likewise to express so great a care *not to infringe our privileges*. And we desire your Majesty to believe no subjects ever had a more tender regard, than ourselves, to the rights of your Majesty, and your Royal Prerogative; which we shall always acknowledge to be vested in the Crown, for the benefit and protection of your people. And therefore for the clearing all doubts that may arise in your Royal mind, upon this occasion now before us, we crave leave humbly to represent unto your Majesty, That it is the undoubted right of the Commons to have the free election of one of their Members to be their Speaker, and to perform the service of the House: And that the Speaker so elected, and presented according to custom, hath by the constant practice of all former ages, been continued Speaker and executed that employment, unless such persons have been excused for some corporal disease, which has been alledged, either by themselves, or some others in their behalf, in full Parliament. According to this usage, Mr. Edward Seymour was unanimously chosen, upon the consideration of his great ability and sufficiency for that place, of which we had large experience in the last Parliament, and was presented by us to your Majesty, as a person we conceived would be most acceptable to your Majesty's Royal judgment. This being the true state of the case, we do in all humility lay it before your Majesty's view; hoping that your Majesty, upon due consideration of former precedents, will rest satisfied with our proceedings, and will think fit not to deprive us of so necessry a Member, by employing him in any other service; but to give us such a gracious answer, as your Majesty, and your Royal predecessors, have always done heretofore upon the like occasions; that so we may, without more loss of time, proceed to the dispatch of those important affairs, for which we were called hither: Wherein we doubt not but we shall so behave ourselves, as to give an ample testimony to the whole world of our duty and affection to your Majesty's service, and of our care of the peace and prosperity of your kingdoms.

To this Representation the King immediately gave this short answer:

Gentlemen,

All this is but loss of time; and therefore I desire you to go back again, and do as I have directed you.

This giving no satisfaction to the House, the next day, March 12th, the Commons, after a warm debate, drew up this following Address:

Most Gracious Sovereign,

Whereas by the gracious answer your Majesty was pleased to give to our first message in Council, whereby your Majesty was pleased to declare a resolution, *not to infringe our just rights and privileges,* we your Majesty's most dutiful and loyal Commons were encouraged to make an humble representation to your Majesty upon the choice of our Speaker, which on Tuesday last was presented by some of our Members: We do, with great trouble and infinite sorrow, find by the report made to us by those Members, at their return, that your Majesty was pleased to give us an immediate answer to the same, without taking any further consideration; which we are persuaded, if your Majesty had done, what we then offered to your Majesty would so far have prevailed upon your Royal judgment, as to have given your Majesty satisfaction in the reasonableness of our desire; and preserved us in your Majesty's favourable opinion of our proceedings. And since we do humbly conceive, that the occasion of this question hath arisen from your Majesty's not being truly informed of the state of the case; we humbly beseech your Majesty to take the said representation into your further consideration, and give us such a gracious answer, that we may be put in a capacity to manifest our readiness to enter into these consultations which necessarily tend to the preservation and welfare of your Majesty and your kingdoms.

Upon reading this address to the King, he immediately gave this quick and sharp return: *Gentlemen, I will send you an answer to-morrow.* Accordingly, as he had often done before upon great difficulties, he resolved to put an end to the dispute; and on the next morning, being Thursday the 13th of March, he came to the House of Peers, and sending for the Commons, he immediately prorogued the Parliament till Saturday following, after the Commons had sat without a Speaker but six days. And thus the King found a way to gain his point, but with very little advantage to his own business and affairs.

On the appointed day, March 15th, his Majesty came to the House of Peers in his Royal robes, and the House of Commons attending, his Majesty was pleased to put both Houses in mind of what he said to them at the opening of the Parliament: And then the Lord Chancellor, by the King's command, directed the Commons to return to their House, and to proceed to the choice of a Speaker. And being returned, the Lord Russel put the House in mind of the King's commands, and immediately recommended William Gregory Sergeant at law, *as a person, for his great learning and integrity, fit for the employment.* And Mr. Sergeant Gregory being unanimously called upon to the chair, he in a short speech modestly excused himself, and desired of the House, that another might be nominated; but no excuse being admitted, he was formally conducted to the chair, by his two intimate friends, the Lord Russel and the Lord Cavendish, and there confirmed in the place.

"On the Monday following, he was presented by the Commons to the King, in the House of Lords, who without hesitation approved of the choice."*

---

*Sir Edward Seymour having so often been mentioned in this debate, it may not be amiss to take some notice of his character as drawn by Burnet, and of his behaviour as Speaker: "In pride he had neither shame nor decency: He was violent against the Court till he forced himself into good posts: He knew the House, and every man in it, so well, that by looking about he could tell the fate of any question: He was the most assuming Speaker that ever sat in the chair: If any thing was put when the Court party was not well gathered together, he would have held the House from doing any thing by a wilful mistaking or misstating the question; by that he gave time to those who were appointed for that mercenary work to go about and gather in all their party, and he would discern when they had got the majority, and then he would very fairly state the question when he was sure to carry it." It is most likely that in favour of such a man the Court party would exert all their influence to get him chosen, and very improbable that being chosen the Commons would so strenuously have opposed his rejection, if they had not thought it illegal and a dangerous precedent; but from this very instance it appears to demonstration how essential it is to the regularity, freedom, and just issue of national debates, that no such Speaker should by any means be obtruded, or one of a contrary stamp be rejected. The Commons maintained their claim as long as they were suffered to continue, and till a prorogation put an end to all their proceedings. At the next session they might be the more unwilling to revive their former choice because they could easily fix upon a better man; Gregory was then chosen, and in the two succeeding Parliaments that very Williams who had asserted that the presenting the Speaker to the King was a bare compliment; the King did not shew any resentment, but approved of him without hesitation. The true reason of Seymour's rejection, who had been Speaker before, was this: The Earl of Danby expected to be prosecuted for things done by the King's order; the King, in order to secure him, granted him a pardon in a very illegal manner; Seymour was looked upon as Danby's

I shall not make many remarks on these accounts, but I cannot forbear observing that the only instance where a Speaker appears rejected by the Crown was in the reign of a Stuart, when there was a settled design against the religion and liberties of the nation, which is far from being a presumption favourable to such a claim; even then the King does not reject *ex plenitudine potestatis,* but assigns *as a reason* that Sir Edward Seymour was proper for other services; and yet the Commons tell the King, that to chuse their Speaker without being deprived of their choice is their undoubted right. When Charles recommended another as one who he thought would be very acceptable and serviceable to them, they cried, No, no, and never would nor did chuse him; the King wisheth then to find an expedient, did not insist on his nomination, but prorogued them for a single day, which was plainly done to compromise the matter; when they met again, he recommended nobody, but Lord Russel, who afterwards fell a martyr to liberty, nominated Gregory, who was unanimously chosen, and formally conducted to the chair, and there confirmed in the place, and Monday after the King approved of him without hesitation. Burnet, in his memoirs, expressly saith the point was settled, that the right of electing was in the House, and that the confirmation was a thing of course.

The argument, that if the King has no right to reject he may be under a necessity of admitting disagreeable persons into his presence, as persons may be chosen disaffected to his Majesty's person and government, of which Wilkes being made Sheriff is given as an example, I cannot think of any great strength. I suppose the law calls no man disaffected who takes the oaths prescribed by law, and if any should be personally disagreeable to the King there is no necessity for his coming into his presence. Wilkes I believe never did, but I conceive the Constitution disables no man to serve his country in any place not in the gift of the Crown merely because he may be disagreeable to the King. The same Parliament that chose Seymour deputed Lord Russel to the King, who never was a friend to the King's measures, and yet Charles had more

---

enemy, and it was thought too dangerous that upon this occasion he should be Speaker; hence the King rather excused himself for not admitting than harshly rejected him; and thus it appears that this rejection was made with a manifest view to obstruct publick justice, and as the right of rejection was never claimed nor contended for but upon this single occasion, it does not seem to derive any merit from the only instance when it was pleaded.

grace than to receive him otherwise than politely. The right of rejecting a disagreeable person can be of no manner of service to the Crown, unless it may be exercised as often as a disagreeable person is chosen. Supposing the case to happen, it can hardly be expected that a House so ill disposed as to chuse a disagreeable person at first would become so good-natured, by the afront of a rejection, as to chuse a person more agreeable in a second election; or, supposing elections were repeated till the Commons gave way and chose a person perfectly agreeable to the Crown, what must be the natural consequence to the people? it can be no other than an express introduction of a Member would have to represent the King. The Speaker is not the King's Representative, but if the Crown insists none shall be Speaker but one that will obey the orders, or, which may be just the same, is agreeable to the King, he might as well; in that case the King would have an Officer in the House, introduced, not by bribery and corruption, but by refusing to approve any other, and he might have the casting vote in a place where he ought to have no vote at all.

That *to present a Speaker for approbation implies a right of rejection* has been alledged with greater shew; but that it is the Commons choice, and not the King's approbation, that constitutes the Speaker, seems very plain, because he is placed in the chair immediately after the election, and sometimes acts as such some days before he is presented and approved of by the King. It would be very indecent to vest him in the office, and place him in the chair, if after all the King's negative might set aside the choice; and I would apply here what Sir R. Atkins saith with regard to a form observed at the same time when the Speaker is presented, *"That humble and modest way of the people's addressing their Sovereign,—for granting privileges,"* (of which the right to chuse and have a Speaker seems necessarily one) *"shews great reverence and becomes the majesty of the Prince to be addressed to; but let it not be made an argument that either the laws thereupon made, or the privileges allowed, are precarious, and merely a favour, or may be refused them of right."* There are many presentations in law which allow not of rejection. The usual privileges, without which the House cannot act nor subsist, must be asked for; but as this is a petition, not of favour, but of right, so it seems the approbation of a Speaker is as much so. If the Constitution requires some applications to the King it also obliges the Crown never to put a negative on some applications. The new Speaker humbly *prays* for the privileges of the House, but should any Prince be so ill advised as to look upon that application as a matter which he may refuse, he might perhaps be informed that such a refusal implied no less than a breach of the original contract between him and his people, and that in this case it would be in vain to say that the power of giving (or approving) also implies a power of refusing.

It has been said that this claim of the Crown was but once denied by Parliament; I believe it was always denied; but it might as well have been said it was but once claimed by the Crown. Some weight is laid on the circumstance that a Speaker was recommended as acceptable to the King, but it seems the King also recommended a man as one whom he supposed very acceptable to Parliament. When a superior recommends to an inferior it is no argument that those to whom he recommends have not a final choice. That a person (*caeteris paribus*) is acceptable to the King may be no improper recommendation to or motive with his electors.

To establish this claim of the Crown, it has been observed, that Speakers have been disallowed, like Sir John Popham; but the case amounts to no more than his excuse was admitted; formerly every Speaker begged leave of the House that he might excuse himself to the King; this request of leave seems rather a proof that the election of the House is looked upon as final than otherwise, and Popham, though his excuse must have been very good, appears the only instance in which it was admitted, and cannot be of much weight against so many instances where no excuse was allowed. It is very certain the King did not approve Seymour, but it is not less so that, in order to get rid of the choice, he was obliged to prorogue the House, and that all he gained is, that the commons did not revive the dispute. The acquiescing of the Representatives of New England under a negative put on their choice is entirely owing to the tenor of their charter, and I am still of opinion that what rights the King reserved to himself in that charter are not such as are the undoubted prerogative of the Crown, but such as every Assembly or Parliament has a just claim to where the contrary is not expressly stipulated by charter.

It has been advanced, that *"when the King gave the Commons leave to chuse a speaker he reserved to himself the right of rejecting a Speaker that might be disagreeable to him, and that there was a compact between the King and Commons for that purpose."* This would be a strong argument indeed; but when and where was that compact made? What author or historian speaks of it? What authority is cited in proof of it? *"Why it is natural to conclude,"* but is it not as natural to conclude that, because no traces of any such compact are to be found, and that the Commons always regularly chose their own Speaker, and that not even an attempt was ever made to reject him, but in the case of Sir Edward Seymour, and that then the King never made any mention of such an original compact, but submitted to have his own nomination treated with a negative, and approved of one chosen in opposition to his own former recommendation, that therefore no such compact ever existed? And as this country is very "scarce of books," I am clearly of opinion *that* book is not on this side of the water where this compact stands upon record, but if a copy, or direction where this compact may be found, is left with the Printer, it shall be duly acknowledged, and, if the owner chuses it, a promise given that his name shall not be mentioned.

I ought to take notice of one argument more, (*Georgia Gazette* June 24:) "*If the Massachusetts-Bay hold their provincial Legislation under charter, do not we in this province hold it under his Majesty's commission and instruction to his Representative? And if that charter has reserved the power of negation upon their choice of a Speaker, will not the commissions and instructions to the Governor of this province have the same effect?*" I conceive a very great difference between his Majesty's instructions and charters; an Englishman I should think entitled to English laws, which I suppose implies Legislation any where and every where in the British dominions; that this right is prior to any charter or instruction, and is held not by instructions to a Governor, but is his natural right, which nothing but outlawry can deprive him of. Whatever is not law cannot be binding upon a British subject, and I suppose no man will say that, because the King has an undoubted right to instruct his servants, that therefore he has also a right to give instructions contrary to the Constitution, or derogatory of the right of the subject; such an instruction a Governor might look upon as a law to himself, but it is only the King can do no wrong, and the reason is plain, because the King can do nothing against law or the Constitution.

It has been said that a Speaker may have an undue influence to the prejudice of the Crown; but he can *have* no undue influence as Speaker before he is really such, and it *cannot* appear that he has any undue influence before he has actually entered on his office, and in this case the Crown is sufficiently guarded by its indisputable negative on every act of Legislature, and of dissolution whenever it shall be thought necessary. By this also it would seem as if the Crown had a right to reject a Speaker actually approved of whenever his influence should become disagreeable, which doctrine I believe is entirely new, perhaps not free from danger.

The Assembly of this province sometimes consisted only of 19 Members; 9 then made a House, and 5 a majority; as the number of Representatives increased it was thought necessary that the number to constitute a House should be increased in proportion; 19 now make a House, and 10 a majority, to do any business relating to the province. The remark that the strenuous advocate of the right of negative makes upon this alteration is this: "Such resolutions (which by the way were unanimous) could be made with no other view than the putting it in the power of a few leading men to impede the publick business by a secession whenever they pleased; which remark, as I suppose it had not been made had any Assembly subsisted, so every reader will judge with what justice and temper it was made. That he wishes 5 men might have the power rather than 10 is self-evident, and that 1 man may more easily influence 4 or 5 than 9 or 10 need not be doubted.

I shall conclude with a citation from a debate in the House of Lords in 1675:

> *The Lords plainly spoke out, That men had been, might and were likely to be, in either House, too much for the King, as they called it, and that whoever did endeavour to give more power to the King than the law and Constitution had given,— might justly be said to do too much for the King, and to be corrupted in his judgment by the prospect of advantages and rewards, though when it is considered that every deviation of the Crown towards absolute power lessens the King in the love and affections of his people,—a wise Prince will not think it a service done him.*

Pamphlet 5

THE LAW OF LIBERTY

1775

In the summer of 1775 political events moved rapidly in America, and in Georgia. British soldiers and American "minutemen" had already clashed at Lexington and Concord, and Massachusetts, in armed resistance to British authority, had appealed to her sister colonies for military support. Goaded by Whigs in other colonies and embarrassed by their previous timidity, Georgia "patriots" attempted to wrest effective political control of the colony from Governor Wright and the British party by organizing a provincial congress and sending delegates to the Continental Congress.

On 4 July 1775, the Second Provincial Congress in Georgia met to organize itself. After the meeting, the delegates adjourned to hear John Zubly, one of their number, preach a sermon from James 2:12—"So speak, and so do, as they that shall be judged by the law of Liberty." On the strength of this sermon and his other writings, Zubly was selected by the Georgia congress as one of the colony's delegates to the Second Continental Congress. Zubly preached moderation on both sides, but his counsel was ignored by both sides. At the Continental Congress the Americans made Massachusetts' cause their own, formed a Continental Army, and without fully realizing the implications of those actions, began the inexorable march toward independence. Meanwhile, in Georgia the Whigs rapidly consolidated their hold on the colony and left little room for moderates like Zubly to act. Armed conflict bred an "all-or-nothing" attitude which would, in time, devour Zubly and his appeals for restraint.

In his sermon Zubly insisted that the law of God represented the only perfect law and that liberty required the regulation of law to prevent licentiousness. He warned rulers not to abuse their power, for Christianity required obedience only so long as the magistrates acted for the common good. Zubly trotted out the old argument that the king was badly served by his advisors, and counselled his readers to await patiently the king's recognition of the true state of affairs. He reminded Americans that precipitate action would bring only condemnation and that oppression, not law, was their enemy. Zubly remained convinced that the colonists could preserve their constitutional rights within the empire.

Zubly's sermon was published as *The Law of Liberty* by Henry Miller in Philadelphia. The pamphlet included an address Zubly had sent to the Earl of Dartmouth, Secretary of State for the American Department, at the behest of the Georgia Provincial Congress; his sermon; and an appendix relating the history of the Swiss struggle for independence. The pamphlet was reprinted in London in 1775 and in Philadelphia in 1778 under the title *A Sermon on American Affairs*. . . . Zubly's address to the Earl of Dartmouth appeared separately in the *London Magazine* in 1775, and as a pamphlet entitled *An Address to the Right Honourable Earl of Dartmouth* in 1775, printed by Henry Miller in Philadelphia. In the same year Miller brought out a German version of the appendix: *Eine Kurzqefasste historische Nachricht von den Kämpfen der Schweitzer für die Freyheit*. The various editions and the Philadelphia and London publishers made *The Law of Liberty* Zubly's most widely circulated pamphlet.

Source: Rare Books Room, University of Georgia Library

A
SERMON

on

AMERICAN AFFAIRS,

Preached

at the Opening of the PROVINCIAL
CONGRESS of GEORGIA.

Addressed

to the Right Honourable
The EARL of DARTMOUTH.

With an Appendix,

Giving a Concise Account of the Struggles of
Swisserland to Recover Their Liberty.

By John J. Zubly, D. D.

Isaiah 11:13. EPHRAIM SHALL NOT ENVY JUDAH,
AND JUDAH SHALL NOT VEX EPHRAIM.

Philadelphia:
Printed by Henry Miller. 1775.

To the Right Honourable

WILLIAM HENRY,

Earl of Dartmouth.

MY LORD,

Your Lordship's appointment to be Secretary of State for the American department, by numbers that respected your Lordship's religious character, was looked upon as a very providential and happy event. Your patronizing of religious undertakings, confirmed the general opinion, and we were happy in the expectations of your Lordship's conscientious regard to justice and equity, as well as to the civil and religious liberties of this great Continent; we expected the cause of liberty and religion would meet with the strongest support under your administration, and in your Lordship would ever find a constant and successful advocate with your royal master.

Unhappily during your administration, measures have been pursued very contrary to American hopes, and we easily conceive your Lordship may think it not less strange that many friends of religion in America should be so uneasy under laws which had your Lordship's concurrence and approbation.

It is to the Man and to the Christian I wish to be permitted to address myself: Your Lordship ranks among the highest subjects, and has a large share in all public measures, but anxiety for what may distress, and zeal for the welfare of the empire, can be no crime even in the meanest; and when a house is once in flames, every man is inexcusable, or must at least be so in his own breast, that does not contribute whatever he may think in his power to their being extinguished. The effects of the present measures are visible, and it requires no sagacity to foresee what may be the consequence, should they be continued. Your Lordship may do much towards restoring and perpetuating the tranquility of a great empire; persons of my station have nothing to offer but hints and wishes, should these be beneath your notice, or stand in need of forgiveness, my sincere wish to contribute any thing towards a just, happy and perpetual connexion between a parent state and an infant country growing apace to the most astonishing importance, must be my only apology. *Pulchrum est bene facere reipublicae, sed & bene dicere non est absurdum.*

The question, My Lord, which now agitates Great-Britain and America, and in which your Lordship has taken such an active part, is, whether the Parliament of Great-Britain has a right to lay taxes on the Americans, who are not, and cannot, there be represented, and whether the Parliament has a right to bind the Americans in all cases whatsoever? Whatever may be said, or whatever the good people in Great-Britain may believe, this is the whole subject of the dispute. All the severities hitherto exercised upon the Americans professedly have no other view than to enforce such a dependance, and nothing less than a claim destructive of all natural and national liberty, could possibly have united all America in a general opposition, or have aroused them to join all like one man in their common defence. Let a declaratory bill be passed, that any law and usage to the contrary notwithstanding, America is entitled to all the common rights of mankind and all the blessings of the British constitution, that the sword shall never be drawn to abridge, but to confirm, her birthright, and the storm instantly becomes a calm, and every American thinks himself happy to contribute to the necessities, defence and glory of Great-Britain to the utmost of his strength and power.

To bind them in all cases whatsoever, my Lord, the Americans look upon this as the language of despotism in its utmost perfection. What can, say they, an Emperor of Morocco pretend more of his slaves than to bind them in all cases whatsoever. Were it meant to make the Americans hewers of wood and drawers of water, were it meant to oblige them to make bricks without straw, were it meant to deprive them of the enjoyment of their religion, and to establish a hierarchy over them similar to that of the church of Rome in Canada? it would, say they, be no more than a natural consequence of the right of binding them (unseen, unheard, unrepresented) in all cases whatsoever.

My Lord, the Americans are no ideots, and they appear determined not to be slaves. Oppression will make wise men mad, but oppressors in the end frequently find that they were not wise men: there may be resources even in despair sufficient to render any set of men strong enough not to be bound in all cases whatsoever.

Grievous is the thought, my Lord, that a nobleman of your Lordship's character should be so zealous to make war, and to imbrue his hands in the blood of millions of your fellow-subjects and fellow-christians: Pray, my Lord, is it possible that those, who at three thousand miles distance can be bound in all cases, may be said to have any liberty at all? Is it nothing in your Lordship's eye to deprive so considerable a part of the globe of the privilege of breathing a free air, or to subjugate numbers and generations to slavery and despotism? Can your Lordship think on these things without horror, or hope they must be productive of any thing but detestation and disappointment? Your Lordship believes a Supreme Ruler of the earth, and that the small and great must stand before him at last: Would your Lordship be willing, at the general meeting of all mankind, to take a place among those who destroyed or enslaved empires, or risk your future state on the merit of having, at the expence of British blood and treasure, taken away the property, the life and liberty of the largest part of the British empire? Can your Lordship think those that fear the Lord will not cry to him against their oppressors, and will not the Father of mankind hear the cries of the oppressed? or would you be willing that their cries and tears should rise against you as a forward instrument of their oppression.

I know, my Lord, that this is not courtly language, but your Lordship is a professor of religion, and of the pure, gentle, benevolent religion of Jesus Christ: The groans of a people pushed on a precipice, and driven on the very brink of despair, will prove forcible, till it can be proved that any power, in whose legislation the Americans have no part, may at pleasure bind them in all cases whatsoever; till it can be proved that such a claim does not constitute the very essence of slavery and despotism; till it can be proved that the Americans (whom in this view I can no longer call Britons) may, and of right ought, to be thus bound; abhorrence of such assertions is only the language of truth, which in the end will force its way, and rise superior to all the arts of falshood and all the powers of oppression.

Right or wrong, my Lord, in all cases whatsoever, but more especially when the fate of nations is concerned, are words of infinite moment. Your

Lordship doubtless believes that the weighty alternative must have very solemn and different effects here and hereafter; but waving the right or wrong of this vile unhappy dispute, let me entreat your Lordship's attention to consider at what an infinite risk the present measures must be pursued, even were it not demonstrable that they are in the highest degree wrong, cruel and oppressive.

The bulk of the inhabitants of a continent extending eighteen hundred miles in front on the atlantic, and permitting an extension in breadth as far as the south sea, look upon the claim, to bind them in all cases whatsoever, as unjust, illegal and detestable, let us suppose for a moment that they are grossly mistaken; yet an error imbibed by millions, and in which they believe the all of the present and future generations lies at stake, may prove a very dangerous error; destroying the Americans will not cure them, nor will any acts that condemn to starve or be miserable, have any tendency to persuade them that these acts were made by their friends. The people in England are made to believe that the Americans want to separate from them, or are unwilling to bear their part of the common burden. No representation can be more false; but, my Lord, a nation cannot be misled always, and when once the good people of Great-Britain get truer notions of the matter, they will naturally wreak their resentment on those by whom they have been grossly misinformed or wretchedly deceived.

Review, my Lord, the effects of the present measures; the past and present will inform your Lordship of what may be to come.

With an unparalleled patience did the Bostonians bear the annihilation of their trade, the blocking up of their harbour, and many other distresses, till at Lexington an attack was made upon their lives, and then they gave sufficient proof that their patience was not the effect of timidity, but of prudence and an unwillingness to shed British blood. This attack convinced all America that the British ministry and troops were athirst after their blood, and the behaviour of both parties on that day, and in many little skirmishes since, must convince all the world that in the cause of liberty the Americans are not afraid to look regulars in the face, and that in an unjust and oppressive service British troops are far from being invincible.

The burning of the innocent town of Charlestown, after it had been left by its inhabitants, is a piece of such wanton cruelty as will fix an everlasting disgrace on the British arms. In the long civil war in Great-Britain nothing of the kind was attempted by either party, and this barbarity cannot fail being condemned by all civilized nations.

If at the battle on Bunker's hill the Americans have been surprized, superiority has cost the regulars dearer than the Americans what is called their defeat, one or two more such defeats of the Americans would forever put it out of the power of the present regular army to gain a victory.

The rejecting of the New-York petition has effectually silenced all those who pleaded for, or hoped any good from, petitioning. The cannonading of that town in the dead of the night, and without the least previous warning, as it has shewn what the inhabitants are indiscriminately to expect, will in history stand as a lasting monument of such wantonness of cruelty as nations not remarkable for humanity would be ashamed of.

The destroying of the New-England fishery laid all those who were deprived of their bread and occupation at sea, under an absolute necessity of seeking it in the American army, and the sense of the injury done them will doubtless exert itself in the day of battle.

The endeavour to stir up popish Canadians and savage Indians against the Colonists has been productive of the taking of the important pass of Ticonderoga, which has been effected without the loss of a single life on either side.

Detaining the inhabitants of Boston, after they had, in dependance on the General's word of honour, given up their arms, to be starved and ruined, is an action worthy of the cause, and can only be equaled by the distresses of Protestants driven under the walls of Londonderry, at which even a James relented.

Proposals publicly made by ministerial writers relative to American domestics, laid the southern provinces under a necessity of arming themselves; a proposal to put it in the power of domestics to cut the throats of their masters, can only serve to cover the proposers and abettors with everlasting infamy.

The Americans have been called "a rope of sand;" but blood and sand will make a firm cementation, and enough American blood has been already shed to cement them together into a thirteenfold cord, not easily to be broken.

My Lord, the violence of the present measures has almost instantaneously created a continental union, a continental currency, a continental army, and before this can reach your Lordship, they will be as equal in discipline as they are superior in cause and spirit to any regulars. The most zealous Americans could not have effected in an age, what the cruelty and violence of administration has effectually brought to pass in a day.

The regular army employed on this errand, with four able generals, now lies no better than besieged within the ruins of Charlestown and Boston, unable to procure the necessaries of life, obliged to import their bread from Europe, and fuel from Canada, pining away with disease, and affording daily martyrs to cruelty and arbitrary power, while every day adds to the improbability of their ever obtaining those unhappy ends. A strange situation for a British army!

Restraining the trade of the Colonies, will effectually annihilate all their trade with Great-Britain. The numbers that crossed the atlantic, or re-exported American commodities from Great-Britain, the manufacturers that wrought for America, or worked up her raw materials, will now be at full leisure to know and feel whether the American trade be an object of any importance, and how much the nation is obliged to a ministry that has so effectually laboured its destruction.

The present dispute has made every American acquainted with, and attentive to, the principles of the British constitution: In this respect, as well as in a strong sense of liberty, and the use of fire-arms almost from the cradle, the Americans have vastly the advantage over men of their rank almost every where else. From the constant topic of present conversation, every child unborn will be impressed with the notion: It is slavery to be bound at the will of another in all cases whatsoever; every mother's milk will convey a detestation of this maxim. Were your Lordship in America, you might see little ones acquainted with the word of command before they can distinctly speak, and shouldering the resemblance of a gun before they are well able to walk.

When millions of free people at once turn their thoughts from trade, and the means of acquiring wealth, to agriculture and frugality, it must cause a most sensible alteration in the state. My Lord, this is the case at present in America; every new act of violence will strengthen and confirm the spirit that taught them the necessity of being frugal and virtuous, that they might remain free, and become invincible.

Admit, my Lord, (for suppositions now become probable in proportion of their being astonishing and violent) that a British fleet may effectually guard every harbour, river, creek or inlet on the American coast; admit also that her troops destroy every town, village or hut along the seashore, what then will be the consequence? Why, my Lord, it will be the destroying the property of thousands in Great-Britain, and of a few on this side of the water, whom your Lordship calls your friends; perhaps the attempt may not succeed, but supposing it should, the Americans, injured beyond a possibility of reparation, and irritated to the highest degree, will retire where they are inaccessible to troops and ships; instead of trade and navigation, you will have a desolate sea-coast, the trade of America will be lost, and with it the sinews of war: And, my Lord, in the natural course of things America, in less than half a century, will contain more inhabitants than Great-Britain and Ireland; and that period, my Lord, is not so far distant, to put the present treatment entirely out of remembrance. America and Great-Britain joined in arms together, may grow confident against the world besides; but if Britain continue her arms against America; if her troops can be persuaded to go on against their brethren and friends, if they will destroy the last asylum of liberty, and a country which has saved so many thousands from starving at home, the Americans will fight like men, who have every thing at stake; the mercenaries with bayonets at their backs, and at the rate of six-pence a day; if they are once defeated, whence will they be resupplied; if they return to Britain victorious, they will be fit instruments to promote that slavery at home which they have been successful in fastening (probably for a very little while) on their fellow-subjects abroad.

In times of public confusion men of all parties are sometimes carried further than they intended at first setting out. History and the knowledge of human nature should inform your Lordship how much it is against all sound policy to secure or strive for punctilios at an infinite risk.

The Americans have always shewn an affectionate regard to the king, and they are truly sensible of the necessity and advantage of a perpetual union with the parent state; but undeserved severities cannot be productive of any pleasing returns. The Americans firmly believe that the claim at present endeavouring to be enforced, would render them mere slaves, and it is their general motto, "Death or Freedom." The parliamentary, or, as they say, ministerial, claim is now written in letters of blood, and that will be far from making it more acceptable to American readers.

On the whole, my Lord, should this address be deemed impertinent and intrusive, I hope it may still be excusable from the importance of the cause, and the sincerity of its motive. In the event of the present dispute I look upon all mankind as interested, and though not natural born, his Majesty has not another subject that more ardently wisheth that his own repose and happiness and that of all his subjects may never meet with any interruption. Whether British troops shall now drive liberty from out of the greater part of the British empire, and bury her remains in the American wilderness, or whether that wilderness shall flourish and chearfully contribute to make Great-Britain the greatest empire of the universe, is the question now to be decided, and it is not so unimportant, but it may be expected He that is higher than the highest, and taketh up the isles like a very little thing, will interpose in the decision. The whole American process, my Lord, is liable to a revision, and when righteousness and judgment to come once make an impression, many a Felix will tremble.

To restore peace and harmony nothing is necessary than to secure to America the known blessings of the British constitution. This may be done in a moment, and without any disgrace or risk. Let the Americans enjoy, as hitherto, the privilege to give and grant by their own representatives, and they will give and grant liberally; but their liberty they will never part with but with their lives. The day that restores their liberty, restores every thing to the former channel; to enforce the contrary claim, ages may be insufficient, and every day encreases the danger of "a mother's being dashed to pieces on her own children."

That your Lordship, in the hand of Providence, may be a happy instrument to bring the present unnatural contest to a speedy, just and honourable issue; that you may live to see much of that happiness which must be the result; is no less my fervent prayer, than that God would blast every counsel and measure that may have a contrary tendency,—that would separate Britain and America, whom God has joined together,—that would abridge the rights, liberties and happiness of the nation, our rightful Sovereign (whom God ever preserve), or any of his subjects.

I am, my Lord, Your Lordship's most humble servant,

September 3, 1775   J. J. Zubly.

A SERMON, &c.

James 2:12.

So speak ye, and so do, as they that shall be judged
by the Law of Liberty.

There was a time when there was no king in Israel, and every man did what was good in his own eyes. The consequence was a civil war in the nation, issuing in the ruin of one of the tribes, and a considerable loss to all the rest.

And there was a time when there was a king in Israel, and he also did what was right in his own eyes, a foolish son of a wise father; his own imprudence, the rashness of his young counsellors, his unwillingness to redress the grievances of the nation, and the harsh treatment he gave to those who applied for relief, also brought on a civil war, and issued in the separation of the ten tribes from the house of David. He sent his treasurer to gather an odious duty or tribute, but the children of Israel stoned him that he died; and when he gathered one hundred and four score thousand men, that he might bring again the kingdom unto Roboam, God sent them a message, "ye shall not go up, nor fight against your brethren, return every man to his house, for this thing is done of me" God disapproved of the oppressive measures and ministry of Roboam, and that king's army appears more ready to obey the command of their God, than slay their brethren by orders of a tyrant. "They obeyed the voice of the Lord, and returned from going against Jeroboam." 2 Chronicles 10:18; 11:4.

The things that happened before are written for our learning. By comparing past times and proceedings with these that are present, prudence will point out many salutary and religious lessons. The conduct of Roboam verifies the lamentation of his father, "Woe to thee, o land, when thy kind is a child." Ecclesiastes 10:16. A very small degree of justice and moderation might have preserved his kingdom, but he thought weapons of war better than wisdom; he hearkened not, neither to the people, nor to some of his more faithful counsellors, and the consequence was that, instead of enslaving the ten tribes who stood up for their liberty, God gave Judah to be servants to the king of Egypt, that they might learn the difference between his service and the service of the kingdoms of the nations. A people that claim no more than their natural rights, in so doing, do nothing displeasing unto God; and the most powerful monarch that would deprive his subjects of the liberties of man, whatever may be his success, he must not expect the approbation of God, and in due time will be the abhorrence of all men.

In a time of public and general uneasiness it behoves both superiors and inferiors to consider. It is easy to extinguish a spark, it is folly to blow up discontent into a blaze; the beginning of strife is like the letting out of waters, and no man may know where it will end. There is a rule given to magistrates and subjects; which, if carefully attended to, would secure the dignity and safety of both; which, if not duly regarded, is usually attended with the worst consequences. The present, my hearers, will easily be allowed is a day of trouble, and surely in this day of adversity we ought to consider. When a people think themselves oppressed, and in danger, nothing can be more natural than that they should enquire into the real state of things, trace their grievances to their source, and endeavour to apply the remedies which are most likely to procure relief: This I take to be the design of the present meeting of persons deputed from every part of the country; and as they have thought proper to open and begin their deliberations with a solemn address unto God, and the consideration of his holy word, I most chearfully comply with their request to officiate on this occasion, and shall endeavour, as I may be enabled, to point out such directions from the holy scriptures as may make us wise in the knowledge of time, and direct us how to carry ourselves worthy of the character of good subjects and Christians: Whatever may be necessary for this purpose, I take to be comprehended in the apostolical rule, which I have laid down as the subject of this discourse, "So speak, and so do, as they that shall be judged by the law of liberty."

There are two things which properly come before us, viz.

I. That we are to be judged by the law of liberty; and

II. The exhortation to act worthy, and under the influence, of this important truth on every occasion.

A law is a rule of behaviour, made under proper authority, and with penalties annexed, suitable to deter the transgressions. As all laws suppose man to be in a social state, so all laws ought to be made for the good of man: A law that is not made by such as have authority for so doing, is of no force; and if authority makes laws destructive in themselves, no authority can prevent things from finally taking their natural course.

Wherever there is society, there must also be law; it is impossible that society should subsist without it. The will, minds, tempers, dispositions, views and interests of men are so very different, and sometimes so opposite, that without law, which cements and binds all, every thing would be in endless disorder and confusion. All laws usually wear the complexion of those by whom they were made, but it cannot be denied that some bad men, from a sense of necessity, have made good laws, and that some good men, from mistake, or other weaknesses, have enacted laws bad in themselves and pernicious in their consequences.

All human laws partake of human imperfection; it is not so with the laws of God. He is perfect, and so are all his works and ways.

The law of the Lord is perfect, converting the soul. The testimony of the Lord is sure, making wise the simple. The statutes of the Lord are right, rejoicing the heart. The commandment of the Lord is pure, enlightening the eyes. All his judgments are truth, and righteousness altogether. Psalm 19.

Among men every society and country has its own laws and form of government, which may be very different, and cannot operate beyond their limits; but those laws and that form of government is undoubtedly best which has the greatest tendency to make all those that live under it secure and happy. As soon as we consider man as formed into society, it is evident that the safety of the whole must be the grand law* which must influence and direct every other: Men did not pass from a state of nature into a state of society, to render their situation more miserable, and their rights more precarious. That government and tyranny is the hereditary right of some, and that slavery and oppression is the original doom of others, is a doctrine that would reflect dishonour upon God; it is treason against all mankind, it is indeed an enormous faith that millions were made for one; transubstantiation is but a harmless absurdity, compared with the notion of a divine right to govern wrong, or of making laws which are contrary to every idea of liberty, property and justice.

The law which the apostle speaks of in our text, is not a law of man, but of Him who is the only lawgiver, that can save and condemn, to whom all owe obedience, and whose laws none can transgress with impunity.

Though all the laws that God ever gave unto man are worthy of God, and tend to promote the happiness of those to whom they were given, yet we may observe a very striking variety in the different laws which he gave at different times and to different people. "He shewed his word unto Jacob, his statutes and his judgments unto Israel; he has not dealt so with any other nation." Psalm 147:18. 19.

To the generality of mankind he gave no written law, but yet left not himself without a witness among them; the words of the law were written in their hearts, their conscience also bearing witness, and their thoughts the mean while excusing or else accusing one another: It cannot be said they were without law, whilst what they were to do, and what they were to forbear, was written in their hearts.

Salus populi suprema lex.

To Israel God came with a fiery law in his hands, it was given with the most awful solemnity upon mount Sinai; and as the sum and substance of all their ceremonial, political and moral law centered in the ten commandments, so the sum and substance of these is comprehended in love to God and love to man which, as our Lord himself informs us, contains all the law and all the prophets.

All manifestations of the will of God have been gradual, and it is probable the means of knowing God will be progressive through different ages, till eternity gives the good man a full sight of God in his immediate presence. During the dispensation of the old testament and the ceremonial law, a spirit of bondage obtained unto fear, the law was a schoolmaster to bring us unto Christ; neither did the law make any thing perfect, but the bringing in of a better hope: Grace and truth was brought to light by Jesus Christ, and hence the dispensation of the gospel, under which we live, is called the law of Liberty.

Though there is a manifest distinction between law and gospel, and sometimes these two things are even opposed to one another, yet the doctrine of the gospel is also called "the law of faith;" Romans 3:17. partly because it was usual with the Jewish writers to call every doctrine a law, and partly also because the doctrine of the gospel presents us with a rule of life, which all its professors are bound to obey; hence they are said to be "not without law, but under the law of Christ;" 1 Corinthians 9:11. and hence our apostle speaks of a royal law, which, though we cannot obey in perfection, nor derive any merit from our imperfect obedience, we cannot neglect without danger, nor disobey without shewing our disregard to the doctrine of the gospel in general.

It deserves very particular attention that the doctrine of the gospel is called a law of Liberty. Liberty and law are perfectly consistent; liberty does not consist in living without all restraint; for were all men to live without restraint, as they please, there would soon be no liberty at all; the strongest would be master, the weakest go the the wall; right, justice and property must give way to power, and, instead of its being a blessing, a more unhappy situation could not easily be devised unto mankind than that every man should have it in his power to do what is right in his own eyes: well regulated liberty of individuals is the natural offspring of laws, which prudentially regulate the rights of whole communities; and as laws which take away the natural rights of men, are unjust and oppressive, so all liberty which is not regulated by law, is a delusive phantom, and unworthy of the glorious name.

The gospel is called a law of liberty, because it bears a most friendly aspect to the liberty of man; it is a known rule, *Evangelium non tollit politias*, the gospel makes no alteration in the civil state; it by no means renders man's natural and social condition worse than it would be without the knowledge of the gospel. When the Jews boasted of their freedom, and that they never were in bondage, our Lord does not reprove them for it, but only observes, that national freedom still admits of improvement: "If the Son shall make you free, then are you free indeed." John 8:16. This leads me to observe that the gospel is a law of liberty in a much higher sense: By whomsoever a man is overcome, of the same he is brought into bondage; but no external enemy can so completely tyrannize over a conquered enemy, as sin does over all those who yield themselves its servants; vicious habits, when once they have gained the ascendant in the soul, bring man to that unhappy pass that he knows better things and does worse; sin, like a torrent, carries him away against knowledge and conviction, while conscience fully convinceth him that he travels the road of death, and must expect, if he so continues, to take up his abode in hell; though his decaying body clearly tells him sin breaks his constitution, as well as wastes his substance, though he feels the loss of credit and wealth, still sin has too strong a hold of him to be forsaken, though he faintly resolves to break off, yet, till the grace of God brings salvation, when he would do good, evil is present with him; in short, instead of being under a law of liberty, he is under the law of sin and death, but whenever he feels the happy influence of the grace of the gospel, then this "law of liberty makes him free from the law of sin and death;" Romans 8:2. it furnisheth him not only with motives to resist but with power also to subdue sin; sin reigns no longer in his mortal body, because he is not under the law, but under grace. By this law of liberty he is made free from sin, and has his fruit unto holiness, and the end of it eternal life. There is another reason why the gospel is called a law of liberty, which is to distinguish it from the ceremonial law under the Mosaic dispensation; a yoke, of which an apostle saith, neither they nor their fathers were able to bear; it was superadded on account of their transgressions, and suited to the character of a gross and stubborn nation, to whom it was originally given; they were so prone to idolatry, and so apt to forget their God, their notions were so gross and carnal, that a number of external rites and ceremonies became necessary, to put them in mind of him, and to attach them to some degree of his worship and service. This, however necessary, was a heavy burden; it bid them "touch not, taste not, handle not;" it required of them expensive sacrifices, and a costly and painful service; it was attended with the most fearful threatnings, if any man brake Moses law, he died under two or three witnesses; and the very spirit they then received was a spirit of bondage unto fear: Whereas the gospel dispensation breatheth a spirit of confidence, and under the law of liberty we call upon God as Abba Father. By this law of liberty the professors of the gospel will be judged.

Every man is a rational, and therefore accountable, creature. As a creature he must needs depend on his Creator, and as a rational creature he must certainly be accountable for all his actions. Nothing is more evident than that man is not of himself; and if once we admit that he holds his existence, his faculties and favours from God, that made him, it becomes a very obvious conclusion, that his Maker must have had some view in giving him existence, and more understanding than to the beasts of the field, neither can it be a matter of indifference to him whether man acts agreeably or contrary to his designs. The Creator of the natural world, is also its moral ruler; and if he is now the proprietor and ruler of intelligent beings, at some time or other he must also be their judge.

If God had not made his will known unto man, there could have been neither transgression nor judgement. If it should be said that God has not manifested himself alike unto all men, and that some have much smaller opportunities to know his will and their duty than others, it is enough to observe, that no man will be judged by a rule of which it was impossible he should have any knowledge. Every work and every man will be brought into judgment, and the judgment of God will never be otherwise than according to truth; but those that never had the law of liberty, will not be judged by that law, and those that have been favoured with the revelation of the gospel will be more inexcusable than any others, if they neglect the day of their visitation. "As many as have sinned without law, shall also perish without law, and as many as have sinned in the law, shall be judged by the law." Romans 2:12. All men are under some law, they feel they are conscious, that they are so; the thoughts which already excuse or condemn one another, are an anticipation of a final and decisive judgment, when every man's reward will be according to his works.

That all those who heard and professed to believe the gospel, will be finally judged by that, we have the fullest assurance. God will judge the secrets of men by Jesus Christ according to his gospel. "The word that I have spoken," saith Christ, "the same will judge them that heard it, on the last day." John 12:48. It greatly interests us clearly to know what is the import and consequence of being judged by the gospel as a law of liberty; and it contains the following things,

The general character, all the thoughts, words and actions, together with the general conduct of all those who professed the gospel, will be brought to the test, and tried by this rule. Man's own opinion of himself, the good opinion of others, will here stand him in no stead; his character will not be determined by his external appearance, but by his inward reality. "Man looketh on the outward appearance, but the Lord looketh on the heart." I Samuel 17:7. The self-righteous pharisee will be rejected, notwithstanding his fair appearance and boasting; the penitent publican will be received, though he has nothing to plead but Lord have mercy on me a sinner. The law is spiritual, and no law more so than the law of the gospel; it requires not merely an external obedience, but an internal conformity to the will of God; it demands truth in the inward part, it looks not only to the actions that are done, but to the principle from which they flow; we must judge of man's inward disposition by his visible action, but God judges of the actions of men according to their invisible spring; thoughts are out of the reach of human cognizance, but they are the first object of divine notice; there is not a word that drops from our tongue but what our judge hears, whatever we do, or whatever we neglect, is all under his immediate eye, and he not only attends to our general character, but also to every thought, word or action, and the prevailing complexion of all these taken together form our true and real character.

In the judgment, according to this law, our character, words, thoughts and actions will be brought to the test of this rule, our conduct will be compared with these precepts, this is the balance of the sanctuary, in which the professors of the gospel shall be weighed, and as they shall be found approved or deficient, their case must be determined. Those whose temper and actions shall be found conformable to the law of liberty, will be acquitted, graciously accepted, and made ever happy, and those who turned the grace of God into wantonness, and made the liberty of the gospel a cloak for their sins, will be finally rejected. The gospel informs us, that a day is already appointed for that purpose; it acquaints us with the person of our judge, and every circumstance, as well as the rule according to which he will proceed in judgment. Perhaps on that day when all nations shall appear before the judge, and he will divide them as a shepherd divideth the sheep from the goats, distinct places will also be allotted to those who are to be judged by natural conscience and the law of nature, and those who have been favoured with a divine revelation, and especially with the light of the gospel: The people of Niniveh will arise against empty professors of the gospel, and will condemn them. Those who have been exalted above others in means and privileges, will sit proportionably lower than those who have made a better improvement of lesser means; and notwithstanding the fondest hope and finest profession, it is a determined rule of the law of liberty, that "except our righteousness shall exceed that of the scribes and pharisees, we shall in no case enter into the kingdom of heaven."

It deserves our peculiar attention, that the apostle considers the gospel as a law of liberty, at the same time when he sets it before us as the rule by which we are to be judged. We are not to imagine because the gospel is a law of liberty, therefore men will not be judged; on the contrary judgment will be the more severe against all who have heard and professed the gospel, and yet walked contrary to its precepts and doctrine. As the transgression of a law of liberty must be more inexcusable, than the transgression of a law unjust or oppressive in itself, or even the ceremonial law, which was given only for a certain period, and to answer temporary purposes, so their judgment and doom must be proportionably heavier, who have sinned against love and liberty, as well as against power and justice.

According to this law the fate of men will not only be determined, but sentence will also be put into execution. God sitteth on the throne of judgment every day, and judgeth righteously, but he hath moreover appointed a particular day when he will manifest his power and justice before the whole creation; when the dead both small and great will stand before God; when those that acted agreeable to the law of liberty, will attain the fulness of glory of the freedom of the sons of God, and when he will also take vengeance on all that have not known God, and have not obeyed his holy gospel. This naturally leads to the second thing proposed, to take a nearer view of the importance of the exhortation, "So speak, and so do, as they that shall be judged by the law of liberty."

It seems as though the apostle had an eye to some particular branch of the law of liberty, i.e. the love which we owe unto our neighbour, and that his design is to obviate the mistake as though men might be considered as fulfilling the law of Christ, in paying respect to some of its commands and prohibitions, at the same time that they were entirely regardless of the rest. He assures them, that "whosoever shall keep the whole law, but shall transgress in one point" (e.g. having respect of persons) "is guilty of all." On this principle the apostle builds the general exhortation, "So speak, and so do, as they that shall be judged by the law of liberty." This implies:

1. Be thoroughly convinced of the certainty of a judgment to come, and that it extends to you, to all your thoughts, words and actions. There is not any truth of greater moment, nor perhaps more easily forgotten. The belief or unbelief of this important doctrine must have the most sensible effects. All the apostles frequently put their hearers in mind of a judgment to come; and there is not any truth more necessary to be frequently inculcated and daily thought on, and wherever this truth is really believed and felt, it will have a constant and natural influence on the behaviour of those who truly believe it.

2. See to it that in judgment you may stand. All men will be brought into judgment, but few will be able to stand; none will be excused, or be able to withdraw, and only those who have acted worthily, will meet with the divine acceptance. The difference will be amazing and beyond all conception: An eternity of happiness, which eye has not seen, ear has not heard, and which never entered into the heart of any man, lies on the one side, and despair, misery and torment on the other. Those that are able to stand, will meet with the smiles and approbation of their judge, and to all the rest the king will say, "These mine enemies that would not have me to bear rule over them, bring them here, and slay them before mine eyes." Those that believe and are convinced of this awful alternative, should certainly make it their care that they may be able to stand in judgment; neither should the persuasion of this only influence their conduct in general, but these words ought to be considered as a rule, which we ought to have constantly before our eyes in all our discourses and every undertaking; we should ever "so speak, and so act, as they that shall be judged by the law of liberty."

I shall draw a few inferences, before I conclude with a more particular address to the worthy Gentlemen at whose request I preach on this occasion.

1. *The gospel is a law of liberty.*

A late writer * asserts, "Every religion countenances despotism, but none so much as the Christian." This is a very heavy charge against religion in general, but bears hardest on the Christian. Whether it proceeds from malice, ignorance, or misapprehension, it is needless to

---

*See a tract, entituled, "Chains of slavery." Printed London. 1775.

determine; but if christianity be a law of liberty, it must be obvious how ill-grounded is such a charge against it. It cannot be denied but some Christian writers have wrote against the rights of mankind. All those who stand up for unlimited passive obedience and non-resistance, may have given but too much cause for such surmises and suspicions; but the truth is, that both those which make this charge, and those who gave occasion for it, were alike ignorant of the spirit and temper of Christianity; and it may well be doubted whether the venders of such odious doctrines, who foisted tenets, so abominable and injurious to mankind, into the system of Christian religion, have not done that holy religion greater hurt under the pretence of friendship and defence than its most barefaced enemies by all their most violent attacks. Some Christian divines have taught the enormous faith, that millions were made for one, they have ascribed a divine right to kings to govern wrong; but what then? Are such abominable doctrines any part of christianity, because these men say so? does the gospel cease to be a law of liberty, because some of its professors pervert it into an engine of tyranny, oppression and injustice.

The assertion, that all religion countenances despotism, and christianity more than any other, is diametrically opposite to fact. Survey the globe, and you will find that liberty has taken its seat only in Christendom, and that the highest degree of freedom is pleaded for and enjoyed by such as make profession of the gospel.

There are but two religions, which are concerned in this charge; the Jewish and the Christian. Natural religion writers of this kind I suppose would not include in their charge; if they do, they set all religion at variance with the rights of mankind, contrary to the sense of all nations, who are generally agreed, that, abstractly of a world to come, religion is of real service and necessity to mankind, for their better government and order.

As to the Jewish religion, it seems really strange that any should charge it with favouring despotism, when by one of its express rites at certain times it proclaimed "liberty throughout the land, to the inhabitants thereof." Leviticus 25:10. It required their kings "not to be lifted up in their hearts above their brethren." Deuteronomy 17:20. And the whole system of that religion is so replete with laws against injustice and oppression, it pays such an extraordinary regard to property, and gives such strict a charge to rule in justice and the fear of God, and to consider those, over whom they judge, as their brethren, even when dispensing punishments, and forbids all excess in them, that it is really surprising any one acquainted with its precepts, should declare it favourable to despotism or oppression.

The Christian religion, while it commands due respect and obedience to superiors, no where requires a blind and unlimited obedience on the part of the subjects; nor does it vest any absolute and arbitrary power in the rulers. It is an institution for the benefit, and not for the distress, of mankind. It preacheth not only "glory to God on high," but also "peace on earth, and good will among men."

The gospel gives no higher authority to magistrates than to be "the ministers of God, for the good of the subject." Romans 13. From whence it must surely follow, that their power is to edify, and not to destroy: When they abuse their authority, to distress and destroy their subjects, they deserve not to be thought ministers of God for good; nor is it to be supposed, when they act so contrary to the nature of their office, that they act agreeable to the will of God, or in conformity to the doctrine of the gospel.

The gospel recommends unto masters to forbear threatnings, and to remember that they also have a master in heaven; it assures them that the eye of God is equally upon the servant and the master, and that with God there is no respect of persons: It commands masters, from the most solemn considerations, to give unto servants that which is just and equal; it saith to the meanest slave: "Art thou called being a servant, care not for it, but if thou mayest be made free, use it rather." 1 Corinthians 7:21.

The doctrine of the gospel has that regard to property, that it commands even soldiers, "Do violence to no man, and be content with your wages." Luke 3:14.—that a Paul sent back a run-away slave, though now converted, and belonging to his intimate friend, and at a time when he seems to have stood in real need of his service, from a delicacy that he would do nothing without the owner's mind, less his benefit should appear as if it were of necessity, and not willingly. Philemon 14. From the same spirit of justice a Zacheus, after his conversion, restored fourfold what before he had taken from any by false accusation: Surely then the spirit of the gospel is very friendly to the rights and property of men.

The gospel sets conscience above all human authority in matters of faith, and bids us to "stand fast in that liberty wherewith the Son of God has made us free." Galatians 5:1. Freedom is the very spirit and temper of the gospel: "He that is called in the Lord being a servant, is the Lord's freeman. Ye are bought with a price, be ye not the servants of men." I

Corinthians 7:22, 23. At the same time that it commands us to submit to every ordinance of men, it also directs us to act "as free, and not using liberty as a cloke of maliciousness, but as the servants of God." I Peter 3:13-18.

Those therefore that would support arbitrary power, and require an unlimited obedience, in vain look for precedents or precepts for such things in the gospel, an institution equally tending to make men just, free and happy here, and perfectly holy and happy hereafter.

2. *The main design of the gospel is not to direct us in our external and civil affairs, but how we may at last stand with comfort before God, the judge of all.*

Human prudence is to be our guide in the concerns of time; the gospel makes us wise unto salvation, and points out the means to be pursued that it may be well with us in the world to come. As rational creatures we are to make use of our reason; as Christians we are to repent and believe the gospel. Motives of a worldly nature may very properly influence us in our worldly concern, we are created not only for eternity, but also for time: It is not at all improper for us to have a due regard for both. The gospel will regulate our desires and restrain our passions as to earthly things, and will raise us at the same time above time and sense, to objects of a nature more worthy of ourselves. A due regard for, and frequent meditation on, a judgment to come, will greatly assist us in all our concerns; and this very consideration the gospel holds out to us in the clearest manner. It not only affirms as a truth, what reason and conscience might consider only as probable, but it takes away as it were the veil from between us and things to come; it gives us a present view of the future bliss of saints, and the terrors and despair of sinners;—rather a historical account than a prophetic description of all the proceedings of the dreadful pleasing day; it clearly points out the road to destruction, and the way to escape; it affords us a plain and general rule to obtain safety and comfort, when it bids us, "So speak, and so do, as they that shall be judged by the law of liberty."

This general rule may also be of considerable service in extraordinary and particular cases. It is impossible to provide express directions for every particular case, and in the course of things circumstances may happen when a good man may be at a loss to know his duty, and find it difficult so to act as to obtain his own approbation. There may be danger of going beyond, and danger in not coming up to, the mark. To act worthy of God, who has called us, is the general rule of the Christian at all times, and upon every occasion, and did we but always follow this rule, what matter of persons should we then be! But in cases of intricacy we may still be in doubt what may be most for the glory of God, and most consistent with our duty. Sometimes also our relative duties may seem to come in competition with one another, and we may hesitate in our own mind which for the present has the strongest call. We would fain obey our superiors, and yet we cannot think of giving up our natural, our civil and religious rights, nor acquiesce in or contribute to render our fellow-creatures or fellow-citizens slaves and miserable. We would willingly follow peace with all men, and yet would be very unwilling that others should take the advantage of a pacific disposition, to injure us in hopes of impunity. We would express duty, respect and obedience to the king, as supreme, and yet we would not wish to strengthen the hands of tyranny, nor call oppression lawful: In such a delicate situation it is a golden rule, "So to speak, and so to do, as they that shall be judged by the law of liberty." Nothing has a greater tendency to make men act wrong than the disbelief of a future judgment, and nothing will more effectually restrain and direct them than the full persuasion that such an event will certainly take place; nothing would have a happier tendency to make us act with prudence, justice and moderation than the firm persuasion that God will bring every work into judgment, and every secret thing, whether it be good or bad.

Neither could I think on any direction more applicable to the design of our present meeting, or which I might more properly recommend to the respectable Gentlemen, now met together to consult on the recovery and preservation of the liberties of America, and who chose to begin their deliberations with a solemn act of worship to almighty God who has established government as his ordinance, and equally abhors licentiousness and oppression; whose singular blessing it is if subjects enjoy a righteous government, and under such a government lead a quiet and peaceable life in all godliness and honesty.

You are met, Gentlemen, in a most critical time, and on a most alarming occasion, not in a legislative capacity, but (while the sitting of the usual representation is not thought for the king's service, or necessary for the good of this province) you are chosen by the general voice of this province to meet on their behalf, to consult on such measures as in our local circumstances may be most to the real advantage and tend to the honour of our gracious sovereign, as well as the good and safety of this province and of all this great continent. For the sake of the auditory, I shall briefly state the immediate causes that have given rise to this Provincial and a general American Congress, and then offer such humble advice as appears to me most suitable to our circumstances.

To enforce some Acts for laying on a duty to raise a perpetual revenue in America, which the Americans think unjust and unconstitutional, which all America complains of, and some provinces have in some measure opposed.* A fleet and army has been sent to New-England, and after a long series of hardships by that province patiently endured, it is now out of all question that hostilities have been commenced against them; blood has been shed, and many lives have been taken away; thousands, never as much as suspected of having any hand in the action which is made the pretence of all the severity now used against that province, have been and still are reduced to the greatest distress. From this other provinces have taken the alarm; an apprehension of nearer foes, not unlikely to appear as auxiliaries in an unjust cause, has thrown our neighbours into arms; how far and wide the flame so wantonly kindled may be permitted to spread, none can tell; but in these alarming circumstances the liberty of this continent, of which we are a part, the safety and domestic peace of this province will naturally become a subject of your deliberations; and here I may well adapt the language of old, "There was no such deed done nor seen from the day that America was first settled unto this day; consider of it, take advice, and speak your minds." Judges 19:30. I mean not to anticipate and direct your counsels, but from your desire I should speak on this occasion; I take it for granted you will permit me to offer such hints as may appear suitable to the place and design of our present meeting.

In the first place, as there is no evil in a city in which the hand of God may not be seen, so in vain is salvation looked for from the hills and from the mountains, but can come from him only who has made heaven and earth. This undoubtedly is a day of trouble, but God saith to his people, "Call upon me in a day of trouble, and I will deliver thee." Psalm 50:15. "What nation has God so nigh unto them, as the Lord our God is in all things that we call upon him for." Deuteronomy 4:7. If this be our first step, if first of all we look unto him from whom our help cometh, we may

---

*This opposition in some provinces consisted in sending the tea on which this duty was to be paid, back to England, not suffering it to be sold or landed in others, and in Boston, when they were prevented from sending it back, it was entirely destroyed, but no person hurt, nor any blood shed.

hope all will be well at last. Let us be thoroughly convinced of this, we must stand well with God, else it can never be well with us at all; without him and his help we can never prosper. The Lord is with you, if you are with him; "if you seek him, you will find him, but if you forsake him, you will be forsaken by him." 2 Chronicles 15:2. If God be for us, who can be against us? if he be against us, who can be for us? Before we think on, or look any where else, may our eyes be unto God, that he may be gracious unto us. Let us humbly confess and speedily turn from our sins, deprecate his judgment, and secure his favour.

> Rent your hearts, and not your garments, and turn unto the Lord your God, for he is gracious and merciful, slow to anger and of great kindness, and repenteth him of the evil, who knoweth if he will return and repent, and leave a blessing behind him, even a meat-offering and a drink-offering unto the Lord your God. Joel 2:13, 14.

Let it be a standing rule with every one that is to sit in council upon this occasion, "so to speak, and so to do, as one that is to be judged by the law of liberty." Let us most carefully avoid every thing that might make us incur the displeasure of God, and wound our own consciences. The effects of your deliberation may become very serious and extensive, and the consequences extremely important: Think therefore before you speak, deliberate before you execute, and let the law of liberty, by which you are hereafter to be judged, be the constant rule of all your words and actions: Far be it from us to be reduced under laws inconsistent with liberty, and as far to wish for liberty without law; let the one be so tempered with the other that when we come to give our account to the supreme lawgiver, who is the great judge of all, it may appear we had a due regard to both, and may meet with his approbation.

Such always hath been, and such is still, the attachment of America to the illustrious house of Hanover, that I need not put you in mind of our duty to the king as supreme. By our law the king can do no wrong; but of his present Majesty, who is universally known to be adorned with many social virtues, may we not justly conclude that he would not do any wrong, even though he could. May we not hope that to the greatness of a monarch, he will superadd the feelings of the man, the tenderness of a father. May we not hope that when the truth of things, the tears of his suffering subjects, the distresses caused by Acts extremely ill advised, once reach his notice, a generous pity will force his heart, and that pity, when he feels it, will command redress. "The heart of the king is in the hand of the Lord, as the rivers of water, and he turneth it as he pleaseth;" Proverbs 21:1. most earnestly therefore let us pray that in this great and most important matter also God may give unto the king an understanding heart, that power may be governed by wisdom, and the wheels of government roll on with justice and moderation.

Should you think that all our present distress is owing to evil counsellors, nothing need to hinder you from praying that God would turn their counsels into foolishness; you may make it your earnest request both in public and in private, that the wicked being removed from before the king, his throne may be established in righteousness, that the rod of the oppressor may be broke, and justice and equity take place of tyranny and oppression.

It may be owing to nothing but the firm attachment to the reigning family that so many Americans look upon the present measures as a deep laid plan to bring in the Pretender. Perhaps this jealousy may be very groundless, but so much is certain, that none but Great Britain's enemies can be gainers in this unnatural contest.*

Never let us loose out of sight that our interest lies in a perpetual connection with our mother country. Notwithstanding the present unwise and harsh measures, there are thousands in Great-Britain that think with us, and wish well to the American cause, and make it their own; let us convince our enemies that the struggles of America have not their rise in a desire of independency, but from a warm regard to our common constitution; that we esteem the name of Britons, as being the same with freemen; let every step we take afford proof how greatly we esteem our mother country, and that, to the wish of a perpetual connexion, we prefer this only consideration, that we may be virtuous and free†

---

*Were it designed to give the Pretender an opportunity; to raise divisions in Great-Britain, starve the manufacturers, send away troops from Ireland and Scotland, and breed civil war in America, must all be circumstances too favourable, and I may say, very tempting to promote such a project.

†The idea of a separation between America and Great-Britain is big with so many and such horrid evils, that every friend to both must shudder at the thought. Every man that gives the most distant hint of such a wish, ought instantly to be suspected as a common enemy; nothing would more effectually serve the cause of our enemies, than any proposal of this kind; all wise men and all good men would immediately speak, write and act against it; such a proposal, whenever it should be made, would be an inlet to greater evils

Let me intreat you, Gentlemen, think cooly, and act deliberately; rash counsels are seldom good ones: ministerial rashness and American rashness can only be productive of untoward compounds; inconsiderate measures, framed on the other side of the atlantic, are the cause of all our mischiefs, and it is not in the least probable that inconsiderate measures in America can be productive of any good. Let nothing be done through strive and vain glory; let no private resentment or party zeal disgrace your honest warmth for your country's welfare: Measures determined on by integrity and prudence, are most likely to be carried into execution by steadiness and moderation. Let neither the frowns of tyranny, nor pleasure of popularity, sway you from what you clearly apprehend just and right, and to be your duty. Consider how much lies at stake, how greatly your religion, your liberty, your property, your posterity, is interested. Endeavour to act like freemen, like loyal subjects, like real Christians, and you will "so speak, and so act, as they that shall be judged by the law of liberty." Act conscientiously, and with a view to God, then commit your ways to him, leave the event with God, and you will have great reason to hope that the event will be just, honourable and happy.

And now, Gentlemen, you have the wishes and prayers of every thoughtful person, that your deliberations may be carried on with candour, unanimity and prudence, may be blessed to preserve the quietness of this province, and co-operate in restoring the rights and tranquility of all America, as well as promote the prosperity of the whole British empire. This will afford you a heartfelt satisfaction, and transmit your name to posterity with honour, when all those who had opposite views, and sought their greatness in the ruins of others, will be held in abhorrence and detestation.

I have but a few hints to give to my hearers in general.

The times are evil; this is a day of adversity, and in a time of adversity we ought to consider. It may perhaps soon become impossible, even to the most indolent, to continue unconcerned, and those that wish no more than to hide themselves in quiet obscurity, may not always have it in their power to remain neuter: To know the signs of the time, is a considerable

---

than any we have yet suffered: But what America detests as the greatest evil, a British ministry has taken the greatest pains to effect; has wasted British blood and treasure to alienate America and Great Britain; the breach is growing wider and wider, it is become great like a sea, every moment is a loss that is not improved towards bringing about a reconciliation.

part of human prudence, and it is a still greater to walk circumspectly, and redeem the time, because the days are evil. Whatever part you may think yourselves obliged to take, "So speak, and so do, as they that shall be judged hereafter, and judged by the law of liberty."

In these times of confusion I would press on my hearers a most conscientious regard to the common laws of the land. Let our conduct shew that we are not lawless; by well-doing let us put to silence the reproaches of our adversaries. Let us convince them that we do not complain of law, but of oppression; that we do not abhor these acts because we are impatient to be under government, but being destructive of liberty and property, we think them destructive also of all law. Let us act "as free, and yet not make liberty a cloke of maliciousness, but as the servants of God."

While it is yet peace and quietness with us, let us not think ourselves inaccessible to the evils which are already come upon others; there are some evils which we would rather deprecate in private than speak of in public, against which being forewarned, we should be forearmed; every trifling report should not alarm us, but it would be folly still greater not to be on our guard against sudden dangers.

Remember them that suffer adversity, as being yourselves also in the body. Think on those who are driven from their habitations and all their conveniencies of life, or confined in their own houses by an enraged soldiery, to starve in their own country, in the midst of property and plenty, not permitted to enjoy their own, and distressed in every connexion, and this without any cause alleged against numbers of them, without complaint, suspicion or a legal trial: The like was never heard since the cruel siege of Londonderry, and is a species of cruelty at which even that hardhearted bigot James II relented.

Above all, let every one earnestly pray that He that is higher than the highest would soon make a righteous end of all their confusion; that he would incline the king to hear the cries of his subjects, and that no more innocent blood may be shed in America.

One thing more: Consider the extreme absurdity of struggling for civil liberty, and yet to continue slaves to sin and lust. "Know ye not to whom ye yield yourselves servants to obey, his servants ye are, to whom ye obey, whether of sin unto death, or of obedience unto righteousness." Romans 6:16. Cease from evil, and do good, seek peace, and pursue it, who will hurt you while you follow that which is good; become the willing servants of the Lord Jesus Christ, hearken to and obey the voice of his gospel; for "where the spirit of the Lord is, there is liberty;" and "if the Son makes you free, then, and not till then, *shall you be free indeed.*"

From the similarity of the subject, an extract from another sermon is added:

The question between Great-Britain and America, which has already been productive of such alarming effects, is, "Whether the parliament of Great-Britain have any power or authority to tax the Americans without their consent?" Every impartial man will allow that this is the foundation of the whole dispute. It is evident that in this question conscience is deeply interested, and in this view it becomes a very proper subject for the pulpit. If any thing is required of subjects which in conscience they are bound to pay, give or do, the refusal of it is not only a crime against the state, but also a sin against God: I think it therefore not only not improper, but my duty, to point out unto my hearers such hints and precedents as may illustrate this matter from the Word of God.

The case I would state thus, "Whether any duty or impost supposed to be laid on in an illegal manner, and inconsistent with natural and civil rights, from motives of conscience ought nevertheless to be paid?" and to elucidate this, I observe, the general rule is this: "Render therefore to all their dues; tribute to whom tribute is due, custom to whom custom; fear to whom fear, honour to whom honour." Romans 13:7. There is something due to government which cannot be refused without injustice, and more than which cannot be demanded without tyranny and oppression. When our Lord was asked, "What thinkest thou, is it lawful to give tribute unto Cesar or not?" he gave a very wise and general answer, "Render therefore unto Cesar the things which are Cesar's, and unto God the things which are God's." Matthew 22:17, 21. We are informed, that upon another occasion he paid the tribute-money, and that, after asking Peter of whom do the kings of the earth take custom or tribute? and Peter answering of strangers, he remarked, "Then are the children free;" and yet nevertheless, as a voluntary act, ordered Peter, "Take a piece of money, and give unto them, for me and thee." Matthew 17:25-27.

On these passages I shall make but two remarks, which are very obvious, and will apply themselves: 1. How far soever the power of the magistrate and the submission of the subject may be extended, it is plain that by these rules and precedents property is left to the subject. To render, give, or pay, supposes property. Those who may be justly deprived of what they possess, at another's pleasure, cannot be said to be possessed of any property; and therefore they can neither give, pay, or render; they are themselves the property of another. I would further observe, 2. That from the answer our Lord gives unto Peter, it appears that sovereigns ought to treat their subjects as children, and that children ought to be free. O the free and benevolent spirit of the gospel!

By some it is urged, that sovereigns have a right to take away what their subjects possess, at pleasure. This right they ground on the following passage, I Samuel 8:10—

> This will be the manner of the king that shall reign over you, he will take your sons, and appoint them for himself, for his chariots, and to be horsemen, and some shall run before his chariots—and he will take your daughters, to be confectionaries and to be cooks and bakers; and he will take your fields, and your vineyards, and your oliveyards, even the best of them, and give them to his servants; and he will take the tenth of your seed, and of your vineyards, and give to his officers and his servants; and he will take your men-servants and your maid-servants, and your goodliest young men, and your asses, and put them to his work; he will take the tenth of your sheep, and ye shall be his servants.

Here then, according to some, is the warrant of divine right for arbitrary power. Those however, who found authority to do what is wrong in a representation, meant to deter the Jews from putting it in any man's power to treat them thus, would do well to consider that from the text itself it plainly appears, this was not to be considered as a right, but as a grievance, which their folly had brought on themselves. "You shall cry in that day, and the Lord will not hear you." Your misery will be the effect of your own folly. We have another precedent, which seems somewhat in point: Rehoboam was a foolish son of a wise father; it seems he laid a tribute on Israel: (2 Chronicles 13:18.) The people applied unto him, presented their grievances, and prayed redress: "Thy father made our yoke grievous, now therefore do thou make it lighter, and we will serve thee." This the council of the old men advised him to do; they said, "If thou wilt speak good words unto them, they will be thy servants forever." But more violent counsels prevailed, the acts were enforced, "I will add to your yoke, I will chastise you with scorpions." This the deluded monarch probably considered as firmness and dignity; but what was the event?

When all Israel saw that the king hearkened not unto them, they said, "What portion have we in David? to your tents, o Israel! now see to thine own house David." A kind and just answer might have prevented this; and what did the king himself gain? "The king sent Adoram, who was over the tribute, and all Israel stoned him, that he died, and the king fled to Jerusalem" Thus far tyranny was very unsuccessful. But this is not all; when the army of Judah was now ready to fall upon the ten tribes, God himself interposed, "Ye shall not fight against your brethren, the children of Israel; return every man to his house, for this thing is of me." Thus this matter ended in a separation of the two kingdoms, and this very Roboam himself afterwards became a servant, and tributary to the king of Egypt.

I leave the application of all these things to those whom it may concern; but would further observe,

Every government must be supported, and what is necessary for the support of government, is also justly due, and ought to be given with readiness and willingly.

Those that think their superiors have a right to take away their property, or any part of it, without their consent, upon their own principle are guilty of sinful resistance and rebellion, if they do not comply with whatever government may demand.* Those that think, every government has no further right than according to the laws and constitution of its respective country, should be very careful nevertheless to obey not only for wrath, but also for conscience sake, and under whatever grievances they may labour never to make use of any methods of redress unjust in themselves, nor of any remedies that may be worse than the disease.

[Appendix to *The Law of Liberty*]
A Short and Concise ACCOUNT of
the STRUGGLES of *SWISSERLAND* for LIBERTY

To a benevolent mind taking a survey of the globe, it must be a very melancholy consideration that liberty, which is the birthright of man, is still confined to a few small spots of our earth: All Asia and Africa are out

---

*King James the First asked the bishops Nelson and Andrews, whether he had a right to raise money on his own authority? The former affirmed it, because your Majesty is the anointed of the Lord, and the breath of our nostrils. The latter replied, "I think your Majesty has a good right to my brother Nelson's money."

of the question; in the southern hemisphere of America it is unknown, and astonishing pains are now taken to drive it out of this northern Continent. In Europe Great-Britain is commonly viewed as the seat of it; but if the conjecture of the bishop of St. Asaph be not void of foundation, even there it hath a sickly countenance; Swisserland, by that great man, is the only country which deserves to be called free, and even Voltaire pronounceth it happy. By what means the Swiss recovered and preserved their freedom, is the subject of the following narrative.

The three countries (usually called cantons) of Ury, Switz and Underwalden, which first entered into a confederacy that laid the foundation of the republic of Swisserland, are but of small extent, all the three cantons together do not exceed seventy miles in length and about thirty in breadth; they are also very thinly inhabited, owing to their situation among the Alps, many of which are covered with everlasting snow, and inaccessible to man or beast; it is usually said of the climate, that there is nine months winter and three months cold. At the time of their revolution the country was not nearly so well cultivated as it is at present, and at present all the inhabitants of the three cantons, capable of bearing arms, are not estimated above 12,000 men; a small number to make head with, as they did against the very powerful house of Austria. Power and number do not prove the justice of any cause, and it is more honourable to be defeated in the cause of virtue and justice, than to erect trophies to injustice and oppression. All Swisserland was subjugated by Julius Caesar; it became afterwards subject to different Lords, and had a nobility which treated their inferiors with great petulancy and violence. The three cantons chose Rudolph of Habsburg to be their captain, and on his being chosen Roman emperor in 1273, the nobility complained against these countries before him, and called them rebellious; but when the emperor saw their charters, he acquitted them, confirmed their privileges, and gave them governors that were not inhabitants of these countries, and were not to tyrannize over, but only from time to time to come among them, to administer justice. Thus the country was quiet, submitted to their governors; and had they been always treated with equal justice, probably would have continued so to this day, but *Nullum violentum diuturnum*, "Nothing that is violent lasts long."

After the decease of Rudolph of Habsburg, Adolphus of Nassau was chosen emperor; he confirmed their liberty, and they continued in submission to his government. Adolphus was slain in battle by the own hands of his rival, Albertus of Austria, son of Rudolph; and it has been observed that neither this Albertus, nor any that were active against Adolphus, died of a natural death.

Albertus of Austria, having a numerous family of children, projected the establishment of a new principality in Swisserland which then was a part of the empire; many imperial fiefs he apropriated to the house of Austria, purchased some jurisdictions which belonged to monasteries, and having made himself master of some strong places, he thought to subdue these three cantons also, and sent ambassadors to Ury, Switz and Underwalden, requesting that they would surrender themselves to him and the house of Austria, under many very fair promises. When his ambassadors arrived among them, the cantons produced their charters, and also sent an embassy to the emperor, praying that they might be confirmed, and that they might not be torn from the empire, and put in subjection to the then new house of Austria. Instead of being gratified, as they had hoped, they were not only refused, but the emperor also would not take the least notice of their complaints against their governors, but appointed two new governors over them, which from day to day proceeded to new and unheard of acts of violence. The design was, by such means to excite an insurrection among the inhabitants, and then, under pretence of being rebellious, to make war upon them, and entirely to bring them under the yoke. These are the express words of an historian, and in different times and places, tyranny makes use of the same arts. The tyranny and cruelty of these governors continually encreased. At that time there lived in Underwalden an aged and honest inhabitant, whose name was Henry de Melchdall. The governor ordered two oxen to be taken from his plough, without even charging him with any crime; the honest man wanted at least to know what had been his fault; but the governor's officer answered it was the will of the governor that henceforth the peasants should work in the plough themselves, and took away the oxen by force; the son of the farmer, enraged at so much injustice and violence, gave the officer a blow with a stick, and wounded his finger, and then fled the country immediately. The governor put his aged father in prison, and wanted to oblige him to deliver up his son; he excused himself that he did not know what became of him, but the governor ordered both his eyes to be put out, and took from him all he had.

The castle of Rozberg was occupied by the governor's deputy of the family of Wolfenshiess, the same seeing a very handsome woman, wanted to constrain her to gratify his brutal lust; under some pretence she withdrew, met her husband, who being informed of it, gave the governor a back-stroke with an axe, and also immediately fled the country.

Werner Stauffacre, a respectable man in the canton Switz, was building a handsome new house; the governor riding by, enquired of him whose it was? Stauffacre, aware of some design if he should dare to call it his own, replied, My noble governor, the house belongs to my king and you, and it is my fief. This frustrated the governor's design, but he told him withall, I will not suffer it that peasants should build houses for themselves as though they were lords, I will bridle you more closely.

Governor Grisler, of Ury, could not help perceiving the dissatisfaction of the people, and that he might discover the malecontents, he placed a hat on a pole at Altdorff, and gave strict orders, that every one should pay that hat the same honour as if he were present himself; he also placed some spies to observe who should pay obeisance to his hat and who should neglect it. This insolence wrought so effectually on the people, that even some of the nobility declared it impossible any longer to endure such tyrannical proceedings. Among numbers that thought so in their hearts, there was one that had courage to refuse submission to such a badge of abject slavery. William Tell passed several times without pulling his hat; he was informed against, and after some imprisonment, condemned, at the distance of one hundred and twenty yards, with his bow and arrow to take off an apple off the head of a beloved child of his, about six years old, and threatened with death in case he missed. No remonstrance availed, his life and that of his son was threatened in case of refusal; the afflicted parent most tenderly took his leave of his child, the spectators melted in tears, but he providentially hit the apple without doing any injury to his child. This happened October 30, 1307; and romantic as it may seem, public monuments to this day confirm the truth of the fact. The people congratulated Tell on his success; but the governor observing he had another arrow in his quiver, asked him the meaning. Tell at first excused himself with the common custom of marksmen: but this not satisfying the governor, and he solemnly promising him his life if he should declare the truth, Tell very frankly said, that had he had the misfortune to have done any injury to his child, he was determined to send the next arrow to the heart of the tyrannical governor. The governor condemned him to imprisonment for the rest of his days. Tell was permitted to bid farewell to his family, and then bound to be carried across a lake to the place of his captivity, and in the same vessel the governor also passed with his attendants. The lake of Lucerne is very liable to severe and sudden tempests, a storm of this kind brought them all into the most immediate danger: in this extremity Tell, who was known to be a good pilot, was ordered to take the helm, and he laboured so effectually that he brought the vessel near the shore; which he had no sooner effected, than he jumped out, and pushed the vessel off. The governor, with great difficulty, landed at some distance, but in the way to his castle he was waylaid by Tell in a narrow road, who placed the reserved arrow in his heart that he instantly fell dead from the horse; and Tell had time to fly to some of his friends, and give them notice of this event. These were Werner Stauffacre, Walter Fürst and Arnold de Melchdall; these were partly sorry to hear of this event, as it had been agreed upon to do nothing before the first of January, 1308, when an attempt to recover liberty was to be made by the three cantons at once; they apprehended the killing of the governor before they were ready to follow the blow, would frustrate their attempt, and bring matters to a crisis before they were prepared; but tyrants frequently hasten their own doom by their own measures.

The oppressive governors were possessed of three castles, and unless these were reduced, the oppression must become every day more intolerable: One of the confederates had an amorous connexion with a servant-maid in the castle of Rozberg; she, as usual, furnished him with means of entering, and he introduced twenty of his friends, who seized the castle and the governor without difficulty. The castle at Sarnen was taken by another stratagem: It was customary on new year's day to bring presents to the governor; twenty confederates accordingly appeared at the castle gates early in the morning, and made the governor the usual compliments, armed with nothing but long staves; the governor was just agoing to mass, and as he saw them without arms, ordered them to carry their gifts in to the castle. They had no sooner entered, but they fixed irons which they had concealed to their sticks, made prisoners of the garrison, and the castle was demolished. The governors betook themselves to flight, and nobody offered to pursue them. Thus in one day all the strong holds were taken and destroyed, and the next day the three cantons solemnly swore to each other for the space of ten years: This small beginning laid the foundation of the republic of Swisserland, which has maintained its freedom and independency until this time, and nearly survived the liberty of most states of Europe.

The emperor Albert had now obtained his wish, viz. a pretext to reduce the cantons by open war, under pretence of rebellion. He immediately repaired to Baden, *stopt all commerce with these three cantons, and ordered his vassals to declare war against them*; but while he meditated war against an oppressed people, he was himself murdered by his nephew, whose inheritance he unjustly detained from him; his murderer hoped to find a place of retreat among these cantons, but the Swiss, zealous for their liberty, were incapable to secure it by giving an asylum unto criminals; his widow was so bent upon avenging the death of her husband, that she took no measures against the Swiss, who had resisted the oppressions of their tyrannical governors.

Leopold, the son of Albert, when he came of age, determined to make war against the three cantons, and collected an army of 20,000 men for that purpose; his plan was to attack the confederates the 15th of November, 1311, at a place called Morgarden, situate between a lake and a mountain. In expectation that the inhabitants of Underwalden would come to the assistance of the confederates, the Count of Strasberg and the city of Lucern were to invade the cantons at the same time and at two different places. At dinner he asked the opinion of his jester, who replied, "All advise how to enter into the country, it seems to me necessary to consider how to come out again." His advice was despised, but verified by the event. A brave and virtuous people may be attacked, but woe to tyrants that cannot retreat.

The plan was exactly followed; Leopold made a false attack at Arth, and perhaps the confederates would have placed all their little force there, if they had not received an information to "beware at Morgarden." To that place the cantons Ury and Underwalden sent 700 men, and the canton Swiss an equal number, who were posted on a mountain called the Saddle. On the day appointed the duke of Austria advanced at the head of his cavalry, his troops marched in great confidence, "sure to obtain an easy victory upon peasants, badly armed, and without military discipline." Accordingly they proudly pressed into a defile, when they were stopt by 50 men, who had been banished the cantons for crimes, and whom, notwithstanding their request, the confederates would not think worthy to fight for liberty, even upon this pressing occasion. These men, however, by generously exposing themselves for their country, hoped to deserve the pardon of former crimes, they posted themselves on a very steep hill, above a narrow path, where the Austrian army could not march above two men a-breast; they suffered them very quietly to advance, but when a considerable number were now engaged in these narrow roads, they sent such a shower of stones and rolled large pieces of timber among the Austrian cavalry, that they were soon put in confusion; which the Swiss no sooner perceived, than they fell upon them with such fury, that they were obliged to retreat towards the plain; to gain ground to form the order of battle, the infantry opened their ranks, to let the cavalry pass; at this moment the confederates broke in upon them, and standing on rising ground, their halbards did most dreadful execution. A contemporary author saith, it was not a fight but a massacre. The prince lost near 1,500 of his horse, the loss of the infantry could not be ascertained, but 52 men from Zuric, then in the interest of Austria, were all found slain in a heap; the loss of the confederates was incredibly trifling: Meanwhile the count of Strasberg, with 4,000 men had also invaded Underwalden, who send to their friends at Morgarden, and 400 of the victorious Swiss instantly fled to their relief; they came up with a body of their own people, with whom they attacked the count, who seeing colours among them that had been at Morgarden, judged his master was defeated, and so fled. The Swiss killed about 300 of his men in the retreat. After this battle gained, the three cantons entered into a perpetual alliance, which no power has since been able to break, and which heaven has remarkably preserved.

One of the next greatest battle the Swiss fought in defence of their liberty, was in the year 1386. Leopold, duke of Austria, personally repaired to Swisserland, in order to carry on the war with greater vigour. The duke had resolved to lay siege to Sempach; the confederates had intelligence of it, and both opposite armies arrived before this little town the very same day. The Austrian advanced guard consisting of about 1,400 men, committed all manner of violence on their territory: One of their officers mounted a cart loaded with halters, and threatened to hang all the inhabitants before sunset. The Austrians insulted the Swiss, it being in the time of haymaking, they came so near the walls to speak with them, and desired they would send dinner and wages to their mowers. The Swiss replied, it was not the custom of the Swiss to pay wages till they were earned, and that they would prepare a dinner for them, that many spoons should drop out of their hands. The duke's army consisted of about 4,000 picked men, and among them many princes and noblemen, armed from head to foot. The confederates were about 1,300 men, badly armed, and all on foot; they had no arms, but halbards, and fastened pieces of wood on their arms, to fend off and break the blows of the enemies; their order of battle was very close, and represented an angle, one soldier was followed by two, two by four, and so on; in this order this handful of men courageously advanced against the enemy. Before they begun the engagement, as was usual with them, they fell down to prayers, which made the duke's jester say, "Leopold, my countrymen" (for he was a Swiss) "have all lift up their hands, and sworn to almighty God, to kill thee." An Austrian officer, observing their undaunted countenance, advised to delay the battle till next day, but a nobleman declared, "He would deliver that handful of boors before supper into the hands of the duke roasted or boiled, as he should best like them." The nobility was so eager to engage, that they dismounted, gave their horses into the care of their servants, and would not suffer any but noblemen to share in the honour of the day. It happened that a young nobleman, in cutting off the long point of his shoe (as all the rest did) wounded his toe, which made him cry, whereupon the nobility ordered him out of the rank, as unworthy to fight. His brethren were all slain, and his life was saved. The battle begun, the superior power of the Austrians in men and arms soon appeared, 60 confederates were killed before they could make the least impression on their enemy; in this distress a brave knight of the family of Winkelried resolved to sacrifice his life for his country, he accordingly advanced boldly, and with his arms grasped and bent down as many of their long pikes as he could hold, the others pressed after him with irresistable fury, broke in with their halbards upon the Austrians, and made dreadful havoc.

It is said, that before the engagement they proclaimed that every man that thought himself insufficient to encounter ten Austrians, might withdraw, and that about 300 withdrew accordingly; but when these saw the Austrians order of battle broke, they hastened to assist their brethren, and the nobility lost courage, gave way to the Swiss, and many of them, from the heat of the day and severity of the engagement, were suffocated by the weight of their own armour. The duke was several times entreated to withdraw, but seeing his banner in danger, he generously advanced to rescue it, but fell in the attempt. When the servants, who had been ordered in the rear with the horses, saw the defeat of their masters, they mounted their masters horses, and left their masters to shift for themselves. It is supposed the loss of the Austrians amounted to 2,000 including 667 of the nobility, and among them 350 with crowned caskets. The Swiss lost about 200, who were all carried to their respective homes. The third day they permitted the enemy to carry off their dead, among whom the duke was the principal; he was carried off the field of battle in a great box (still extant), which, 'tis said, had been full of halters, to hang the confederates. The Swiss, in hopes of obtaining peace, were sparing of the blood of the Austrians, and did not pursue them in their retreat; they had reason to repent their lenity, but the continuance of the war served only to increase the victories and fame of the Swiss confederates. The sons of the defeated Leopold made great preparation for a war, and many imperial cities joined with them against the Swiss; a truce was indeed concluded, which the Austrians badly kept, and by surprize and secret intelligence made themselves masters of Wesen, the possession of which laid the whole canton of Glaris open to their ravages. The Swiss confederates advised that canton to get the best terms possible, but those proposed by the Austrians were so excessive severe, that that treaty came to nothing. The Austrians proposed themselves to invade that country with about 8,000 men; the inhabitants had cast up an entrenchment, which was guarded by about 350 men; when the Austrians advanced, these finding themselves too weak to resist, retreated to a rising ground, the Austrians penetrated into the country, and burned the village of Nafels, and then attacked the above-mentioned handful of inhabitants, who received them with a shower of stones; the Austrians having retreated a little to put themselves under cover, the Swiss seized the favourable moment, and fell upon them with such fury, that after an engagement of five hours, they were forced to fly. The Swiss pursued and came up with them at a bridge, where about 700 Swiss had gathered; the Austrians, in their confusion not aware that the bridge was broke, pressed on, and numbers were drowned. The loss of the Austrians was computed at 2,000, while that of the Swiss did not exceed 55 men.

The dukes of Austria again consented to a truce, by which the Swiss were to remain in possession of all their conquests; this truce in 1314 was renewed for twenty, and in 1412 for fifty years longer. The Swiss made use of these times of tranquility to give stability and perfection to their military disciplines. In 1393 they agreed upon the following regulations among themselves: 1. No church nor chapel to be attacked, unless it is made use of as an asylum to the enemy. 2. No woman to be violated or insulted. 3. *Every Swiss engageth to sacrifice his substance and life for his country.* 4. No Swiss to forsake his post, even tho' wounded. 5. Forbids to pillage without leave of the commander, and orders the spoils to be equally divided. 7. All that send provisions to the Swiss shall be protected. 8. No canton to make war without the consent of the rest. 9. No Swiss to take away any thing by violence from another, neither in time of war nor peace.

The Swiss carried their military discipline to such perfection, that Machiavel pretends no nations ever exceeded them in that respect, except the Romans.

On the whole then we may conceive the rise and progress of liberty in Swisserland thus: 1. They had some rights and liberties granted them by emperors, which do not appear very considerable. 2. The emperors of the house of Austria endeavoured to separate them from the Roman empire, and bring them in subjection to the then rising house of Austria. 3. Against this the Swiss remonstrated, petitioned and pleaded their charters. 4. Governors were sent among them, who were to, and did, oppress them, in order to drive them to some act of despair, which their enemies intended to term rebellion, and under pretence of it reduce them by force of arms. This, 5. at length produced confederacies, first only of three men, by degrees of three small countries, which encreased gradually to *thirteen* cantons, besides some confederates. 6. To subdue them, a stop was first put to their trade, and afterwards they were attacked by force. 7. When attacked, they defended themselves with incredible bravery, and under every possible disadvantage resisted every attack, and at last obliged their enemies not only to desist, but to declare them a free state; and surrounded by Austria, France and Savoy they have continued free and brave ever since, and may they do so to the end of time.

[Printer's advertisement]

The following Tracts are to be had at the Printer:

> The Christian's Hope in Death, exemplified in the last Hours of several pious Persons. 3s.
>
> A Sermon on the Repeal of the Stamp-Act. 6d.
>
> A funeral Sermon for the Rev. Mr. Whitefield. 6d.
>
> Pious Advice of an affectionate Father. 3d.
>
> A Sermon on Faith, with an Appendix in Vindication of the Rev. Mr. Harvey. 1s.
>
> A Letter to the Rev. Mr. Frink, on Fees demanded of Dissenters, 3d.
>
> Thoughts when the day of Judgment may be expected. 9d.

Also to be had:

> Great-Britain's Right to tax the Colonies, placed in the clearest Light, by a Swiss. 1s.

OTHER WRITINGS

TO THE GRAND JURY OF
THE COUNTY OF CHATHAM

1777

John Zubly returned from the Second Continental Congress in 1775 under suspicion for his unwillingness to endorse the full range of Congress' military and political proposals and for his secret correspondence with Governor James Wright of Georgia, supposedly revealing the inner workings of the Continental Congress. From the time of his return to Savannah until 1777, Zubly devoted himself to his religious duties, revising two pamphlets on theological questions and delivering a healthy round of sermons in Georgia and South Carolina. Zubly avoided his political enemies as much as possible, but in the heat of war this became increasingly difficult to do. A clash was inevitable.

It came in 1777. The Georgia patriots insisted on oaths of loyalty as political tests because of the uncertain loyalties of so many people in the state. Like other provincial governments in the southern states, the Georgia government clamped down upon moderates in an effort to ferret out British sympathizers. To isolate and expose friends of the British, and so enemies of the new American governments, the southern rebels in the Carolinas and Georgia especially resorted to loyalty oaths requiring all free adult males to swear allegiance to the United States and to the state in which they lived, and thereby to repudiate any allegiance to the British crown. Failure to comply with the oath requirements meant banishment and confiscation of one's property. Fierce fighting between Loyalists and Whigs in the southern states intensified old personal and political hatreds and increased the likelihood that those in power, of whatever side, would seek harsh reprisals for injuries suffered. Some Georgians of doubtful loyalty to the rebel cause avoided confrontations by fleeing the state; some submitted to the loyalty oaths for reasons of expediency; and others refused to take the oaths and suffered the penalties. Zubly fit the latter case.

Short of money and unwilling to test its own power by levying taxes, the Georgia rebel government relied on confiscation to raise a revenue and to force loyalty to the Whig cause. When Zubly refused to take an oath of allegiance to the United States government in 1777, he became a public enemy. Zubly did agree to take an oath of allegiance to the state of Georgia, but the Whigs were not satisfied. They banished him from the state and confiscated half of his estate.

The irregular proceedings against Zubly and other suspected "Tories" drove Zubly to write his appeal *To the Grand Jury of the County of Chatham* in 1777, protesting his banishment and the loss of his property, but, more than that, warning that the Whigs' suborning of constitutional rights and common justice posed a greater danger to American liberty than any British action.

Source: Georgia Historical Society

To the GRAND JURY
of the County of Chatham,
State of Georgia.

Gentlemen,

On the Point of being (unjustly as I conceive) banished from this Country, I think it a Debt due to those whom I shall leave behind, to point out the very fatal Precipice towards which this State is, I think, now verging, and which, in my Opinion, must soon compleat the Ruin of the State, and of every Individual. I cannot address myself to any one more properly than to you, who are of the Grand Inquest, and if Things take their present natural Course, will probably be the last Grand-Jury that will have an Opportunity to enquire into Grievances, present them for Redress, and judge whether a Man shall be put to the painful solemnity of a tryal.

You must be convinced, Gentlemen, that no Grievance can more properly demand the Attention of a Grand-Jury, than that which strikes at the very Root of its Existance. That nothing can be more injurious to Freemen in a popular Government, than to be declared Subjects.

That nothing can be more alarming, than the Establishment of a Power to take away Liberty and Property out of the usual and due Course of Law, by a Power distinct from and in Opposition to the only legal and constitutional judiciary Department.

You must be convinced, Gentlemen, that if the Constitution, by which a People are to be governed, may be altered, infringed, or taken away, or acted contrary against, at the Pleasure of those who may chuse to do so, Constitutional Government is at an End.

If we must swear an Oath of Allegiance to other States, who are not by Oath bound to support, nor Claim any Right to rule over us, the Independancy of *this* State is at an End.

If a Man may be taken up without any previous Accusation upon Oath, all Liberty is at an End.

If a Man may be condemned without any public Tryal, or Pretence of Violation of a Law, all Law is at an End.

If he may be determined against by his known and professed Enemies, whom he is not allowed to except against, all Appearance of Justice is at an End.

If a Man cannot preserve Liberty and Property, without taking an Oath, which cannot be known whether it be true, and in Part is known to be false, all Decency is at an End.

And in a Word, where the Constitution is not a Law to Rulers, when Judges and Powers are set up in manifest Opposition to it—where natural Justice, which condemns no Man without a Crime proved, is disregarded—where a Set of Men, not sworn to act according to law, and to do justice, are vested with discretionary Powers, to harass or spare whom they please, I ask, what Constitution, what Law, what Liberty or Property can the People possibly hope for, what Motive can they have to swear, or what Benefit can they expect from an Oath of Allegiance? What great Blessing can those, who may be ruled without, or contrary to law and the Constitution, expect from their Rulers, and what can those who rule contrary to a Constitution, from which they derive all their Authority, and which they have sworn to support, expect from the People?

I submit it, Gentlemen, whether the Treatment I have received comes within any of these Cases, but as the Gentlemen who were called upon before me, were Prisoners on parole, (which it seems is not to be held sacred) I look upon myself as the very first Victim singled out to feel the Effects of a Power which will greatly affect every Man in this State.

If any Government in its proper Channel may require an Oath of the People, I must yet look upon it as a great Stretch of Power, that no Man shall be permitted to swear, unless he produces two Vouchers, this I conceive equally dishonourable to Government, the Vouchers that are to be presented, and the Person that is to take the Oath.

If a Government cannot acquiesce in the highest Assurance they can receive, an Oath, it marks very strong Diffidence, which is usually the Effect of fear, as that is of something else.

If two Persons vouch for one, and he is to swear notwithstanding, it is plainly treating the Vouchers like Men that cannot be credited.

If no Man is to be admitted to swear without Vouchers, it plainly implies a Supposition that he would forswear himself, this I apprehend a most ungenerous illiberal Presumption, *(unworthy of a wise Government and intolerable to a virtuous People).*

In free Government no Person can be compelled to appear before any but the lawful Judge, and in Case of Refusal and Contempt, may be proceeded against and outlawed. I have been ordered to appear before Judges who have no Existance in our Constitution, under the moderate Penalty, not of being proceeded against and outlawed, but of an IMMEDIATE Forfeiture of my Effects, and of being sent to any Gaol without Bail or Mainprize.

When I appeared, I was not indeed required to take an Oath, but had the Alternative set before me, either to take it, or be banished in forty Days—that I had some Scruple—and had heard that the Committee themselves had altered the Oath, availed me nothing. The Chairman told me that if they acted wrong, they were liable to be called to an Account, by the Assembly, I suppose, who will not meet till after I am banished, and so shall have it out of my Power to prefer a Complaint.

A Power to tender an Oath, to deprive a Man of Half his Estate, and banish him from every endearing Connection, is lodged in seven Men, without Appeal, without Check, without Challenge. I verily believe this State is the only one which hath trusted so few Men with so much Power—a Power which annihilates Grand Juries altogether, and effectually renders Petty Juries useless. Formerly in a Tryal, the Issue of which might not be above Ten Pounds, we had a Jury of twelve Men, any of whom might be challenged, who must be Freeholders, and unanimous in their Verdict. As the Matter is now mended, every Man's Person and Half his Property lies at the Mercy of seven Men, who need not have any Qualifications, need not receive or produce any Accusation, or hear any

Evidence, nor judge of the Breach of any Law, but only swear, that they will judge and determine to the best of *their* Knowledge, without Favour or Affection.

Besides the Civility of hearing a short Defense without Interruption, I must do the Committee the justice to acknowledge that they have proceeded against me more formally, than against the two Gentlemen heard before, or as far as I know, against any that were heard after me. They exhibited some Charge, a very enormous one indeed, a parallel to which, I doubt whether the most experienced Lawyer will find in any Law Books new or old. The Chairman, by desire, most gravely and solemnly asked me *"Whether, before I went to the Continental Congress as a Delegate, I had ever signed the Association?"* and must it not be evident that a Person, who may but be asked so important a Question, must be a suspected Person of course, and deserve to be banished as an internal Enemy of the State? You may be informed by Numbers who were present, that this great and mighty Charge was the Sum total of all that was offered to be alledged against me.

I offered to swear, that while I enjoyed the Protection of the State, I would in all Things do my Duty as a good and faithful Freeman.

Would give no Intelligence to, nor take up Arms in Aid to the Troops of the King of Great-Britain.

And that I had received no Letters of Protection since the War.

But all this would not answer the Purpose.

I have begged to be excused from swearing myself a Subject, till the Assembly had reconsidered whether we ought to be Subjects of Freemen.

I have hesitated to take an Oath of Allegiance to other States, who are bound by no Oath to us.

I have refused to swear that I have received no Protection from the King of Great-Britain, because every one who knows me, must know it to be false.

And for this I am now to be banished, and have Half my Estate taken from me. By the Act, no Provision is made to transport any that may be thought Enemies, but have no Estate or Means to transport themselves, probably because it is found by Experience, that those who have the least to lose, are always the best Friends to their Country.

I will not take up more of your Time, but embrace this seasonable Opportunity, Gentlemen of the Grand Jury, before I am driven out of this Country, to leave with you upon Record, that in my Opinion, no People can be more miserable than those who may have Laws made for them without any Regard to a Constitution, who may be judged without Evidence, or the Tryal by a Jury of their Peers, deprived of Liberty and Property without any Accusation made or proved against them, who must submit to their Enemies as their Judges, and to Men, who without any Disguise, alter the Constitution from which they derive their Authority, and which they have sworn to support, as their Rulers.

To be punished for no Crime, even pretended to be committed, always carries a strong Appearance of Injustice, but there may be Cases in which Banishment may be a greater Injustice than Hardship.

J. J. ZUBLY

Savannah, Oct. 8th, 1777.

P.S. I should be glad to know upon what Principle, natural, humane, divine, moral, legal, equitable, or conscientious, any Jury upon Oath, or any impartial Barbarian, could possibly condemn a Man as an internal Enemy, against whom no Crime has been alledged, whose Veracity is not disputed, and who offers solemnly to swear not to give any Intelligence to, nor take up Arms to assist an Enemy, and in all Things to do his Duty as a good and faithful Freeman of the State.

To be had of William Lancaster *and Dr.* Zubly. *Price* 1s.

"HELVETIUS" ESSAYS

1780

In 1778 the British shifted their military focus to the southern states. The promise of significant Loyalist support, the inability of the American forces to reinforce the area because of British control of the sea lanes, and the military stalemate in the northern theater combined to push the British in a southerly direction. The British offensive in Georgia and South Carolina scored a stunning success when most of Georgia fell into British hands in 1779 and Charleston surrendered in 1780. Governor James Wright returned to Georgia to resume his duties, and the British settled in for a long occupation of Savannah and the hinterlands. American military reverses in 1780 brought on the "dark days" of the cause. The American armies dwindled due to desertions and casualties, and the Congress wrangled with generals, diplomats, and itself.

The presence of royal troops in Georgia strengthened Loyalist sentiment there and served as a magnet drawing Loyalists from other states. Georgia Loyalism had been slow to form as an effective political or military force because the men who became its most able leaders had been Whigs who had supported the American resistance until independence. Now emboldened by numbers and British military successes, and still seething over sufferings at the hands of the rebel governments, the Loyalists panted for revenge. In 1780 Governor Wright and his supporters instituted their own policy of confiscation to punish rebels. The Disqualifying Act of 1780 provided for suits against rebel estates and for the sale of absentee (read rebels who had fled) property. Tit for tat ruled as the political order of the day.

An ugly civil war between Loyalist and Whig militia and partisan forces ravaged the southern states during the British occupation. In Georgia the Whigs retained control of Wilkes County, and such rebel leaders as Elijah Clarke, Benjamin and William Few, and James Jackson used the county as a base to launch raids against the British and Loyalists. In the summer and fall of 1780, Clarke led a small group of Georgia rebels against the British in Augusta, but they failed to take the town. The Loyalist leader Thomas Brown supposedly responded by hanging twelve of Clarke's men whom he had captured. Loyalists and Whigs traded atrocities, or reports of them, throughout 1780.

Zubly used the sorry state of Whig fortunes in 1780 to lecture them on their own responsibility for their sufferings and to try to induce uncommitted Americans and lukewarm "patriots" to come over to the British side. From July through October of 1780 Zubly wrote a series of essays for James Johnston's *Royal Georgia Gazette* in Savannah. Writing under the pseudonym "Helvetius," he scored the Americans for their violation of natural and international laws regarding war and their rejection of the Carlisle Commission's "peace" and reform offers of 1778, played on the Congress' courtship with the French, and reminded the Americans that rebellion destroys all law and brings misery to any society that engages in it. Hurried, awkward, and stilted, the essays yet revealed Zubly's deep attachment to discipline and restraint. He cited Emmerich de Vattel at length, as well as quoting passages from such other authorities on international law as Alberico Gentili and Hugo Grotius, to provide a very limited definition of a just war. Zubly also drew on the history of Europe to show that bravery was no assurance of success, that wars of rebellion degenerated into anarchy, and that war was an ineffectual instrument of positive social change. Zubly compared the American cause with the struggles of the Swiss and the Dutch to demonstrate that humility, forbearance, and dignity were no part of the American Whigs' character. He cited examples of failed rebellions to remind Americans of the awful fate of failed insurgents. He styled the American rebels as desperate men who sacrificed the lives and property of innocent followers for an unworthy cause and who would suffer God's wrath for their crimes against the public peace.

The "Helvetius" essays were the centerpiece of the Loyalist ideological argument in the Georgia press. They probably changed nobody's mind in the contest, but they did allow Zubly, like similar Loyalist essayists in other states, to show that his unwillingness to endorse the American Revolution was rooted in law and honor, not just self-interest as the Whigs charged.

Only six of the originally seven "Helvetius" essays have survived. Number five has been lost. The essays appeared only in James Johnston's *Royal Georgia Gazette.*
Source: British Museum

Number 1

Fortem & tenacem propositi virum,

— — — Non civium ardor prava petentium,

Mente quatit solida.   Hor.

In the beginning of those unhappy times, when men that would rather close than widen the breach advised to coolness of thought and moderation of measures, they were usually answered, "We must not think;" and never was any resolution more strictly adhered to than this by those that formed it. The task of renouncing thought was very easy to such as never considered thinking as any part of the business of life, and perfectly suitable to men of def— [Ed. torn] of thought always appeared a devil coming to torment them before their season. They were told, "they that would not think first must think last;" "that their unthinking principle would involve them and their country in ruin;" but some sought their refuge and ease, and others placed their honour and patriotism in thoughtlessness. Every man that was suspected of thinking became a suspected person, and to think different from people that did not think at all was a crime which exposed to every species of insult, suffering, and injustice. The consequences of all this are now visible; and of numbers that died as thoughtless as they lived it is to be feared they now suffer an everlasting conviction, that tho' it might be a man's choice it is not in his power to be a fool forever, and that he can no more deprive himself of thought, and after thought, however painful, than of his own existence.

It was the universal and professed maxim of that day, "*if we succeed it will be called a Revolution, and deemed a Rebellion if we miscarry.*" On this dreadful alternative, which with the greatest safety to themselves and their country they might altogether have avoided, they ventured blindfold, and like rope-dancers skipped on merrily, and frisked about with the highest unconcern while attempting to pass over the narrow and frightful precipice. As this implied Neck or Nothing, I heard some of the most respectable Carolina officers publickly declare, "We must not look to consequences." This is an easy way to ward off ruin and destruction when it is irresistibly pointed out as coming on apace; but when that ruin and destruction they have been warned against is actually come, what reparation can those make to their country who have wantonly brought it on? And if thoughtless wretches who sported with misery are ever brought to feelings, what must those feel who neither can bear their doom with conscious innocence, nor escape from it, tho' they looked upon their prosperity "as fixed as fate."

Perhaps those who set their country in blood and flames, to have the pleasure of trying whether they could bring about a rebellion or revolution, would now be very loth to admit the authenticity of so hazardous a principle: We have, however, the sanction of their authority when on the summit of glory and power to declare it what it really is. There is not so much of the existence of these quondam states left as to permit a shadow of hope that all their proceedings by the conquerors will ever be called by any other name than that which themselves agreed upon in the beginning. This doubtless will not make them in love with the notion, that miscarriage may be called rebellion; but perhaps also the illusion may cease, and mens eyes may be opened who had no apprehensions till they found themselves in the midst of Samaria; and, now the ground of their infatuation is removed, what should hinder candid men to acknowledge that the madness and knavery of their rulers, and the abject servility of a people that took up arms against themselves in these rulers support, has really been productive of nothing else but a defeated rebellion, and that the utmost of their power, deception, and villainy, caused no other revolution than to give a turn to the wheel by which the virtue of honest men was put to a severe trial, and the very worst rode triumphant, but that their triumph was short and infamous, and the sufferings of men who fear God, and do not meddle with them that are given to changes, last only "till the pit can be digged for the wicked?"

Though, upon the principle on which the chief actors pretended to set out, the case, in these parts at least, is entirely decided, yet particular fears, hopes, and wishes, private thoughts, and publick discourses, may still vary about the name the late transactions may deserve. Could I hope that, while the prosperity of fools destroys them, adversity might lead men to consider, I would willingly even now offer some considerations which will stand or fall by their own weight, and can hurt none but such who, obstinately resisting their own convictions, thereby render themselves inexcusable before God and men here and hereafter. I would leave them with those who are deepest concerned, happy for themselves if they are brought to think seriously at last, tho' it might have saved a world of trouble if they could have been induced to do so at first. Let the cause be argued in their own breast, and their own conscience faithfully record the irresistible verdict.

Upon no other principle than the prospect of success, and that success would abolish the criminality of the means, would men that have any regard for their lives, engage in any desperate action. To set out upon such a plan may be deemed bold and politick; but it is self-evident that a regard to God, to justice, and conscience, have no share in the resolution. Upon this plan men may, and I may say, must place perjury in the room of a lawful oath, to murder must be no crime; rapine and violence hold the place of equity and justice; nor can any design be too dark, or any action too villainous, for men that expect to succeed in wickedness; and that success will sanctify all the measures they have made use of to obtain it.

Rebellion may be hatched in a single breast, but becomes formidable by numbers; a few designing desperate men lay the plan, commence violent patriots, and set up a popular pretence the most distant from their real designs, but the most likely to deceive honest men; the unwary are taken in, the unthinking follow, knaves trouble the water in which they intend to fish, the giddy multitude is led on from step to step till they follow because they see no possibility [Ed. torn] ware of what is coming, the cautious prepare for the worst, the cunning endeavour to be secure in every event, those at the helm begin secretly to dread the general ruin and downfall; despair and violence is the natural consequence; the authors of the mischief "dash," and provide for safety by flight; those that remain pay the cost; and nothing is left of the baseless fabrick but a curse as extensive as the guilt imprecated by the dupes and lighting on the authors of anarchy and rebellion.

What constitutes the latter I may state in some future paper, upon impartial principles received and respected by all civilized mankind.

Helvetius.

Source: *Royal Georgia Gazette*, July 27, 1780. Number 74.

Number 2

Quibus ob scelera & paenae metum maxima peccandi necessitas est, aut quibus ambiguae domi res, & ob magnitudinem aeris alieni afflicta in pace fides, domesticis malis excidium patriae opponere patriae & privata vulnera reipublicae malis oppetire suamque causam libertatis larva & boni publici praetextu velare solent.

Barclay: Argenis.

The question wherein Rebellion consists can never be agitated with apparently greater disadvantage than in a time when opposite parties struggle to the utmost to fix or ward off the odious appellation. The utmost impartiality of an author will not escape blame from those who think they are blamed, or feel themselves blameable, and those who know no rule of justice but to do what they list will ever be ready to condemn and persecute any one that dares to avow principles of justice opposite to their power and usurpation. This however is a question of greater importance than curiosity, the calm discussion of which is never more necessary than when the case is actually supposed to exist; and a writer that has no other view but the publick good is superior to the petty cavils or insidious reflections of party and faction; he may either despise or pity them, but he ought not to suffer himself to be diverted from his honest intentions.

The most favourable name that can be given to commotions where subjects are in arms against their sovereign is that of a civil war; it may be very proper therefore to consider how far war in general is lawful; and surely that kind of war which cannot stand the test of general rules received by all sober men, between two foreign and perhaps naturally rival powers, must stand condemned by all equitable and decent persons if begun or carried on by lawful subjects against their natural prince and legal sovereign. I proceed to lay down some of these rules, and shall not be very pointed in their application to particular cases.

No war can be lawful without a just cause, and unless there is no easier and safer remedy to preserve and obtain peace. As it seems an insult to reason to alledge reasons in proof of such an assertion, I shall content myself to quote some authorities to prove what ought to be said or thought of such on whom no such reasoning can make any impression. "Those who run to arms without necessity are the scourges of the human race, barbarians and rebels to the law of nature, or rather to the common father of mankind." "Those disturbers of publick peace, those scourges of the earth, who, swayed by a lawless thirst of power, or a haughty and savage disposition, take arms without justice or reason, who sport with the quiet of mankind and the blood of others; those false heroes, however deified by the injudicious admiration of the vulgar, are in effect the worst of enemies to their species, and deserve to be treated as such. Experience shews how very calamitous war is even among nations not immediately engaged in it. War disturbs commerce, destroys the property of men, raises the price of necessities, obliges all nations to be upon their guard, and keep up at a great expence an armed force; therefore he who breaks peace without a cause necessarily injures nations who are the objects of his arms, and by his pernicious example essentially attacks the safety and happiness of every nation upon earth, and gives them a right to join in repressing, chastising, and depriving of a power which he has so enormously abused." These are the impartial thoughts of a very great man whom I shall often have occasion to cite, the respect for whom and his country has induced me to adopt the signature of Helvetius. *Vattel's Law of Nations.*

It is not less certain that, even where there may be a just cause, justice forbids war, unless every possible method and hope of obtaining redress fails. As war is the greatest evil nations can be afflicted with it ought not to be rushed into while there is any possiblity to avoid or prevent it. *Est fortasse boni principis aliquando bellum gerere sed tam denique posteaquam omnibus frustra tentatis huc adigit extrema necessitas:* It may be the duty of a good prince sometimes to engage in war, but then only when, having tried all other means in vain, he is compelled to it by extreme necessity, *Alberic Gentilis de Jure Belli, lib.* i, *cap.* 17. *Bellum est res tam horrenda, ut cam* [Ed. illegible] *summa necessitas aut vera charitas honestam officere nequeat:* War is so horrible that nothing but extreme necessity can excuse it, *Grotius de Jure Belli & Pacis.* It is clear therefore that war begun when it might safely be avoided is always unjust, and that those who begin it under such circumstances must be considered as the authors of all the mischiefs that flow from it. "The Law of Nature recommends peace, concord, and charity, and obliges to attempt the mildest methods of terminating differences," *Vattel, p.* 243. Beside, there may be just cause for complaint where yet there is no cause of war; it is safer and more honourable for a time not to insist upon a dubious right, or to submit to some temporary injustice, than, by flying to arms, to risk every thing and use remedies infinitely worse than the disease. This is a maxim which all humane and prudent nations adopt, and infinitely more safe and honourable before God and man than theirs who upon the smallest pretence light the flame and spread everywhere slaughter and desolation.

It will be difficult to controvert these assertions in any instance, and still more so to deny that in a civil war they are applicable with a double force.

The relation between subjects who depend on their governors is of a very different nature from that between different independent states;

they compose but one body, and to attempt the dissolution of that differs as much from war against foreigners as man-slaughter from suicide, and self-defence from common murder. What may justify a war against a different nation may not even be a plausible pretence for taking up arms against our own sovereign, or any part of the state of which insurgents have hitherto been members. Subjects are under the most solemn oath to their sovereign, and the strictest ties to each other, they have pawned their souls for their fidelity, and called upon the Supreme Ruler of all to punish them with everlasting destruction should they disregard the oath of their God. Whatever can operate upon men, the fear of God, the happiness of their country, the regard for family and posterity, ought to restrain them from breaking in upon the publick tranquility. "All violences (saith Vattel) disturb the publick order, and are crimes of state; N. B. even when arising from just causes of complaint—Every citizen should even patiently suffer supportable evils rather than disturb the publick peace." If those who begin a war against a foreign state are the pests of mankind, who ought to be rooted out of the earth by the common interest and efforts of all nations, there cannot be worse beings in hell, or out of it, than those who begin and keep up a war in the nation of which they are a part without cause, and they (without previous repentance) must appear conspicuous and next in rank, on the last day, to Lucifer and the fallen angels, who without any cause introduced rebellion in the creation. Whosoever therefore resisteth the power resisteth the ordinance of God, and they that resist shall receive to themselves damnation, Romans 13:2.

There are bounds to all human power, and these neither sovereigns nor subjects can break thro' without injustice and impunity. The doctrine of non-resistance and passive obedience has long and deservedly been exploded, but its opposite, like some powerful and violent medicines, ought to be handled with the utmost caution, lest it becomes a dangerous weapon in the hands of a madman, and by an untimely or over-dose destroy that very constitution which it ought to preserve. The violation of every law, privilege, and promises, by a poor bigotted, priest-ridden prince, in 1688, brought on a most happy and glorious revolution; the insurrections in 1715 and 1745 were odious rebellions, though not stained with such base motives and knavish financiering as have since disgraced men who acted in direct opposition to every solemn appeal to God on which they set out, and threw themselves and their deluded followers into the arms of a power the most remarkable for despotism and oppression of any in Europe.

The case of Swisserland and the United Provinces has frequently been mentioned during the present contest, and in a manner as shews how little those that would avail themselves of it are acquainted with or desire others should know the truth of the matter.

The Swiss never revolted, never took up arms against their lawful sovereign; they belonged either to the Empire of Germany or some Monasteries in their own country;* the Emperor Albertus, who had a large family, attempted to provide a principality for some of his children in their country; against this they pleaded, petitioned, and appealed to their charters; governors were sent among them to drive them to despair, which their enemies intended to term rebellion; what hardships they suffered contemporary historians declare; yet they did not take up arms till they were attacked, nor did they run when 6, or 60 or 100 men fell, but fought like men, "in hopes of obtaining peace were even sparing of the blood of Austrians, and did not pursue them;" and, so far from taking up arms or revolting against the Roman Empire, to which they then belonged, the Imperial Spread Eagle to this day appears on their gates and coins, and when criminal justice is administered the President still acts under the authority and in the name of the Empire. Their case therefore differs *toto cado* from theirs who without, or even with some cause, took up arms against their sovereign, or make war upon the members of the same body from which they have wantonly revolted.

Let us see next whether the conduct of the Low Countries, when they separated from Spain, affords any patronage to such as make war without any or without a sufficient cause, and reject every offer of peace by which it might have been ended.

About the year 1560 Philip II. of Spain attempted to introduce the Inquisition in the Low Countries, and to exact a general submission to the Council of Trent. No Protestant will deny that this was a mortal grievance. About 1566 a number of the nobility and others presented a petition to the Governess that they might be maintained in their liberties; they received a mild amusing answer; but in 1567 the Duke of

---

See the Appendix of Dr. Zubly's Sermon called the Law of Liberty, addressed to the Earl of Dartmouth, and printed under the eye of the American Congress, of which he was then a Member.

Alva arrived with an army, beheaded the Counts of Horn and Egmond, (both Catholicks) and, after defeating the Princes of Orange, laid on a tax of one per cent. on every estate, five per cent. on all moveables, and ten per cent. on all immoveables, and in 1571 ordered 70 citizens of Brussels to be hanged the next day before their own doors in failure of payment; nay, during the six years of his administration, no less than 18,000 persons lost their lives by the common hangman, and yet the Confederacy wherein the provinces shook off the yoke of Spain, and declared themselves independent, did not take place till 1579, and the war between them and Spain lasted not less than 70 years before the Seven Provinces (for ten after all remained to Spain) were declared an independent people by the treaty of Westphalia. Whoever will read the history of their wars, and the battles of the Americans, will find a remarkable contrast between the "poor distressed States of Holland," as they stiled themselves, and some other people, who, without a copper of their own coin, and hundreds of millions in debt, boast that they are *as fixed as fate, and that all the nations of the earth admire and almost adore their rising glory."*

There is a more recent instance: The Corsicans, by the acknowledgment of the very power that assisted the Genoese, had long been sorely distressed by their government; when they had recourse to arms France privately at least supported them; they maintained the conflict upwards of 40 years, performed prodigies of valour, and probably might have perpetuated their freedom; but alas! *"The French, like true politicians,* after weakening both parties, at last made a conquest of it for themselves, *and seemed convinced that the only means to gain an easy settlement in a conquered island, to which they are sensible they can have no just title, is to get rid of the old and unruly natives by breaking them alive on the wheel, putting them to the sword, or dispatching them by any other means which regal humanity may suggest."** One would think this transaction, which happened while the American Congress was sitting, would not have encouraged them to fly to France; but so it is that they did, and on the very prince who thus treated the poor Corsicans they have bestowed the title of *"Protector of the Rights of Mankind,"* with the same propriety, no doubt, that the Pope stiles a King of England the Defender of the Popish Faith.

From what I have said I might not unjustly conclude, that when subjects take up or continue in arms against their lawful sovereign,

---

London Magazine 1774, page 408.

without a just and sufficient cause, it is Rebellion; but, before I draw any conclusion at all, I mean to offer some further considerations to the serious thoughts of every reader.

Helvetius.

Source: *Royal Georgia Gazette*, August 3, 1780. Number 75.

Number 3

In bellis suscipiendis, quoniam ingentium malorum inducant diluvium oportet omnibus occulis advigilare, nequid temere statuatur. Est fortasse boni principis aliquando bellum gerere, sed tum denique posteaquam omnibus frusta tentatis huc adigit necessitas & necessitatem it [Ed. illegible] *se esse nobis* [Ed. illegible] *bellum inferamus.*

Erasmus Rot. ad Gallim Regem.

I have laid it down as an incontrovertible maxim, that all war begun or continued without a just cause is unlawful, and that this holds with a double force when subjects take up arms against their lawful sovereign. My next I hope will not appear less evident: *It is possible that between two contending nations the right claimed by the one, and the injury pretended to be received by the other, may be very dubious; in that case the laws of nations and humanity require that negociations and every other method be tried before recourse is had to arms.* It is impossible that both parties can be at the same time in the right, but it is very possible that *bona fide* they may think so; we are ever apt to be partial to ourselves, and this partiality will magnify every consideration in our favour, and heighten every prejudice we may harbour against our enemies. Nay, the scale of claims or complaints, of rights or grievances, may seem sometimes so very equally [pressed?] that even an indifferent spectator may find it difficult to determine which preponderates, and that partiality itself will not disallow the opposite party has some plausible reasons for the right it claims, or the grievance under which it complains. In this case, if reason, conscience, and humanity, are consulted, they will very readily determine, that the certain evils of war, which extend themselves much further than could be expected, should never be entered into merely for the support of a claim, or redress from a grievance, which it is possible may be but dubious, may be imaginary more than real. It is folly to make use of remedies worse than diseases, and in morality it is an universal principle, *in dubiis abstinendum.* While we are in doubt whether what we would engage in is just or otherwise, it is our duty to forbear; nor can humanity otherwise than highly condemn the sporting away of peace and lives upon pretences frivolous or dubious in their own natures. "Nature gives us no right to have recourse to force but where mild and pacifick measures are ineffectual. It is not permitted to be inflexible in uncertain and doubtful questions. Who shall dare to pretend that another suddenly and without examination shall abandon to him a litigated right? This would be rendering war perpetual and inevitable. The two contending powers may be equally possessed of good faith; why should the one yield to the other? In such a case," (*to begin a war would at least be running the risk of beginning it unjustly*) "they can only demand a negociation, a conference, an arbitration." *Vattel, lib. iv.* 18, 331. "Every power owes this respect to the happiness of human society, TO APPEAR OPEN TO EVERY METHOD OF RECONCILIATION, when it relates to interests that are not essential or that are of small consequence." (I add, or may possibly be secured without the risk of the horrors of war). "If he exposes himself to some loss by an accommodation, a negociation, or arbitration, he ought to be sensible what are the dangers, the evils, the calamities of war, and to consider that peace is well worth a small sacrifice."

This accordingly among nations is no unusual practice, their formal declarations of war generally pretend that they have recourse to arms with reluctance. "Pretences are at least an homage which unjust men pay to justice. He who covers himself with them shews still some remains of modesty; he does not openly trample on what is most sacred in human society; he tacitly acknowledges that a flagrant injustice deserves the indignation of all mankind." In 1741 the King of Prussia published his manifesto in Silesia, then belonging to the Queen of Hungary, at the head of 60,000 men; in 1745 he offered to make the Courts of London and Petersburgh mediators between him and the House of Austria. In which case did the Monarch appear with greater honour, viewed by humanity or justice? "It is not denied that a prince may attack without all these formalities, as he has no account to give to other nations; but if he abuses this power, he renders himself odious and universally suspected, and when he seems to advance his affairs ruins them sometimes past recovery."

Sovereigns owe each other nothing but justice, and if they have any quarrel, as there is no judge between them to decide, (though impartial mankind will always judge for themselves, and no wise man despise the judgment of impartial mankind) they may have recourse to arms, when their rights or complaints may be but doubtful. The case is far different in subjects taking up arms against their prince. What may justify independent established powers subjects cannot make use of even as a plea. There can be no reciprocal rule or submission between different sovereigns; but without power and authority to rule in governors, obedience and submission in subjects, no government whatever can subsist. Single individuals in no case whatever have a right to resist, or endeavour to subvert lawful government. The cases where resistance may be lawful to the body of a nation are few, and it is the interest of all government they should not be multiplied. An apparent settled plan to rule without or against law can be the only justification of subjects upon such occasions. Could every club and parish betake themselves to arms when they think themselves aggrieved all government would soon be at an end, and mere necessity would oblige the soberer part rather to submit to one tyrant than be tyrannized over by a hundred. What every discontented courtier bawls against may nevertheless not be a grievance, and there may be [Ed. illegible] in government which may render measures necessary, extremely unpopular in themselves, which yet would be, and in after times are applauded, when once their spring and motives are laid open, which, had they been known at the time, might have prevented disruption, but whose [premature?] knowledge would also have defeated the good that was obtained and intended. There may be real grievances, and yet they may not warrant the taking up of arms to obtain redress. You have the rheumatism in your joints, will you therefore cut off your members? You are unjustly deprived of a 1000 of your estate, will you therefore make a sacrifice of the other 999? You are displeased with the administration of the olive tree, the fig tree, and the vine, and so you will say to the bramble, come and rule over us. The fathers of your prince perhaps delivered you out of the hands of Midian, nourished and raised you to greatness, and will you call some son of a concubine to deprive his heirs of their inheritance and be your judge? Government is so sacred, and so absolutely necessary and useful to mankind, that, without the most irresistible evidence to the contrary, the presumption lies always in its favour. Intestine commotions and civil wars are productive of such infinite mischiefs that humanity shudders at their approach, and very great evils and just complaints grow small and unworthy of the resentment they might otherwise deserve, where the evils produced by an intestine war for redress are thrown into the opposite scale of the balance.

The less real reason dissafected persons may have to use the more will they usually pretend. They are obliged to do so; any shew of diffidence in their cause, or its success, would immediately alienate their dupes, and ruin their designs, as no man of the least thought or decency would engage in a cause, of the justice or success of which the very leaders should profess to have but an indifferent opinion. Desperate and wicked men have stifled all conviction, but men happily cannot reach that degree of wickedness at once. *Nemo repente fit* [*turpissimus?*]. Before they arrive to it conscience will now and then force a hearing and make them uneasy. Whatever man does in any circumstance of life contrary to his own conviction, to him it is sin. Even lawful actions assume a different appearance when committed by men who thought them otherwise. The man that meant to transgress the law is undoubtedly a transgressor of the law. If in so small a matter as eating or not eating flesh the Apostle passeth so severe a sentence against those who act contrary to their conviction, what are we to think of him who ventures upon resistence to lawful authority, joins to promote all the evils of domestick discord, sheds the blood perhaps of his dearest friend because he remains faithful to his king and country, brings on every species of evil upon the present, and entails them upon the next generation without once considering whether his way may not be perverse before God, and still doubting the justice of that very cause in support of which he runs every risk of time and eternity for himself, and aggravates it by involving his fellow creatures in guilt and ruin. Nothing but the fullest conviction of the justice of the cause, and purity of their intentions, can support an honest man to act under so disagreeable a necessity; but for men to rush into arms, and all their evils, while themselves are doubtful whether the cause is lawful, or the evils unavoidable, is running a high hazard indeed, and of such a one we may well say, he that doubteth is damned, if he eats (or acts) contrary to, or without previous solemn thought and conviction; he is damned, because, contrary to the checks of his conscience, he ventured upon damnation.

It is not to be denied that petitions from America, and overtures from Great Britain, preceded the war in form. It is lamented that the former did not meet more speedily with a favourable reception, and that the latter, by some unhappy delays, were not made till the enemies of both had an opportunity to carry into execution those dark designs which before they ever disavowed and durst not mention. The mystery of iniquity by which independency and a French treaty was hurried on is not yet unravelled, but so early as 1775 the then President of the Congress declared in private: "It does not signify, some men wish to keep up the ball, and I am sorry I cannot except my own province." The respectful reception given to the Delegates from Congress (Franklin, Adams, Rutledge) and the most generous offer made by the King's Commissioner, sufficiently evince Great Britain's desire of a reconciliation, and the haughtiness and stubborn inflexibility of a Franklin and Adams clearly point out what was their original design. Great Britain's condescension will do honour to them as a nation, and bring a blessing on the King's arms; the scorn and contempt wherewith it has been treated will recoil with interest on the authors, and in the end cause them to be trodden down like mire in the street. Every insolent cobler or committeeman would then say, as some wiseacres in our own climate even now affect: "Great Britain's offers came too late;" but they will find in the end that the Declaration of Independency was too soon, and that now it is too late for themselves to have any hopes but in the mercy of that generous power which they have taken so much pains to injure and provoke. In every view of the thing, those Delegates who voted for independency, without express orders from their constituents, were traitors of their country; the time is come, and coming, when they will be declared and treated as such by those whom they have betrayed. It seems the South Carolina Delegates voted against it, and a Georgian boasts that HE gave the casting vote. The miscreant is known, and whether his boast be true or false it is of a piece with the general character of a man whose name ought never to stain paper, unless it be in an indictment, or in the blackest part of the blacklist of those who have been the bane of their country and disgrace of their species.

In the opinion of authors I cited, kings and nations are guilty of a crime against humanity if they engage in war under a doubtful pretence, and without having taken every step to prevent it by amicable means. What would these respectable authors think or say of subjects who take up arms, under very doubtful pretences, against their undoubted sovereign, and avoid and treat with scorn every measure and offer to prevent the measures and crimes into which they are impetuously rushing?

August 4.   Helvetius.

Source: *Royal Georgia Gazette*, August 31, 1780. Number 79.

Number 4

Quo nunc Turnus ovat spolio gaudetque potus
Turno tempus erit magno cum optaverit emptum
Intactum Pallanta, & cum spolia ista diemque
Oderit.

Virgil.

The maxim which I advanced in my last, viz. *"That no war can be lawful without a just cause and unless there is no easier and safer remedy to obtain and preserve peace,"* will not openly be disputed by any that have an idea of justice, or profess some regard for that and their own character. How many truths are admitted, and even contended for, in theory, which are opposed and insulted by practice? Men that have parted with every principle except pride and obstinancy may still pride themselves to be in the wrong, and war against their own convictions; but those that have the courage to avow and follow truth and justice for better or worse will always be victorious in the end, and honourable even under temporary disasters. I readily submit it to every species of my readers whether my next proposition will stand the test of truth and justice; it is that:

A just and lawful war no longer continues just and lawful than the cause continues that made it so; and whenever just and equitable offers of peace and reconciliation are made by either party, the whole guilt and all the consequences of the war rest soley with that party by which they were rejected. This assertion is virtually contained in the preceding one and cannot be consistently denied or opposed by any that admit the former; but what is there that some men will not object against? If reason is against them they will be against reason of course; they can easily work up themselves or persuade their dupes into a belief or disbelief of what most affects their fears or wishes; they may confound what they cannot confute; men that suffered themselves to be persuaded out of their former strongest principles, nay their very property and possessions, may easily also be persuaded out of their senses, and have that palmed upon them as an object of hope and pleasure which is only a preface to certain destruction.

That war, even justly begun, can no longer be just than while the cause continues that made it so, is as certain and self-evident as that no effect can exist longer than the cause by which it is produced, *cessante causa cessat effectus*; how can that operate, or even furnish a pretence, which has no existence, or that continue a grievance which has been absolutely removed? War and misery must either continue forever, or must end in the entire destruction of one or both parties, or in a reconciliation between them. If a nation will not hearken to or receive any proposals of peace they renounce human nature, and offend against mankind at large; if they scornfully reject just and favourable ones, the least bad consequence to themselves will probably be, that at last they may be glad on their knees to beg for what they haughtily rejected. Many have scorned peace when it was offered who afterwards sued in vain for it when it was not to be had. Some would have thought hard terms granted by a conquerer very favourable who once had it in their power to make peace on their own terms before they were made a conquest. To desperate men war may be necessary, and doubtless they will impose every lie that suits their purpose, and make large promises of plunder and booty to engage men as desperate as themselves; they will talk loftily after a defeat, and reserve sullen affectation after every thing failed; they may be as proud as Lucifer, and as fixed as fate, but God resisteth the proud, himself is at war with them and those whom neither sense, reason, nor religion, can humble, *"he knoweth how to abase."* I shall quote the opinion of two authors on this subject, the first of which has drawn after him all the fierce men in America, and the other has the approbation of all men of candour and humanity wherever they are to be found.

"Men of passive tempers, still hoping for the best, are apt to call out, *'Come, come, we shall be friends again for all this;'* But examine the passions and feelings of mankind, bring the doctrine of reconciliation to the touchstone of nature, and then tell me whether you can hereafter love, honour, and faithfully serve, that power that has carried fire and sword into your land.—But if you say you can still pass the violation over, then I ask, 'Hath your house been burnt, your property been destroyed before your face? Are your wife and children destitute of a bed to lie on, or bread to live on? Have you lost a parent or child by their hands, and yourself the ruined and wretched survivor?' If you have not, then you are not a judge of those who have: But if you have, and can still shake hands with their murderers, then are you unworthy of the name of husband, father, friend, or lover, and whatever may by your rank in life, you have the heart of a coward and the spirit of a sycophant." *Common Sense, page* 41. Passionate language this for one who declares, page 51, that he has been no sufferer. My readers may observe that all the sufferings declaimed against in this bombast are no more than what are common, and indeed unavoidable, in every war, and that, according to him, nations that have been at war once ought never again to think of reconciliation and peace; a principle which strikes at the root of humanity, and proves nothing but that this author and his admirers are distinguished from the fiercest beasts of prey only by the immortality of his and their hatred. But let us submit to the drudgery of quoting from him another passage:

"There are injuries which Nature cannot forgive; she would cease to be Nature if she did. The Almighty has implanted in us these inextinguishable feelings for good and wise purposes. They are the guardians of his image in our hearts; they distinguish us from the common herd of animals. The social compact would dissolve, and justice be extirpated the earth, or have only a casual existence, were we callous to the touches of affection; the robber and murderer would frequently go unpunished, did not the injuries which we sustain provoke us to justice." *Common Sense, page* 61. A rare discovery this, but worthy of a cause it is intended to serve, and a striking proof of the improvement of the times in political and religious knowledge. No other brains could have produced so exotick a plant, and no other ground or season could have nursed and fostered it to maturity. Now, when it is considered that this pamphlet was printed as the "Common Sense" of America, and had private and publick sanction by individuals and legislatures, what he advances must be deemed as a national sentiment, and experience has but too clearly proved how universally it has been adopted. The nations of the universe may hence learn what in futurity they may expect should the ambition of these new fangled states to figure among them prove successful, or any disagreement happen between them in time to come. Peace and reconciliation after war seems no part of their system; like the Algerine pirates they mean to fasten upon others; inextinguishable animosity is avowed as a national character, and they glory in it even while their existence is but in embryo; this vindictive temper is to establish their rank among civilized nations, whom they probably mean by "common herd of animals," and raise them above the ordinary condition of men. Happily must the image of God be guarded in beings thus nearly resembling devils, and superior to beasts by a diabolical temper only! None but this author taught others to pride themselves in such a distinction; no devil before uttered the blasphemy of putting the image of god into wardship and appointing inhuman rancour and immortal malice to be its guardians. Blush forever, if you are yet capable of blushing, all you that by such execrable blasphemies could be led to prefer a continuance of war and wretchedness to that peace and happiness which you were so generously offered.

After quoting a declaration which teems with war, vengeance, and rancour, in every word, it is a relief to transcribe and read a passage from an author who breatheth peace on earth and good-will to men in every syllable:

"A rational being is to terminate his differences by rational methods, whereas to decide them by force is proper to beasts. If one of the parties should reject pacifick measures of accommodation the other is empowered to take up arms for reducing him to an agreement. War does not decide the question. Victory only compels the conquered to subscribe to a treaty." *Vattel lib. iii. p.* 14. "If a nation, on an injury done it, is induced to take up arms, not by the necessity of procuring a just reparation, but by an unjust motive, it abuses its right. The injustice of the motive disgraces its quarrel, which otherwise had been just. War is not made for the primary lawful cause which the nation had to engage in it, that cause is now no more than the pretence. What right has the head of the nation to expose the safety of the state, with the lives and fortunes of the citizens, to gratify his passions? These passions are the arrogant desire of command, the ostentation of power, the thirst of riches, the avidity of conquest, hatred and revenge." *Idem, p.* 12, *passim.* I shall add but one passage more: "Were the rules of an exact and precise justice observed at making peace, each party punctually receiving all that belongs to him, a peace would become impossible; first, with regard to the very subject which occasioned the war, one of the parties must acknowledge himself in the wrong, and condemn his own unjust pretensions, which he will hardly do unless reduced to the last extremities; but if he owns the injustice of his cause, all he has done in support of it likewise falls under condemnation; he must restore what he has unjustly taken, reimburse the charges of the war, and repair its damages. . . . . Who shall make a just and exact calculation of all this? Thus, as it would be dreadful to perpetuate the war, to prosecute it till the total ruin of one of the parties, and as in the most just cause we are never to lose sight of the restoration of peace, are constantly to tend towards this salutary view, no other way is left than to agree on all the claims and grievances on both sides, and to extinguish all differences by the most equitable convention the juncture will admit of." *Vattel, lib. iii.* 120.

I shall not now enlarge to shew how much stronger all this holds where members of the same state and subjects against their natural sovereign are the contending parties, but shall conclude this paper with two or three questions which will hereafter be found very interesting. I ask the most zealous American: Supposing an American legislature had laid on a tax of a million per month, and enacted other laws which the people at large should have thought grievous; supposing the inhabitants had petitioned, remonstrated, and at last taken up arms, against the enforcing of such laws; supposing thereupon the legislatures had not only repealed a [Ed. torn] of, but also gave assurance that no such law should be passed in future; and supposing the people should continue nevertheless in arms, aim at nothing less than the overthrow of that government, and the destruction of all its friends, and call in foreign aid and a common enemy to effect their purpose, by what appellation would the government and its friends dignify such proceedings, and how far does this supposition affect the cause between America and Great Britain?

Is it not a most notorious fact that Great Britain not only repealed every law and grievance complained of, but also made the most generous offers to Congress, and each state separately, and that those offers have been treated with a scorn and contempt which would be deemed intolerable between private individuals, and with an insult that violates the laws of all civilized nations?

Is it a just and lawful plea against generous offers of peace, that they cannot be accepted because those to whom they were made called in a perfidious power to support their opposition against their natural sovereign? And may those who trust such a perfidious power reasonably expect more assistance and fidelity than the nation with whom such a power perfidiously broke through every tie sacred among men, to reap an advantage from the rebellion of its subjects?

It will be an easy matter to curse or evade any such questions, but they go to the essence of the cause, and though men may flatter themselves with impunity, or even success, yet God at last will make inquisition for blood, and *"there is no* [Ed. illegible] *above."*

August 11.   Helvetius.

Source: *Royal Georgia Gazette*, September 7, 1780. Number 80.

Mr. Johnston,   Sept. 22, 1780.

Since I sent you my last number, dated Sept. 13, an event has happened, which, as it must defeat the last hope of Rebels, ought to fill every loyal subject with the warmest gratitude to Providence, and the highest esteem for those brave and worthy men whom it has made the instruments of their defeat, and, I trust, of our future tranquility. Good news then prevented you from giving it a place, and I shall always be happy to be thus agreeably prevented, but wish you may have it in your power to insert it in your next verbatim as you received it before we heard of the enemy's intended invasion and disgrace. No person can more sincerely lament the fate of that gallant youth Capt. Johnston, but he died gloriously in his King and Country's cause, and HE has lived to a noble purpose who lived and died for the good of his country, and secures an immortal name almost as soon as he appeared on the stage of action.

Your's,

Helvetius.

Number 6.

An evil man seeketh only rebellion, therefore a cruel messenger shall be sent against him.   Proverbs 17:2

In my former numbers I have insinuated that unlawful resistance to lawful government is rebellion, and that as all war is unjust that has not a just cause and object, so a civil war must be superlatively so, when grievances, real or pretended, are actually removed, and men nevertheless still pretend to levy or continue war against their sovereign, or the body of which they have been members. Cool and impartial men of all nations will not hesitate to admit the truth of my several propositions, and allow that in them tyranny is not flattered, and true liberty not opposed, tho' licentiousness also, and opposition to law, order, and government, are not encouraged. I have also produced a case from holy writ, by which what is deemed rebellion in scripture is most clearly determined, and from which all those that profess regard and obedience to the scriptures may learn under what specious pretence and appearances men may nevertheless incur the greatest guilt, and involve themselves, their country and posterity, into ruin, when they think every thing pleads in favour of their proceedings. I have been very sparing in applying either this fact, or the general maxims I had advanced, to the present unhappy times, because, with readers that have been led astray by ignorance and mistake, rather than by disloyalty and malice, arguments simply offered may cause conviction, whereas it is a forlorn hopeless labour to write for the reclaiming of such as will hearken to nothing but their own rage and delusion, and appear evidently under the power of a reprobate mind, or the most unhappy delusion. Pity may be due, but all pity is lost upon those who will have no pity for themselves.

A most unhappy war still subsists between sovereign and subjects, between brethren and brethren, and by men whose aim is nothing less than the good and interest of either has been spun out to an unexpected length. Thousands have perished by the sword, many of hunger and want, some sank with a broken heart under injuries they could not sustain, and too great a number have fallen a sacrifice to the desperate fury and cruelty of those who were not satisfied to sport away the lives of their fellow creatures in military service, but would also enjoy the triumph of wickedness in consigning better men than themselves to an ignominious death. The infamy rests not upon the martyr, but upon the unrighteous judge. There is not a province in America, nor district within the disunited states, which is not more or less stained with the blood, sufferings, and violence, of its inhabitants, nor a spot of this once delightful part of the globe that bears not visible marks of the curse and misery introduced by their present or late factious rulers. The parent state has held out friendly offers after every victory, and Congress and states are grown more oppressive and outrageous after every defeat. Blows recover some to their senses, (*Phryges plagis emendantur*) but no judgment of God, nor calamity and distress that man can bring on themselves, has hitherto proved sufficient to cause them to make a pause and think. They see their country ruined, all misery produced by their tyranny, and losses the mere effects of folly and madness stare them everywhere in the face, but you may as well expect to find bowels in a stone, or sense in an oyster shell, as pity, thought, or mercy, in the leading men of this generation. After being in every respect fallen themselves, their last delight is to involve others in their guilt, and, if possible, to substitute them in their room in the day of punishment. They have bargained and sold their country and dupes to France, and wish now, with the assistance of that arbitrary perfidious power, to seize, deliver, and make good the bargain. They know what they deserve, and what the De Witts, for the mere suspicion of something similar, met with; and it is now even natural for them to wish that France, the Pope, or any one, should be the possessor of America, rather than they should meet with their deserts. The independency of a country mortgaged to a foreign power, and stupidly inviting that very power to foreclose every method of redemption, is now out of all question. This is not even denied, but whatever may be the pretence, while the Congress already totally depends on France, and must be glad to do any thing they are commanded, this is all the Congress can contend and Americans hope for, and is there no man, or body of men, within all your states, that dares assert your natural rights and re-offered privileges against those that betrayed you? O Americans! do you not yet feel the unworthiness and vanity of your pursuit? and how long will you be made tools of to make war against your own bowels rather than return to a connexion in which even your betrayers cannot deny you have been always and superlatively happy? You that have refused every offer of peace, and made use of every artifice to continue the war, "you are chargeable with all the evils, all the horrors of war, all the effusion of blood, the desolation of families, the rapine, the violence, the ravages, the burnings, are your works and crime. You are guilty towards those you call enemies of attacking, oppressing, massacring them, without cause. You are guilty towards your own people of drawing them into acts of injustice, exposing their lives without necessity, without reason; towards that part of your subjects whom the war has ruined, or who are great sufferers by it, of losing their lives, their fortunes, or their health. You are guilty towards all mankind of disturbing their quiet and setting a pernicious example." All this complication of guilt hangs over the heads of the late or present governors of any of the states ever since they rejected Britain's too favourable offers; every counsellor and assemblyman, every general and volunteer, is implied in this charge, tho' it falls heaviest upon that worst set of bad men (clergy or laity) who have been the principal authors and fomenters, whose basest work to their constituents, but happiest to Britain and America, was the rejection of proposals of terms which would still have left power and a degree of importance in inauspicious hands, destitute of all merit but what they could derive from a fixed resolution to establish themselves upon the ruins of either or both parties. These are the gods which have brought you thus far, and these are the works which characterize their administration. "Shocking catalogue of miseries and crimes! dreadful account to be given to the King of Kings, to the common father of men!" *See Vattel, lib. iii. cap.* II. §184. If any person thinks the proposition, that resistance and carrying on war against a lawful sovereign, when every grievance has notoriously been removed, is rebellion, controvertible, his objections candidly proposed shall be fairly considered; as to those who deny what the scriptures positively assert, while they reject the authority of the Bible, it is not worth while to plead with them in support of any authority.

Exclusive of Congress, generals, and the leading men of the faction, war is *intended* to be kept up by all that choose to be either prisoners of war or upon parole, when they had the offer of being admitted British subjects. This speaks for itself, and we may with great propriety look upon the generality of such men living among us in this character, and observing our situation, as more ready to join our enemies, should it be in their power, than to approve themselves our friends and fellow citizens while it might be attended with some danger. Those that were liberated upon their parole still more fully discovered their real inclination; and it has been observed, that, at the late approach of the American army, of which they had undoubted intelligence, the very appearance of what is sacred among all men became so burthensome to them that they could not help betraying their real dispositions, and by a premature rejoicing in what they ought to have detested shewed themselves unworthy to be trusted and most truly detestable.

There are persons among us whose delicacy and tenderness does not permit them to call those who have overturned our government, and to the utmost of their power fought the lives and destruction of all its friends, by the odious name of Rebels. Doubtless they have their reasons for this civility, tho' these reasons may not be universally known; it remains however an indisputable maxim, No man can serve two masters, and he that is not for us is against us; nor can he be said for us who is not against those who are against us. I would not wish to *affect* calling any set of men by odious names, however they may deserve it, but while any are scrupulous, after all the mischief done and endured, to call things by their true name, they must admit that their negative loyalty cannot entitle them to be thought and treated as hearty friends and zealous subjects of the government which in many instances at least passed over their frailties and affords them protection.

It is the nature of some men when they suffer to be angry for their sufferings with those whom they injured, or who have forewarned them, rather than with themselves who are the sole cause of their sufferings. They meant to set only their neighbour's house on fire, but theirs also caught, and now they are vexed that they should be scorched a little by the flames. Perhaps they feel the want of the bread that they formerly eat, and now they are outrageous against him whose bread they did eat and found sweet, tho' themselves trampled both upon the bread and the giver. Poor creatures, it is now low with them, but they choose rather to quarrel with and abuse their former friends and benefactors than acknowledge they have been so foolish as to quarrel with their own bread and butter.

You that still are, have been, or wish to be in arms in such a nefarious cause, I never was a personal enemy to any of you, tho' no man has a greater abhorrence of your proceedings. I never attempted to destroy, but ran very great risks, and suffered most heavy losses, to prevent your destruction. I never lifted arms against you, tho' possibly I planted daggers in your souls. You so fully enjoyed your career that you either thought God Almighty was not at home, or that it would be as easy to you to banish him, and all justice, honesty, and religion, out of the world, as it was to banish the few individuals who would not worship the beast and his image because they knew the triumph of the wicked is short. Wisdom, truth, honour, and justice, will at last prove better and more forcible than all your weapons of war. It is hard for man, even upon the most irresistible evidence, to give sentence against himself, but the justice of God and his injured country will do it for him and leave him in an utter incapacity to avoid the consequence. If in thought, word, or deed, you wish well to a cause, of the desperate vileness of which you have a witness in your own bosom, and the destructive wickedness of which you cannot but behold wherever you turn your eyes, then that you may suffer the penalty due to obstinate rebellion in this life is a trifle not to be mentioned with what you must expect when all the ghosts of the slain, every drop of innocent blood you spilt, every act of violence and injustice which you concurred in or committed, all the confederates of your crime whom you have forced or seduced, every injured widow's groans, and every orphan's tear, whom you have ruined, the spoils of the honest and innocent whom you have robbed, every friendly warning which you rejected, will at once arise in judgment against you, and render you as compleatly miserable as you have rendered yourselves distinguishingly wicked.

Before it comes to this most dreadful extremity, how dreadful is the case of any person or people of whom it may be said: "They have eyes to see and see not, they have ears to hear and hear not, for they are a rebellious house." How little reason is there to hope that, by a speedy and sincere repentance and humiliation, they might mitigate or prevent their final doom, while they still feed upon delusions, and will not admit the evidence of their own eyes, ears, or feelings; yet would humanity indulge a wish for them, and charity would hope, "*It may be they will consider though they be a rebellious house.*" Ezekiel 12:3.

Sept. 13.   Helvetius.

Source: *Royal Georgia Gazette*, September 28, 1780. Number 83.

Number 7.

Ecce rescindendum est immedicabile vulnus ne pars sincera laedatur.

Whoever considers the natural attendants of Rebellion, and the dreadful effects which must unavoidably follow, will readily admit that a greater crime cannot easily be committed against the Supreme Ruler and Judge of all, nor any that spreads greater misery, and therefore deserves severer punishment among men. Perjury is its beginning; murder, bloodshed, rapine, and violence, mark its progress; injustice and cruelty are its characteristicks; and of perjury, murder, violence, injustice, and cruelty, what else but temporal and eternal destruction can be the end?

Rebellion frequently begins in triumph, but seldom fails to end in infamy. It furnishes a colour for every vice; but woe unto them who cannot alledge even rebellion as a sanction for their proceedings and who have not even the warrant of an idol to furnish a pretence where all authority is wanting! This is the case of all such as attempt war without a commission, or carry it on contrary to the rules established among all civilized nations. "A nation attacked by such sort of enemies is not under any obligation to observe towards them the rules of war in form; IT MAY TREAT THEM AS ROBBERS. The city of Geneva, after defeating the attempt of the famous Escalade, hung up the Savoyards over their walls whom they had made prisoners, as robbers who had attacked them without any cause. Nobody offered to censure this proceeding, which would have been detested in a formal war." *Vattel part.* ii. *pag.* 26. These Savoyards, of whom about 500 were killed, were all regularly commanded, had commissions from their Prince, who himself was at hand; but the treacherousness of his proceedings could not excuse their attempt, nor mitigate their fate; and surely pirates and persons acting without any commission at all are still upon a worse footing if they fall into their hands whom they intended to make a prey of.

Men who under pretence of publick war commit private robberies, and form themselves into bodies that they may the better effect their villainous purpose, are no better than highwaymen, and deserve no better treatment; if the guilt becomes general, the punishment must be in proportion. In 1745, "the King of Prussia had advice that the inhabitants of the mountains began to be suspected, and sent a general to repress these robbers, the chief of whom had disappeared on his approach, so that he found only some miserable wretches, whom he pardoned, *burning several cabins of those who had made their escape, and gave a general order to all the inhabitants not to suffer the fugitives to return,* but to seize them, stating that they should be liberally rewarded for their obedience, and on the contrary suffer the same punishment, and have their hamlets demolished, if the least disorder should happen among them, or if it should be found that these insurgents were entertained in their country." *Campaigns of the King of Prussia,* p. 54. "In the distance of a short league we saw eleven bodies hanging on gibbets, which, beside the disagreeableness of the sight, had also a most shocking smell. These had been robbers, who under colour of war, had plundered and murdered a vast number of people." *Ibid. p. 93.*

But revolted subjects, who have conquered, submitted, received to mercy, and revolted again, as they are the very worst of men, are the unfittest to be endured in society, and therefore, by the consent, nay, and demand of all mankind, liable to every severity.

"In the year 1738, after the surrender of Meadia, Deputies came to the camp from the inhabitants of Almas, *to declare their sorrow for having been obliged to take arms against the Emperor.* Upon an examination it appeared that they had been guilty of the basest treason; because, in defiance of the duty which they owed to the Emperor as his subjects, they declared for the enemy at the beginning of the campaign, gave them directions how to take Meadia, and made incursions into the Bannat of Temeswaer killing and slaying all the Emperor's subjects who were for persevering in their loyalty. Such a criminal behaviour being reckoned worthy of the severest punishment, Col. Helfrich was sent with a detachment of the Duke of Tuscany's regiment of foot into the territory of Almas, to cut off all the inhabitants, without distinction of age, sex, or quality, in order to keep the rest of the Bannat of Temeswaer in their duty, and deter them from shewing the least favour to the enemy." *Gent. Mag.*

"The Prussian General Jasmund marching to the relief of some Saxons, came too late, but because the peasants had fired upon him, and he understood they had assisted in the massacre of the Saxons, together with their wives and children, he made reprisals, and extirpated all the inhabitants without distinction of age or sex." *Prussian Campaigns, p.* 37.

In the year 1705 the Bavarians, always remarkable for their attachment to their Prince, his whole country being subdued by the Imperial arms, rise *in favour of their Sovereign,* and at first made some progress; but the Emperor's troops coming against and defeating them, their leaders were hanged and quartered, and all of them treated as Rebels. Their Prince doubtless lamented their ill success, but never complained that they had been treated unjustly.

Men who sported with an oath may still have a regard to what they call their honour, but upon those who have broke their parole, and honour also, there can be no further tie, and consequently society can no longer endure them. All mankind are concerned in it that such men may be treated as they deserve; no honest man can possibly say any thing in their favour, and every one's principles and person may be justly suspected who speaks of them otherwise than with detestation.

The speedy and exemplary justice executed upon a number of persons who had taken the oath of allegiance, and then joined Clark and his bandits, will probably preserve the lives of numbers, on whom fear at last may operate, tho' hitherto they proved callous to every principle. The lenity of the civil and military has hitherto emboldened men to act as tho' their return was a meek favour, and arrogance rather than penitence has been the most usual companion of those that returned. Thus some have not only avowed themselves void of fear or shame for taking the wages of rebellion, but many could not conceal their joy at any glimpse of hope that might distress the government they had lately again sworn to support, but which it was, and probably still is, their hearts' wish to overset. All those who refuse to become subjects, and prefer continuing upon parole, proclaim to all the world that they still wait and wish for an opportunity to renew the horrors of war, and to re-establish tyranny and confusion among us. Some men have made it their business to spread false reports, and tho' their lies scarce ever outlived a day before they were disproved, scarce a day passed before they were repeated, —and repeated and renewed with impunity.

The more oaths and paroles are trifled with by those by whom they are given, the more it behooves those to be upon their regard by whom they are received; while we are amazed to see men capable of such a breach whom we should never have thought capable of it, charity itself must take the alarm, and call upon justice for preservation. No society can subsist without some tie, and where religion and honour are no more binding all ties are at an end, and there is no remedy left but in the language of any Motto to cut off the rotten that the sound may be preserved.

But never is the violation of an oath more horrible in itself, or more pernicious to the community, than when it is disregarded by judges, jurors, or evidences, in a court of justice; this strikes at the root, and while in other cases the effects may be slow, in this they may be instant, and must always prove extensive. The juror that *acquits* because the criminal is his friend, or because his heart tells him, that, tho' the fact is manifestly proved and illegal, he would to the same case have acted in the same manner himself, (i.e. is really a criminal himself;) and the juror that *condemns*, not because he is convinced the prisoner is guilty of the fact, but because he owes him a particular [soue?]; the witness that gives his evidence, not as he knows it to be true, but as he wisheth to save or destroy him for or against whom it is given; all these in that instant publickly seal their damnation in open court, and call upon the living God to be a swift witness and avenger of their guilt, and a swift witness will he prove against them, for "*He that justifieth the wicked, and he that condemneth the just, even they both are an abomination to the Lord.*"

October 6.   Helvetius.

Source: *Royal Georgia Gazette,* October 12, 1780. Number 85.

BIBLIOGRAPHY AND INDEX

Short Title Bibliography of Zubly's Pamphlets

Leichenpredigt, welche ein Reformirter Prediger in Savannah in Georgia einem alten lutherischen Prediger gehalten, über Offenbarungen, vii, 13: Wer sind diese in weisen Kleidern ... (Germantown: Christoph Saur, 1746). A funeral sermon for the Reverend J. Christian Gronau of the Salzburger settlement at Ebenezer, Georgia. There is a copy at the Historical Society of Pennsylvania. The same sermon also appeared under the title *Leichenpredigt, eines Beruhmten Geistlichen in Georgien über Offenbarung vii. 13* . . . (Germantown: Christoph Saur, 1746), and the title *Eine Leicht-Predigt, welche ein Reformirter Prediger in Savanna in Georgien gehalten über die Worte Apoc. 7. Wer sind diese in Weisen Kleidern, &c.* . . . (Germantown: Christoph Saur, 1747).

Eine Predigt welche ein Schweitzer, ein Reformirter Prediger in Süd Carolina bey Charlestaun gehalten, über die Worte des Propheten Hosea: Sie bekehren sich, aber nicht recht. (Germantown: Christoph. Saur, 1749).

Evangelisches Zeugnuss. Vom Elend und Erlösung der Menschen, in zwey Predigten abgelegt und auf Hofnung Mehrer Erbauung dem Druck überlassen vom Johann Joachim Zublin Prediger bey einer englischen Gemeinde ohnweie Carlesstade in Sud Carolina. (Germantown: Christoph Saur, 1751). This sermon was reprinted under the title, *Evangelisches Zeugniss vom Elend und Ersolung der Menschen, in zwey Predigten abgelegt ... Vierte Auflage.* (Germantown: Peter Leibert, [1792?]). Haverford College has a copy of the 1751 edition.

The Real Christians Hope in Death; or an Account of the edifying Behaviour of several Persons of Piety in their last Moments, with a Preface recommendatory by the Rev. Mr. Clarke ... Collected and published by J. J. Zubly. Minister of the Gospel of South Carolina. (Germantown: Christopher Sower, 1756). There are good copies of this work at the American Antiquarian Society, the University of Georgia, and the Massachusetts Historical Society, among other places.

The Stamp-Act Repealed; A Sermon, Preached in the Meeting at Savannah in Georgia, June 25th, 1766. By J. J. Zubly, V.D.M. Published at the Request and Expence of the Hearers. (Savannah: James Johnston, 1766). The pamphlet was reprinted under the title *The Stamp-Act Repealed; A Sermon, Preached in the Meeting at Savannah in Georgia, June 25th, 1766 ... First published at the Request and Expence of the Hearers. The Second Edition.* (Savannah:

James Johnston, 1766); and under that title again in Charleston by Peter Timothy in 1766 and in Philadelphia by Henry Miller in 1766. Copies exist at the American Antiquarian Society, University of Georgia, the Library of Congress, the New York Historical Society, among other places.

An Humble Enquiry into the Nature of the Dependency of the American Colonies upon the Parliament of Great-Britain, and the Right of Parliament to lay Taxes on the said Colonies. By a Freeholder of South-Carolina. ([Charleston?], 1769). This pamphlet was reprinted in England under the title *Great Britain's Right to Tax her Colonies; Placed in the clearest Light, by a Swiss* (London: J. Delegal, 1774); and in Philadelphia under the same title in 1775 and again in London in 1775. Good copies of *An Humble Enquiry* are at the American Antiquarian Society, John Carter Brown Library, the University of Georgia, the Henry E. Huntington Library, among other places. A good copy of the London 1774 reprint is at the Library Company of Philadelphia.

An Account of the Remarkable Conversion of Jachiel Hirshel, from the Jewish to the Christian Religion ... (Savannah: James Johnston, 1770). There is a copy at the Massachusetts Historical Society.

The Christian's Gain in Death; Representing a Funeral Sermon, Preached at Purysbourg, in South Carolina, Jan. 28, 1770. at the Interment of Mr. Jacob Waldburger. (Savannah: James Johnston, 1770). There is a copy at Harvard University.

A Letter to the Reverend Samuel Frink, A.M. Rector of Christ Church Parish in Georgia, Relating to Some Fees demanded of some of his Dissenting Parishioners. ([Savannah? printed by James Johnston? 1770?]). This pamphlet was reprinted under the title *Letter to Mr. Frink* ... (Philadelphia: Henry Miller, 1775). The Henry E. Huntington Library has a copy of the 1770 edition, but it is poorly trimmed. The copy at the Massachusetts Historical Society is now badly deteriorated, but it was preserved on microprint in the *Early American Imprints* before the deterioration set in.

The Wise Shining as the Brightness of the Firmament ... *A Funeral Sermon, Preached at Savannah in Georgia, November 11th, 1770, on the much lamented Death of the Rev. George Whitefield, A.M.* ... *by J.J. Zubly* ... (Savannah: James Johnston, 1770). The only copy extant, at the Library Company of Philadelphia, is imperfect. The pamphlet was reprinted under the title *A Funeral Sermon on the Death of the Rev. George Whitefield* ... (Philadelphia: Henrich Miller, 1770).

Calm and Respectful Thoughts on the Negative of the Crown on a Speaker chosen and presented by the Representatives of the People: Occasioned by some Publications in the Georgia Gazette, of May and June 1772, wherein the late Assembly of that Province is charged with encroaching on the Rights of the

Crown. By a Freeman. ([Savannah? printed by James Johnston?] 1772). There are copies of this pamphlet at the Library of Congress, Princeton University, and Williams College.

The Nature of that Faith without which it is impossible to please God, considered in a Sermon, on Hebrews xi. 6 ... Together with some Occasional Remarks on some late Writers: Also, An Appendix, Shewing what has been the constant Doctrine of the Protestants in the Article of Faith, and some Vindication of the Reformers, and the late Mr. Hervey, &c. against some Animadversions of the Rev. Joseph Bellamy, D.D. of Bethlehem in New England ... (Savannah: James Johnston, 1772). There are copies of this pamphlet at the American Antiquarian Society, the John Carter Brown Library, the Library Company of Philadelphia, among other places.

The Faithful Minister's Course Finished. A Funeral Sermon ... August the 4th, 1773, in the Meeting at Midway in Georgia, at the Interment of the Rev. John Osgood ... (Savannah: James Johnston, 1773). There are copies of this pamphlet at the Georgia Historical Society, the New York Historical Society, and Princeton University.

The Law of Liberty. A Sermon on American Affairs, Preached at the Opening of the Provincial Congress of Georgia. Addressed to the Right Honourable The Earl of Dartmouth. With an Appendix, Giving a concise Account of the Struggles of Swisserland to recover their Liberty. By John J. Zubly, D.D. (Philadelphia: Henry Miller, 1775). The pamphlet was reprinted under the same title for J. Almon in London in 1775. It also appeared under the title *A Sermon on American Affairs ... by John J. Zubly, D.D.*, published in Philadelphia in 1778. In 1775 Henry Miller brought out Zubly's preface to the original pamphlet as *An Address to the Right Honourable Earl of Dartmouth*, and in 1775 he published the appendix separately in German under the title *Eine Kurzgefasste historische Nachricht von den Kämpfen der Schweitzer für die Freyheit.* There are copies of the *Law of Liberty* at the John Carter Brown Library, Emory University, Library Company of Philadelphia, Princeton University, among other places.

Pious Advice. A Sermon on the Faith ... (Philadelphia: Henry Miller, 1775). No copy of this pamphlet survives.

Exercitatio Theologica de nuptiis Virginis superadultae ... (Charleston: Robert Wells, 1775). An analysis of 1 Corinthians 7:36, this pamphlet was published in Frankfurt in 1776 under the title *Theologisch-Kritische Untersuchung d. Stelle I. Kor., 7, 36.* There is a copy of the Latin version at Princeton University, and a copy of the German version at Yale University.

Index

11; and John Dickinson, 6; education of 7; family of, 7, 8, 26; and Samuel Frink, 12, 84-94; in Georgia Provincial Congress, 20, 121; "Helvetius" essays of 25-26, 172-99; *An Humble Enquiry*, 14, 17, 51-82; *Law of Liberty*, 15, 18, 19, 20, 121-61; on legislatures, 17-18, 22; *Letter to the Reverend Samuel Frink*, 11, 12-13, 83-94; library of, 10, 23; Loyalism of, 23, 24-25, 165-66; ministry of, 7, 8, 9, 12, 86, 165; and politics, 9, 18-20, 20-21, 21-22, 121, 165-66; on power, 15-16; *Real Christians Hope in Death,* 10-11; on religious dissent, 11-12, 83-84, 86-93; religious themes of, 13, 31, 121-22, 131-32; on representation, 14-15, 96; settlement of, in America, 7; settlement of, in Savannah, 8; sources of, in writings, 13-14, 172; on sovereignty, 16-17; *The Stamp-Act Repealed,* 11, 13, 14, 15, 18, 31-49; and Ezra Stiles, 9; *To the Grand Jury of the County of Chatham,* 11, 22-23, 165-70; travels of, in America, 8, 9, 20; on war, 25-26; wealth of, 8-9; and George Whitefield, 8, 9n; and Sir James Wright, 9, 17, 21; writing ability of, 11, 13n

Zubly, John (d. 1780): 8; Whiggism of, 26

DATE DUE

A.L.L. CAT. NO. | 30501